PRAISE FOR

(R)EVOLUTION: THE GIRLS WRITE NOW 2016 ANTHOLOGY

"The courage, passion, and insight on display in *(R)evolution: The Girls Write Now 2016 Anthology* will knock you off your feet. Girls Write Now has created a powerful space for young women writers, and this book gives us a taste of the remarkable work they've done—and the great fun they've had—in the company of their peers and mentors. To read these pages is to feel hopeful and fired up about the future."

—MIA ALVAR, author of *In the Country: Stories* and
Girls Write Now mentor alum

"The voices in this anthology are insistent, urgent, and inescapable. They are girls on the verge of everything. Read them and remember who you were—and who you still want to be."

—CRIS BEAM, author of *To the End of June: The Intimate Life of American Foster Care*

"Nothing less than the future of the world hangs on the ideas and passion of girls. Let us welcome them to the world and rally behind their revolution."

—MARTHA BROCKENBROUGH, author of *The Game of Love and Death*

"The very existence of Girls Write Now is an evolution and revolution, all in one. You need only read the words of the poets, essayists, and fiction writers highlighted in this anthology to recognize what the world would be missing if Girls Write Now did not exist. These young women writers are the epitome of perseverance, and their words remind us all to live more intensely."

—LAURIE JEAN CANNADY, author of *Crave: Sojourn of a Hungry Soul*

"Year after year, Girls Write Now has nurtured young women writers and shown them that their voices matter—and have always mattered. The beautifully talented voices that grace these pages are filled with such insight, passion, and ambition. These young writers are our future leaders and scholars, so savor their words and get to know them well. It's an honor and an inspiration to experience so much talent."

—ANNIE CHOI, author of *Shut Up, You're Welcome*

"The pieces in this anthology aren't just literary expressions. They are words with wings. I can't wait to see what these young women become and what kind of world they will help to shape."

—MEGHAN DAUM, author of *The Unspeakable: And Other Subjects of Discussion*

"During this very important time of social revolution, Girls Write Now is an invaluable support to young women who are finding their voices to tell their stories. As the child of civil rights activists, I know how important it is to include all stories in the national narrative, especially the stories of young people—so this is a critically important project."

—TANANARIVE DUE, author of *Ghost Summer: Stories*

"Writing down how we feel is one of the bravest things we can do. We need our feelings to make a more just and loving world."

—GRACE DUNHAM, writer, poet, and Girls Write Now craft talk speaker

"Thank you to these young women who let us into their worlds through writing that is daring, visceral, and ultimately deeply affirming. And thank you to Girls Write Now for enabling their words to be heard."

—ELIZABETH ECONOMY, author of *The River Runs Black*

"Having your voice be heard is the best form of power I know. Girls Write Now contributed mentors and a platform. These young women contributed their own words: honest, loving, angry, sad, joyful, vivid, and *strong*."

—ANNE FADIMAN, author of *The Spirit Catches You and You Fall Down*

"A girl who learns to speak up for herself will grow into a woman with the capability to do great things in the world. Read Girls Write Now's anthology *(R)evolution*, and get to know the next generation of necessary voices: they are young, they are talented, and they are brave."

—**ANGELA FLOURNOY,** author of *The Turner House*

"Girls Write Now shouts it from the rooftops: I write, therefore I am! This anthology is a remarkable testament to the power of self-expression."

—**MYLA GOLDBERG,** author of *Bee Season* and *The False Friend*

"It's hard to think of a more important endeavor for a girl than learning how to use her voice. Through Girls Write Now, the young women in this book have encountered new experiences, new ideas, new challenges, all of which inform and strengthen their voices. The writing here is fresh and alive. You are about to experience the great joy of reading new artists as they begin to discover themselves and their powers."

—**KAITLYN GREENIDGE,** author of *We Love You, Charlie Freeman* and Girls Write Now mentor

"*(R)evolution* is the perfect title for this bold, important, and galvanizing 2016 anthology. The equation is simple: the more Girls Write Now = the more Women Write Later. I hope and expect to read the singular voices collected inside of this book—at turns tender and tough, but always searching—for years to come."

—**BROOKE HAUSER,** author of *Enter Helen: The Invention of Helen Gurley Brown and the Rise of the Modern Single Woman*

"The spirit and verve of *(R)evolution* echoes the power of young women to reimagine our world with their words. Each and every story in these pages is a testament to the necessity of literary learning spaces like Girls Write Now. Their creative fire will stay with you long after you've finished reading this important, beautiful collection."

—**TANWI NANDINI ISLAM,** author of *Bright Lines*

"Find in these pages whispered, shouted, necessary notes on our present in the voices of girls on their way to becoming women. The world is a better place for the poems and stories contained here, and the relationships of mentorship and creativity among women and girls that these words reflect."

—**NAOMI JACKSON,** author of *The Star Side of Bird Hill*

"This anthology showcases a remarkable collection of what Girls Write Now creates. Unique perspectives, compelling voices, and articulate and energetic accounts of 21st-century female teenage life fill the book. There is something in here for all of us to enjoy and to learn from."

—EMMA GILBEY KELLER, author of *The Comeback: Seven Stories of Women Who Went from Career to Family and Back Again* and *The Lady: The Life and Times of Winnie Mandela*

"My whole life has been supported by the gift of being given the space to tell stories. Seeing these brilliant and driven young women take on the world through words gives me so much hope for the future, both of television and the world."

—JENNI KONNER, coauthor with Lena Dunham of the weekly feminist online newsletter and website LennyLetter.com, and executive producer, cowriter, and showrunner of HBO's *Girls*

"Reading these talented young writers makes it impossible not to feel hope for the future. Their voices are simply that powerful."

—JEAN HANFF KORELITZ, author of *You Should Have Known*

"The development of women's voices and the female perspective remains an important task in our society. The power of the story, wielded by young women, is in itself a form of revolution in the fight for greater equality."

—BOURREE LAM, Associate Editor, *The Atlantic*

"The voices of these girls energize me with their courage, honesty, and vulnerability. They bring me right back to my own teenage years, when writing was a lifeline for me, a way to pull myself to the future while making sense of the past. Their words shine."

—MALINDA LO, author of *Ash*

"These are voices lifted high: girls speak their truths, laugh at their own jokes, create rhythms, invent new worlds. In doing so, they write their own future."

—E. LOCKHART, author of *We Were Liars*

"The stories you will read here ask big, complicated questions about love, death, betrayal, loyalty, friendship . . . those same questions that nag at us no matter our age. That these young writers have braved the terrors of a blank page, and every insecurity that creeps up on every writer, to put their stories onto paper is a testament to their understanding of the power of a story. One story released into the world reaches others and forms a community. What you hold in your hand is an invitation to take part. Welcome."

—MAAZA MENGISTE, author of *Beneath the Lion's Gaze* and writer on the film *Girl Rising*

"Only in telling my story have I been able to step into my power as my own protagonist, so I recognize how vital Girls Write Now is, giving a brilliant generation of young sister-writers the tools, encouragement, and power to see themselves as the heroines of their own stories."

—JANET MOCK, TV host and *New York Times* best-selling author of *Redefining Realness* and the forthcoming *Firsts: A Memoir of the Twenties Experience*

"Girls who read and write grow up to be women who think straight and take on the world with imagination and compassion. I can hardly wait to see what the girls in these amazing pages will do."

—PATRICIA O'TOOLE, author of *When Trumpets Call: Theodore Roosevelt After the White House*

"Girls Write Now is an inspiration. This collection of fresh, new voices reminds us of the girls we used to be, and the women we are trying to become."

—PATRICIA PARK, author of *Re Jane: A Novel*

"In these pages, the young women of Girls Write Now share—generously, courageously, eloquently, dazzlingly—of themselves as they give voice to stories and perspectives that have been too infrequently heard. Listen up!"

—HELEN PHILLIPS, author of *The Beautiful Bureaucrat* and *Some Possible Solutions*

"This anthology shines a bright and irresistible light on some of the most captivating voices in a rising generation of women writers. It is testimony to Girls Write Now's ability to transform inspiration into action, a page-turning showcase of fearless dedication to the craft of writing."

—ELENA PEREZ, author of *The Art of Disappearing*

"By sharing their dynamic voices, these young women join a rich tradition of self-expression that is both transformative and empowering. I am so very inspired by their words and courage."

—**ANDREA PIPPINS,** author of *I Love My Hair*

"The wisdom in the writing of the participants in Girls Write Now shows how important it is for these girls to learn to write. The introspection required to write like this introduces them to deeper, wiser versions of themselves."

—**ROBIN QUIVERS,** author of *The Vegucation of Robin*

"Open this book and you will be allowed into secret worlds of pain, love, tragedy, and triumph. Girls Write Now gives young women the chance to be heard, and we are lucky enough to listen in."

—**LAUREN REDNISS,** author of *Radioactive* and
Thunder & Lightning

"*(R)evolution* is more than a compilation of teen writing. It is a call to action, it is art as activism. It is a generation taking the pen and writing their future. The vulnerable, diverse, and passionate voices here will resonate with young people and adults alike."

—**RENÉE WATSON,** author of *This Side of Home*

"The world would be a better place if more people listened to and truly heard the voices of our girls. These voices are brilliant and daring and playful and coming into their own. They are an absolute pleasure to read."

—**NICOLA YOON,** author of *Everything, Everything*

(R)EVOLUTION:

THE GIRLS WRITE NOW

2016 ANTHOLOGY

Published 2016
Printed in the United States of America
Print ISBN: 978-1-63152-083-9
E-ISBN: 978-1-63152-084-6
Library of Congress Control Number: 2016939325

For information, address:
She Writes Press
1563 Solano Ave #546
Berkeley, CA 94707

Cover design © Julie Metz, Ltd./metzdesign.com
Interior design by Tabitha Lahr

She Writes Press is a division of SparkPoint Studio, LLC.

(R)EVO-
LUTION

THE
GIRLS WRITE NOW
ANTHOLOGY

FOREWORD BY
FRANCINE PROSE

2016

SHE WRITES PRESS

THE GiRLS WRiTE NOW 2016 ANTHOLOGY

Every year the *Girls Write Now Anthology* centers on a theme that speaks to the dreams and ambitions of the young women whose writing we celebrate in these pages. This year's theme, (r)evolution, reflects the very essence of these teenage writers. They have no qualms about turning the world upside down, and doing what they can and must to ignite change within themselves, their communities, and the entire universe. In these pages you will find revolutions and evolutions, and the leaps of imagination that provoke small and large transformations, personal and global.

For eighteen years this organization has been a catalyst for the next generation of women writers. Matching teenagers with writing mentors, the program offers talented girls the chance to express themselves freely, to challenge their own preconceptions and self-imposed limitations. Girls Write Now celebrates the written word, and also believes deeply in creating a safe and loving community where creativity can blossom. Through pair sessions, workshops, portfolio building, readings, and publication, mentees develop the skills and strength they need to navigate a world where political, technological, and cultural revolutions take place every day. When I became a Girls Write Now mentor four years ago, I didn't quite know what to expect but anticipated being a combination tutor-editor. Certainly that turned out to be part of my role as a Girls Write Now mentor—but possibly the least significant. In the two years I was paired with my mentee, Nishat Anjum, we became a team of explorers, figuring out the world as we walked, talked, wrote, edited, snacked, took excursions around the city, and laughed—a lot. Nishat is now in her sophomore year of the Macaulay Honors Program at Brooklyn College, but we both remain connected to Girls Write Now and to one another.

Like most things that are worthwhile, Girls Write Now requires hard work and dedication from both mentors and mentees. The year's activities culminate with the publication of our award-winning anthology, which includes the best writing produced by both mentors and mentees. It is a delight for the girls to see their work in print—official acknowledgment for many of them that they really are writers. With this anthology they become part of a Girls Write Now tradition, young writers featured in a substantial collection that has become an emblem of literary merit. There are a combined 136 mentors and mentees who have contributed to the poetry, fiction, and essays contained in this volume, built on experience and imagination, introspection and action, turmoil and triumph. What better way to meet our mentor-mentee pairs than through their writing? For Girls Write Now, that's where the revolution begins.

—JULIE SALAMON, Anthology Committee Chair

ANTHOLOGY EDITORIAL COMMITTEE

MOLLY MACDERMOT
Editor

JULIE SALAMON
Anthology Committee Chair

NAN BAUER-MAGLIN
LAURA BUCHWALD
RACHEL COHEN
AMY FLYNTZ
CATHERINE GREENMAN
ANN KIDDER
ESTHER KIM
LINDA KLEINBUB
ERICA MOROZ
CAROL PAIK
RACHELE RYAN
MARYELLEN TIGHE

MARIA CAMPO, *Director of Programs & Outreach*
EMILY YOST, *Senior Program Coordinator*
HANNAH LYTHE, *Communications Manager*
MEREDITH CLARK, *Copy Editor*
MARIA CAMPO, CHRISTINA DRILL, MAGGIE MULDOON, LEAH PELLEGRINI, SALMAAN RIZVI, RICHELLE SZYPULSKI, *Photographers*
MAYA NUSSBAUM, *Founder & Executive Director*

CONTENTS

GIRLS WRITE NOW ANTHOLOGY 2016

FOREWORD

FRANCINE PROSE

Before I became a writer, I was a babysitter. When I was in junior high (middle school, we say now) I was paid—not much—to take care of the younger kids on my block in Brooklyn. They were active, they were noisy, they were rebellious—they did what they wanted to do and didn't listen to me. Until I made a useful discovery.

I began to write stories—ghost stories, the scariest and most nightmarish stories I could imagine. I wrote them down and read them aloud to the kids I was taking care of. And they were so scared that they wouldn't move, wouldn't talk. They looked to me for help and guidance and protection from the terrors I had imagined. Suddenly, they would do anything I said. And a writer—me—was born.

In many ways, there's nothing more powerful than writing. We sit at our desk with only a computer, or a notebook, or a pencil and paper. And we can make people fall in love. We can arrange marriages. We can start a war. We can travel back in time. We can destroy the planet and invent a new world, or we can imagine how this world will look centuries from now. When we write, we're so powerful that it's often hard to readjust and recalibrate when we leave our desks. Our characters say what they want them to say, but real people don't. Real people tell us to do things. But when we write, we are the ones in charge. The power that writing gives us transfers over—and makes us more powerful.

The stories, essays, and poems gathered in *(R)evolution: The Girls Write 2016 Anthology* are expressions of, and vehicles to, power. Writing them, the girls discover who they are and who they want to be—and how they want their community and their country to be. They create worlds, turn their friends and family into characters on the page, and reach new understandings. And the power they gather from writing carries over into their daily lives. Writing these pieces, the girls learn how to talk, how to reason, how to express themselves. They learn that what they think and say matters. They learn how to write—and they learn how to be writers in the only way that any of us learns, which is to write and keep on writing.

* * *

Francine Prose is the author of twenty works of fiction. Her novel *A Changed Man* won the Dayton Literary Peace Prize, and *Blue Angel* was a finalist for the National Book Award. Her most recent works of nonfiction include *Anne Frank: The Book, The Life, The Afterlife* and the *New York Times* bestseller *Reading Like a Writer*. Her most recent book is *Lovers at the Chameleon Club, Paris 1932*.

INTRODUCTION

QUIARA ALEGRÍA HUDES

Most days I'm even-tempered and cool.

But some days I find myself bewildered by fury and grief, feeling confused and angry, crying at random moments. On those days, I remember being seventeen, when my heart was saturated with feeling.

First off, I was in love. Madly, crazily. We walked hand in hand through the streets of West Philly, and everything seemed glowing and alive. The irises thrived that year, they were a rich purple. Even the bricks and sidewalk cracks shone bright. I will never forget the first time this person leaned in and kissed me. My whole body felt about to burst.

Secondly, my heart was broken. My father had left years before and built a new family with new kids. We spoke infrequently and I wished he'd call me more, especially on my birthdays. Dad had been my childhood hero until I was six, when he left. I wanted *that* man back. My Wiffle ball partner, my reading coach. When I did visit him on occasion, the little glimpse of his life made my sadness worse; his new family seemed happy and well cared for, and I wasn't a part of it. I sank deep into depression. With the help of counseling and my female mentors I poured my heartbreak into poems, stories, songs. I practiced Chopin nocturnes and Bach fugues for hours every day. I took my despair and *created* and *lived*.

Thirdly, I was wildly loyal. As a biracial, mixed ethnicity person, I felt torn by my middle-ness. Many outsiders, on first glance, sized me up as white, sometimes even showing me preferential treatment over my darker-skinned sister and mother. One time a health care worker was speaking to my Titi Ginny, Aunt Ginny, as though she were an alien, and an idiot alien at that. Ginny was fully fluent in English and Spanish. She was also dark-skinned, had kinky hair and a lovely, lilting accent, and was clearly a brown woman. When I entered the room, Ginny introduced me as her niece who went to Yale and the healthcare worker greeted me with full respect and in a normal voice.

I outwardly resembled the Jewish side of my family, but I felt fiercely loyal to, and increasingly defensive of, my large Boricua family. I danced with them. I feasted with them. And I witnessed the ways they were tagged as different from mainstream society, into which I was regularly welcomed. As I became more aware of the obstacles they faced in our drug-addled, impoverished community, a sort of loyal fury planted itself in my bones. Not just love of one's cousin but protectiveness of one's cousin. Not just affection for one's sister but advocacy for one's sister.

At seventeen I was honored by a local girls group for work I had done involving AIDS and pregnancy prevention. I talked about my younger sister, who was about five years old at the time. She was darker-skinned than me, and like many of our family members, she was already showing herself to be heavyset. One day she ran into my bedroom naked, proudly saying, "Look at my huge belly! It's round like the Mother Earth!" When I gave my speech, I talked about how a girl's self esteem changes as she grows. I was scared for how my sister would view her body a few years down the line, and I reveled in a five-year-old girl admiring her curvaceous belly in the mirror.

So, keeping a tally here: at seventeen I was crazy in love, painfully heartbroken, and fervently loyal. Fourthly, and finally, I was terrified. That September I left Philly for college. I was the first in my family to do this. I left the lover I kissed, the aunts I defended, and my round-bellied sister for the wealthiest, most homogenous place I had ever been: Yale University. I felt desperately alone and yet excited about the dare that lay ahead of me: "make something of yourself." For better and worse, seventeen was an incredible, alive time—full of color-saturated heartbreak, fear, sadness, and joy.

I'm not like that any more. At thirty-seven years old, there's a coolness about me now. A bit of remove. Some might call it repression. Others might call it maturity.

In life and in writing, maturity makes a difference. Passion is ephemeral. One is not better than the other; one is not more enlightened, advanced, or worthy. But they're different, and both worth experiencing.

In other words, keep living and keep writing.

* * *

Quiara Alegría Hudes is the author of *Water by the Spoonful*, recipient of the Pulitzer Prize for Drama. Her musical, *In the Heights*, received the Tony Award for Best Musical and was a Pulitzer finalist. Quiara was the keynote speaker for the Girls Write Now CHAPTERS Reading, June 2015.

JISELLE ABRAHAM

YEARS AS MENTEE: 2
GRADE: Sophomore
HIGH SCHOOL: Edward R. Murrow High School
BORN: Queens, NY
LIVES: Brooklyn, NY

MENTEE'S ANECDOTE: *I've always written stories about characters that I made up and never about myself, but I've started to get more personal this year. My mentor has helped me see things from different aspects while I'm writing and helped me find different ways to write. For example, if I wrote something one way, she would open up gates to another way of writing the same thing without changing the message.*

HEATHER STRICKLAND

YEARS AS MENTOR: 2
OCCUPATION: Communications Manager, American Express
BORN: Philadelphia, PA
LIVES: Brooklyn, NY

MENTOR'S ANECDOTE: *Working with Jiselle has given me multiple opportunities to see things from new angles. She's encouraged me to look at things from new perspectives and challenged me to explore new genres. I've always written fiction and journalism, but we have attended poetry slams together and watched some of her (and my!) favorite YouTube channels, which has opened me to new ways to share the messages that are important to me.*

I HATE YOU

JISELLE ABRAHAM

My personal evolution with my writing began when I started to get personal with my words. This piece, "I Hate You," is about my feelings towards someone whose love was bittersweet.

I hate you so much
As if you dropped my ice cream on the floor
Or if you came into my room
And left
Without closing the door
Or is it deeper than that?
That I let you into my life
And I fucked everything up
I thought we had
Or what it could've been
And I guess I shouldn't be mad
Because I said we should just
Take a step back
And move on with the lives we had
Before
But it wasn't until it was time for me to sleep
And all night long
I thought into things
Deep
What did I do?

I had you
And we had so much ahead of us
If you had just acted
A tad bit interested in me
Instead of always begging for a hickey
Or saying how you couldn't wait for the day
You were going to see me in my pink panties
Instead of pushing me to the side
Why didn't you make me feel wanted?
And now
Me
The person who ended this shit
Because I was tired of feeling so
Temporary
And now I'm in the middle of love and hate
And how I love the way you pinched my cheeks
And how I hate how you can go without talking to me for weeks
And how you can move on to some next girl and call her your sweet baby
And don't bother with the fact that I'm going crazy
Because you were real to me
Talking to you with that boasting personality
Was like sex to me
And if life were a movie
I'd be the idiot to have it unprotected
With you
Because I had no clue
How much I would fucking hate you

THIS ISN'T REAL

HEATHER STRICKLAND

During our first meeting, Jiselle and I said we were both scared of poetry. Two years later, Jiselle has become a confident poet, yet I remain afraid to explore the genre. Inspired by Jiselle and her evolution as a writer, I am sharing a poem in this year's anthology.

I am lying in my bed pretending
That my sheets don't reek of you
Of that sour onion smell of you
Of that salty smell and taste of you
That gets trapped in my mouth like the ocean when I am swimming
And it tastes kind of good until I find myself
Drowning, sucked in by the riptide
Which won't stop
(even though I ask it to)
My skin has itched ever since
I can't rub your salt off
I can't forget that crashcrashcrash of waves
But I can change my sheets
And leave them fresh and lavender-sweet
And lie in bed
Pretending

RACHEL AGHANWA

YEARS AS MENTEE: 2
GRADE: Junior
HIGH SCHOOL:
Queens Gateway to
Health Science
Secondary School
BORN: Brooklyn, NY
LIVES: Queens, NY

MENTEE'S ANECDOTE: *Before this year, I could barely finish one story in the weekly sessions Sara and I had. I'm now proud to say that with her helpful advice and twenty-minute timers, I've been completing more pieces. I learned that even if it takes weeks to conclude, a finished story is better than one left incomplete. I may not quite have the hang of it entirely, but I hope that I continue to progress, with her aid.*

SARA POLSKY

YEARS AS MENTOR: 2
OCCUPATION:
Senior Features Editor,
Curbed
BORN: New York, NY
LIVES: Queens, NY

MENTOR'S ANECDOTE: *Working with Rachel to finish and revise her pieces has been a joy. Some of my favorite times in our pair sessions have been when I've seen Rachel figure out something she wants to say or how she wants one of her stories to end. Writing is hard work so much of the time, but those moments when everything comes together make it worth it.*

A BIG BROTHER, A BIG MOUTH

RACHEL AGHANWA

This poem is important to me because it's dedicated to my brother, who I worry about often due to the struggles we face being black in America. I used to be tentative when speaking on issues regarding my race and identity, but I'm learning how to open up through writing.

I always wished my voice were louder when I was a young child.
Oh dear god, yes I had a big mouth
but what is the use if it moved without purpose?
I wish I were less naïve
when I thought just being myself was enough.
As if there aren't people
who want to see me suffer.
As if there aren't people
who want my brother shot in the street, dead.
I wish I were as carefree as I was when I was a child,
unaware of the trouble life had ahead of me.
Oh dear god, I wish.
--

August 9th, 2014. I didn't see Michael Brown's name plastered all over CNN.
I saw "MY BROTHER," because that's who it could've been.
Oh dear god, I pray every night to keep him safe.
I say, "Thank God my brother isn't six feet, or he'd be six feet under."

THE WALL

SARA POLSKY

*Rachel and I both wrote our pieces in the Spoken Word Poetry
Workshop. I don't usually write work that is overtly political,
but Rachel's poem inspired me to share mine.*

You say, let's build a wall. Let's line our
borders with bricks and barriers. Let's ban
the people who don't look like us. (Your
concept of "us," by the way, could use an
update.) Worse is what goes unsaid: that
you thrive on our anger. That you win with
every thought of *they took what's ours* and *there's
not enough to go around.* That you think hate is
the way to make America great again. That if we
harden our hearts into bricks, you'll be our mortar.
The wall will build itself.

ROSEMARY ALFONSECA

YEARS AS MENTEE: 1
GRADE: Senior
HIGH SCHOOL: High School of Law and Public Service
BORN: New York, NY
LIVES: Bronx, NY
PUBLICATIONS AND RECOGNITIONS: Scholastic Art & Writing Award: Silver Key

MENTEE'S ANECDOTE: *Growing up with a single mother and no siblings made my household feel boring and dull, but joining the Girls Write Now program has helped me to see it all differently. Diane made me realize that sometimes the smallest things can be the most interesting to write about. Having a mother that's not fluent in the language you speak can be troublesome, but Diane is always available to talk. It's been a busy year submitting college applications, keeping up with classes, making time for friends, and having a job. But we always seem to fit in time for each other.*

DIANE BOTNICK

YEARS AS MENTOR: 1
OCCUPATION: Writer
BORN: Akron, OH
LIVES: Cold Spring, NY

MENTOR'S ANECDOTE: *I am a Midwest girl who couldn't wait to go to college in New York City. Rosemary is a city girl—born and bred in the Bronx—who is determined to go to college upstate. It's been a good match. I love that she dreams big and remains utterly practical; that she's lived in the same neighborhood, the same apartment, all her life, and is hungry for new views of the world. I love that she and her mother aren't equally fluent in the same languages. And I love that she can hold such strong opinions and be open to change.*

THE INFAMOUS CATCALL

ROSEMARY ALFONSECA

This piece is a revolution. Living it and writing it changed me as a woman, and hopefully once you read it, you will be inspired to start your own revolution with me.

"Hey beautiful, can I get your number?" is a familiar question I hear in the streets of my neighborhood. I'm walking to the train station when a stranger walks towards me trying to seem attractive but he's failing miserably because his underwear is showing. He gives me that up and down stare that I hate more than anything. I'm being called beautiful, yet I feel anything but beautiful. He glares at my body and I can feel every goose bump on my skin. He doesn't get the hint that I'm beyond uncomfortable.

"Why are you ignoring me, beautiful?"

Here we go with the word "beautiful." I drop my gaze and try to ignore his inappropriate stare.

My first instinct always used to be to look down because I felt responsible. I used to be ashamed when men openly stared at me in public. But last year I decided to join the Sadie Nash Leadership Project, and now I see me, the world, and men differently.

I only joined the program so it would look good on my college resume, and when I found out it was just for girls, I wanted to run for the hills. During the first week of the program, we all felt awkward and shy with each other. But the following week our group leader, Leslie, instructed us to play a game called "Electric Fence." The fence was a rope attached to two walls. It was too high to get over easily, and we weren't allowed to go under it. All the girls had to help each other get over. We had to climb on each other's backs, hold hands, and trust that we would be caught on the other side. No matter what size we were, what language we spoke, or where we came from, we all came together to help each other get to the other side.

At the end of the exercise, we had all made it.

After this experience I knew this program would benefit me. It got me to open up to people that I didn't know very well. What empowered me was when a young girl just like me shared her sexual assault story in our safe space. Every one of us was crying with her. It was like we all felt her pain. Everyone hugged her and was proud that she had been able to let it all out. I felt fortunate that she felt comfortable enough to share such a personal story with me and the others.

Soon after, we took a bus to a reproductive rights conference at Hampshire College. Women from all different states attend this conference once a year. When we arrived on campus we were starving, and they fed us nasty chili and cornbread. Luckily there were chocolate chip cookies, and that's all we ended up eating that night. But once the first event got going, it didn't matter to any of us. It was a gathering of women speaking out on abortion and telling their own personal stories. The audience was asked not to clap or talk but just to listen. I was sitting with some of my Sadie Nash friends, and we were all so touched by what we heard that all we could do was hold hands.

Before I found Sadie Nash, I thought it was normal to be sexually harassed in the streets of New York. Sadie Nash made me aware that catcalling is oppressive to me and other young women. I was inspired to accept my natural hair and stop chemically processing it. My mom said, "*Ese pelo tuyo es feo.*" Ever since I was young I felt like an outcast from my own home because my family had only one view on how hair should be: soft and straight. When I became part of this safe space of women, they showed me that there is no such thing as "good" hair. Not straightening my hair with chemicals is a symbol that not every woman of color has to accept this stigma. When women of color go natural, we are seen as "untamed" and "wild," but I want other women to join me in accepting our looks so that others will, too.

I don't want to be seen as just a "beautiful" girl anymore but rather a strong woman with a college degree and a future. I want every woman to find her own sisterhood, like I have.

I still don't like catcalling or being called "beautiful" by strange men, but it no longer makes me feel bad about myself. Sadie Nash has built my confidence and made me proud of who I am. I will begin to stare down the men who stare at me. They may want me to drop my gaze and lower my head, but I won't. I want to let them know that I see them and they no longer affect me.

I want to empower other young women to do the same.

WEDNESDAYS AT THE LIBRARY

DIANE BOTNICK

Truthfully, I've reached an age where (r)evolution is a lovely memory. Hurt, anger, frustration with the world—those have all quieted, leaving me feeling sometimes complacent, sometimes wise. In the library every week, a place Rosemary picked for us, I wonder if it matters. Life, in all its lovely details, is everywhere.

On Wednesdays, at least, a gentleman—a guard—dressed in a navy sports jacket, white shirt, and tie,
keeps an eye out, walking the floor,
his gray pants pleating over his rubber-soled tie shoes, black and soundless on speckled linoleum,
wire-rimmed glasses sliding down his nose, hair in tidy cornrows.
The first floor is for adults, a one-size-fits-all term.

There's a bank of ten computers with swivel desk chairs, every one taken, today, mostly men.

All their heads are covered—black hoodies, sock hats but mostly baseball caps, one in metallic magenta, the others black. The computers are equipped with good-sized screens, displaying Bible verses, Facebook pages, games, job listings.

Other men sit scattered about, one to a table, not much sharing going on, plugged into iPhones;

two, at separate ends of the room, read books with call numbers on their spines.

One asks another, apparently a stranger, to borrow his ear buds, and he hands them right over.

No one's eating, but I have pretzel fish and string cheese in my bag, in case Rosemary's hungry.

I remember how long those school days felt, how wrung out and pent up and bored, how starved for candy and fresh air and talk I was at the end of them. My hair's gone grey but that much hasn't changed.

She always partakes, but daintily. Maybe careful not to abuse my generosity. Maybe careful to hold down the day's calorie count.

Maybe just careful.

The guard leans against the elevator door. In addition to remaining watchful, he must also remain on his feet.

The librarians are all women. One white woman of about thirty who wears horn-rimmed glasses and ties her mousy hair into a thin ponytail; one a little older, chunkier, browner, a Mayan profile cut right from the ruins. They get to sit.

The librarian with the mousy ponytail spots two boys at a low, round table and heads their way. She has a project for them.

They're okay with cutting pictures from her magazines but won't answer her questions.

She wants to know their names, what they like to do, but they're refusing to answer her questions.

The bathroom and the key to it live on the second floor with the children who suffer the flow of us misfits.

The library sits at a crossroads and beyond the wall of windows a road curves up and away, beckoning. Up and over that hill is the river, I think. How well used this place is, I think.

This is as good a place to be as any, I think.

When Rosemary comes, I'll ask her how her week's been, if she's gone to any parties, if she's gotten any more school acceptances,

and she'll answer my questions and have some crackers and cheese and ask me if she can charge her phone in my computer and complain about a test no one studied for, and I'll prod and she'll offer a little more and we'll plan, and write,

and whatever thoughts or realizations or wishes have made it on record, whatever transformations imagined,

will be put aside, stuffed away, piled up on

for another Wednesday at the library.

ZOE ANTOINE-PAUL

YEARS AS MENTEE: 1
GRADE: Senior
HIGH SCHOOL:
High School of Law,
Advocacy and
Community Justice
BORN: Saint Lucia
LIVES: Brooklyn, NY

MENTEE'S ANECDOTE: *I've only known Catherine a short time, but she's been a great person to work with. She is very patient and supportive and my ideas matter to her. She's been an amazing mentor.*

CATHERINE GREENMAN

YEARS AS MENTOR: 1
OCCUPATION: Author
BORN: New York, NY
LIVES: New York, NY

MENTOR'S ANECDOTE: *When you first meet Zoe, she tends to be quiet and subdued. Her facial expressions do not reveal a lot. But as soon as she starts to talk, especially about writing or music, her two big passions, her eyes zero in on you and her demeanor completely changes. The smart, complex girl emerges. Zoe is a fantastic reminder to me, in writing and in life, of all that lies just beneath the surface, as long as you are patient and open to it.*

BROOKLYN AT 6:30 IN THE MORNING

ZOE ANTOINE-PAUL

I wrote this poem sitting on the front steps of the Central Library. The year 2015 was rough for me, and it seemed the place to turn was nature. A city buzzing with life in early morning could never let you down because all a city has is its beauty.

Brooklyn at 6:30 in the morning:
A quiet sort of victory,
Riding on coattails

Sticky, summer heat.

Brooklynites running, rather than
Walking into their day,
In worn out sneakers and tattered joggers,
A second cup of coffee in their
Slightly shaking hands.

The tulips in the window boxes serve as testament;
A broken perfection in the
Early-morning sun.

At 6:30 in the morning,
A living, breathing thing.
The subway cars rattling through
The tunnels, like blood in veins

And out of the abandoned building
On Lincoln Place; a solemn song.

UP AND DOWN

CATHERINE GREENMAN

*Understanding and communicating the differences in how peo-
ple see things can lead to revolution. It can incite people to act.
Zoe has a unique viewpoint, and she is a great communicator.
Her work always inspires me to take a closer look at what's in
front of me.*

Evelyn waited in the tunnel with the other listless passengers. It was a full
flight, and when she finally reached the threshold of the plane, the beast
that would secret them up into the clouds, her eyes zeroed in on the metal
tag with the model and its birth date. 2006. Not bad! The sun hit the left
wing and shot a blazing glare at her. This plane was shiny and new. But
wait, those scuff marks. On her left, under the cockpit window. Had it
scraped against tundra during an emergency landing?

She found the window seat in her row; she'd moved as far as she
could toward the front of the plane without shelling out extra bucks. A
tall, slim man in a decent suit stopped at her row. He had a beakish nose
and thinning hair and was younger than Evelyn by a few years, maybe, but

still ostensibly old. He pushed his glasses up, smiled politely, and took the aisle seat, arranging his knees. There was one empty seat between them—a safe zone. Evelyn stripped her headset of its plastic wrap and wondered for the billionth time whether she thought about dying more than everyone else did. A flight attendant passed and the man in Evelyn's row raised his hand to catch her.

"Sorry, can you tell me what time we land again?" he asked, as though they'd just discussed it. The flight attendant held a tray filled with little plates of ice cold, beady butter. Evelyn got a whiff from where she was sitting and it surprised her that butter could smell so much, across such a distance. There are so many little, tiny things in life to enjoy, Evelyn thought. I want to forage for mushrooms in a beautiful, black forest with someone who knows what they're doing.

"We don't have an exact time yet," the flight attendant answered. "The pilot will make an announcement shortly."

MISBAH AWAN

Years as Mentee: 3
Grade: Senior
High School: The Young Women's Leadership School of Astoria
Born: Pakistan
Lives: Queens, NY
Publications and Recognitions: Scholastic Art & Writing Award: Gold Key

MENTEE'S ANECDOTE: *Far before the official announcement of Girls Write Now's theme this year, I found myself in revolution within my mind and soul. This is my final year here, but I am glad to close my time as a mentee by continuing the tradition of meeting up at 30ᵗʰ Avenue in Queens and freewriting with my mentor. It is always comforting and acts very much as a release. My mentor has challenged me to write whenever I get the chance and never pressured me into forcing a piece out, and I am grateful for that.*

FRANKIE THOMAS

Years as Mentor: 2
Occupation: Writer and writing tutor
Born: New York, NY
Lives: New York, NY
Publications and Recognitions: "The Naked Party," published in *H.O.W. Journal*; "The Two Faces of Bisexual OKCupid," published on *The Hairpin*; four poems published on *The Toast*

MENTOR'S ANECDOTE: *This year, Misbah and I have been talking a lot about radical vulnerability. We're both facing big changes in our lives: Misbah is going away to college for the first time, while I'm about to get married, finish my degree, and move to a new city. When everything is shifting and evolving around us, how can we remain true to ourselves? The journey won't be easy, but Misbah inspires me every day to tackle life with courage, sincerity, and curiosity. I'm so lucky to know her, and I know she's going to change the world.*

ADHAN

MISBAH AWAN

Given birth to during my college application process, the following narrative fleshed into a personal reflection on what sound is most revolutionary to me.

The sweetest sound I have ever heard is the sound of *adhan* (Muslim call to prayer), especially in countries with large Muslim populations. Hearing it on the streets is a completely different matter than hearing inside a mosque, because that location already implies thinking of worship. However, when I hear it while walking down the streets, I not only find myself relaxed and at peace, but also begin to really see the synchronized unity among Muslims. I found this sense of peace in Pakistan when I was about eight years old. As soon as the *adhan* went off from a high point in the city, it spread across miles, and the imagery around me transformed. Coming from America to visit the motherland became an entirely new experience with that sweet sound. The shops and restaurants and rides came to a slow pause. If there was not a masjid nearby, people prayed inside their shops or outside on the streets.

I am able to feel similar comfort in the bustling community in New York City, though. Although the *adhan* does not reach across neighborhoods, inside the masjid, I feel safe. Usually the masjids, unfortunately, imitate the socioeconomic situations in our communities. Often, they are socially dominated by Arabs in between prayers and gatherings. It becomes cliquey. However, once the *mu'adhin* (the person who calls people toward prayer) intones, "The prayer is due, the prayer is due," everyone—young or old, black or white, poor or rich—lines up behind the *Imam* in rows and begins to pray.

The feeling of comfort I get from that sound, and these communities, has led me to download a Prayer App on my phone to respond to my religious duty. I plan to take it with me to college, because prayer gives me the time to pause life—either to mentally process it or simply to step out of it for the moment.

I am currently going through a metamorphosis; however, the call to prayer is part of my personal revolution. I want to continue to feel for it and want it.

HOW IT ENDED

FRANKIE THOMAS

I wrote this during the Dystopian Flash Fiction Workshop. It's inspired by the Jonestown massacre, because real life is so much more dystopian than anything I could make up.

How long would the elixir take—hours? All night? Some began to tremble, to sweat. The first symptom?

Angry motherly shushes failed to drown out the whimpers of the children; it was forbidden to weep in front of Father Bob.

Suddenly, shockingly, a laugh—harsh—Father Bob himself.

"My beloved children," he said, "I am well pleased in you. This was but a test of your faith in me—and you have all passed."

The crowd cried, "We love you, Father Bob!"

Then the first body hit the floor, and Father Bob laughed again.

LIBRANECE AYALA

YEARS AS MENTEE: 2
GRADE: Senior
HIGH SCHOOL:
Lehman High School
BORN: Bronx, NY
LIVES: Bronx, NY

MENTEE'S ANECDOTE: *In September of 2014, I was a fifteen-year-old writer with talent and skill but no voice or confidence in my writing. I did not fully understand the power of the pen, or of my fingertips on the keyboard. But two years later, at the age of seventeen, after countless cups of coffee and writing sessions on the Upper East Side, I have found my voice as a writer and have gained utmost confidence to use it. And I owe much of that to my empowering and amazing mentor, Alyssa Pelish.*

ALYSSA PELISH

Years as Mentor: 2
Occupation: Writing Consultant, Columbia University
Born: Eau Claire, WI
Lives: New York, NY
Publications and Recognitions:
Publications this year in *Harper's* and *The Smart Set;* finished a memoir of my childhood and adolescence and am taking the next steps toward publication

MENTOR'S ANECDOTE: *It's tough to pick my favorite moment from my two years with Libra. Does it suffice to say that I always leave our writing-and-coffee sessions in a good mood? Well, what about the time that we spent over an hour talking about everyday sexism, what feminism is, Instagram, a seventeenth-century poem about an unwise man who freaks out about women's bodies, and a twenty-first century movie about slut-shaming—and then Libra began thinking hard about writing what is now her Chapters piece (a knock-out poem called "Why I Need Feminism")?*

I'm so glad you're my mentee, Libranece Ayala.

WHEN SHE TALKS

LIBRANECE AYALA

This piece is about an introverted young woman who has not yet gained the ability to speak with confidence or defend her beliefs. But even people like her can still contribute to the (r)evolution.

Everything she says is said submissively. Almost giving a disclaimer every time she makes a statement. If there's a possibility that she's wrong, she wants to clear that up now so that she can't be ridiculed later. She'll say, "I don't think I want to vote for Hillary Clinton," with her left hand on the left side of her face, and her right hand pushing her hair behind her right ear. She doesn't look you in the eye, but she doesn't want you to see how timid she truly is, so she doesn't look into her lap, either. Instead, she pretends to observe her surroundings. First looking to the ceiling, then to her right. Quickly, she'll make eye contact with you—but as soon as you get the chance to notice, she'll look to her left. Her face looks flushed and her hands shake very discreetly as she waits for your response. If you willfully respond with some sort of "pro-Sanders" comment, she'll light up with a sense of relief. Feeling a sense of security, she's glad you don't disagree with her, because then you might ask her to justify her beliefs, and she doesn't want you to be mad at her.

She talks like she's been conditioned to think that her words don't matter or make any sense. Like her voice has been drowned out by that of other people on too many occasions to count. She pauses before making any absolutes. She stutters when her words provoke a look of disapproval on the faces of others.

When she talks, it's obvious she second-, third-, and fourth-guessed herself before opening her mouth. Her lack of confidence is evident when she spews out her beliefs in the form of a question.

When she talks, everybody listens, but it's almost as if she doesn't want them to.

GiRLS TOGETHER

ALYSSA PELISH

This excerpt is taken from the episodic memoir of my childhood and adolescence that I began writing during a regular Sunday writing-and-coffee session with my mentee, Libra. While the chapter is about the tumultuous friendship between two girls, this very last bit is about the significance of their shared history.

[Four years have passed since the narrator and her childhood friend last spoke. This, the final semester of high school, is the last time the narrator will see her.]

* * *

No one would take the first slice of pizza. I remember the giant moment of hesitation, every girl in the room suddenly self-conscious. Uneasy glances. And then how Laura Lummsen flung her arms out, toward the very nice pizza and the plates and napkins, exhorting us all to *Eat! Eat! Is no one going to eat the pizza?* There was something a little bit comic, a little bit ridiculous, about the size of her exasperation and her long, thin arms flung out like a crossing guard's. I remember how my amused gaze and Bobbi's happened to cross at the same time. She no longer permed her hair, hadn't since grade school. Now it was straight and cut to her chin, her face maybe thicker or broader, but still the face I knew from grade school pictures. We both smiled the knowing smile of two people who get the joke but are not part of it.

There is a line in Toni Morrison's *Sula*, a book about two childhood friends who later become enemies: *"We was girls together."* The line comes at the very end of the story, Sula gone for good and Nel, the protagonist, suddenly realizing what's been lost. Overcome by it. *"We was girls together," she said as though explaining something.* Was that it? Was that what that last, shared smile was about?

There is an ocean of time between age thirteen and age eighteen, between the first semester of eighth grade and the last semester of your senior year of high school. Was the smile in recognition of all the gallons and gallons of water under the bridge since we'd last spoken? Was it a recognition of how little, finally, it all mattered? Because it *had* mattered—so much, so terribly much. Maybe we smiled because we were embarrassed to acknowledge just how much it had mattered. I don't know. If it was recognition, it was recognition of a past that had so completely disappeared, was so lost, that we couldn't even explain it to one another. And so maybe the smile was all that could be said: *We was girls together.*

AYANNA BAILEY

YEARS AS MENTEE: 2
GRADE: Junior
HIGH SCHOOL: Urban Assembly Institute of Math and Science for Young Women
BORN: Brooklyn, NY
LIVES: Brooklyn, NY

MENTEE'S ANECDOTE: *Marissa has given me the confidence that I wouldn't have been able to gain otherwise. Her constant encouragement has made me proud to be who I am, and now I don't doubt myself. Meeting her is always the highlight of my week, and I feel like it's a judge-free zone. Her voice is always so modest and genuine and I always love talking to her about her childhood, her experiences, and controversial topics. My relationship with her is one that I know will last for a lifetime.*

MARISSA QUENQUA

YEARS AS MENTOR: 3
OCCUPATION: Freelance writer
BORN: Long Island, NY
LIVES: Brooklyn, NY
PUBLICATIONS AND RECOGNITIONS: Featured by Freerange Nonfiction, *SMITH* magazine (creators of Six-Word Memoirs), and justpressplay.net

MENTOR'S ANECDOTE: *Ayanna gives me hope for the next generation of women scholars. Her determination and interest in the medical field impressed me at our very first meeting. Her desire and willingness to leave New York to attend college across the country for no other reason than to have a totally new experience inspires and delights me. We make each other laugh; we identify with each other because we both came from modest means and had the drive to extricate ourselves from our born circumstances. I'm so proud of her.*

ENVY IN NYC

AYANNA BAILEY

This is a piece I wrote because I found it very interesting to develop a character based on one of the seven deadly sins. I was inspired by my surroundings, and after some help from my mentor, this shows how I've grown as a writer.

Growing up as an orphan isn't bad if you have the right attitude. Living in New York City is always exciting. You get to go to clubs and drink and do whatever you want whenever you want. In my case, I like to borrow without asking. Some call that stealing, but saying "borrowing without asking" sounds a bit less harsh, in my opinion. And no, I don't steal from hobos or poor people. I target the rich people.

I'm supposed to be in school, but school is for people who have a chance at making it out of the ghetto. Today I decided to go around the Upper East Side and watch as the rich people shop.

The Upper East Side is filled with clean roads and sidewalks. There is never any trash or garbage anywhere, and that's because the people who live there respect their environment. The people all look put together. Their gloves match their shoes that match their coats. The cherry on top is the jewelry they have on. Looking at it makes me feel like a raccoon. All I want to do is steal all of the shiny jewelry off of them.

I slowly scan my surroundings and spot a half-bald fat man. I've seen him before, coming out of a restaurant that is crazy expensive. It's a small little store with a red theme for all of its furniture, but the ambiance it gives off shows that they serve high-quality food. And I know he doesn't order anything cheap because of his big belly.

I quickly cross the street and walk a few steps behind him. I wonder where he's going. Hennessy says that rich people always take cars, so I search to see if he's going to try to hail a cab. He comes to a stop and starts looking at his phone. This is my chance.

Seconds later he yells, "Hey! Stop her! She has my wallet!"

I run down into the train station and hop over the turnstile. I hear the train roar as it rolls into the station, so I hurry down to the Bronx-bound train and scurry in just before the door closes.

Parkchester and the Upper East Side are very different. The houses in the Upper East Side are new and beautiful or old and classic. In Parkchester, there are nothing but tall apartment buildings that look older than Earth itself.

When we approach the last stop I get off, leave the train, and slowly drag home. As I walk I look in the man's wallet that I stole. His name is George Perez. He is fifty years old and married with four kids. There's a picture of him, his wife, and his kids; he seems happy. I scan the inside, looking for his cash. He has wads of it, in tens and twenties. I only take the cash, because I know the cards won't work if I try to use them; then I throw the rest of his stuff into a trash can.

As I approach the orphanage, I see a couple walking out with a little kid. Great, another kid gets adopted while I'm stuck in this hellhole. I've been here all my life, and none of the parents who have come have given me a second glance.

When I walk into the building, I'm greeted by the director, Sean. Despite being tall, having a deep voice that can soothe dogs, and his overall masculine physique, Sean is like everyone's mom. Always nice and nurturing, but strict and stern when needed. He's a person that everyone wishes they had in their life. Yet I usually ignore every word that comes out his mouth.

"Livia! Where were you?" he complains.

I sigh, knowing what he's going to say next. "I was out, okay?"

"How was your day?"

"Good," I respond instantaneously.

He pauses, then asks, "And what did you learn in school today?"

Shit! I forgot to take my bag today. At least if I act like I'm going to go to school, he won't lecture me as long. I look at his face and know that if I try to lie he'll know. I stay silent.

He sighs and facepalms himself. I know he's disappointed or whatever, but I'm seventeen now. I'm almost an adult. I know whether I should go to school. And I know I don't need to. They don't teach anything there, and they know that we are all going to end up with minimum-wage jobs serving burgers. So what's the point of going.

Right before he can say anything, Hennessy rushes into the room and jumps on me.

"Hi best friend! Did you miss me?"

I hug her back tightly, glad that she saved me from the lecture I was about to receive.

She giggles. "I guess you did!"

She doesn't even know the half of it.

MY (R)EVOLUTION

MARISSA QUENQUA

This is a piece I wrote for a slam poetry event; it was written during a Girls Write Now Workshop, actually. I was inspired to share my own personal story from childhood to college, and I am very proud to say that this piece was born out of that environment.

I grew up on Food Stamps
blue, beige, yellow, they were actual bills
back in the '90s, *billets*

Mom said, take French,
it is the language of the educated.
Could you live in this apartment? my mother asked,
a dark basement down a narrow set of stairs
it scared me
we could afford it
but at eight years old, I cried
and the look on my face made her say no.
My mother shopped at Kmart for herself
and at Macy's for me.
Sending the best face of our broken family forward
her backward
in shadows, holes in shoes, shirts, teeth
falling out
but I'm so smart
I can change the world.

I went to the most expensive college in the nation
because $40,000 a year meant nothing to me
it felt like a made-up number.
I believed that I deserved the best,
that my dream was worth it.
I just wanted to write in a place that didn't care about math grades
Tudor-style buildings fifteen kids in every class
published authors as my teachers.
The first night I spent at Sarah Lawrence
I cried myself to sleep listening to a cellist practice music
rising up through the floor.

That writing program ripped me apart
my still-beating heart like a fist, royal purple
raw and burning.
I called my mom.

I was no longer the English star I was in high school
In these classes, there were fifteen Marissas in a line.

"This is amazing," I said to her, "I know nothing, my professor
took my paper line by line and said
'Okay, but you didn't prove this,
cite this, go again.'"

Suddenly I was thrust among kids with lots of money
Max Whitney, whose parents owned The Whitney,
and that drunk girl Charlie who smoked too much and
wore a tie, whose grandfather
invented the Dixie Cup.

I am not one of them but I am not like my mother and
father, neither went to college or have any advice.
My mother, who dropped out of high school because her paper
on metaphysical reality and biofeedback was not well received.

She cleans houses, worked at McDonald's
her hopes are on my back knitted to me like a parcel
am I betraying her, being here? I spin in circles.

I cried on the phone then. Lost and afraid
my first year in college.
"But you want all of this from me and have no advice for how to get there!"

Not from you, my mother said.
For you.

ROMAISSAA BENZIZOUNE

YEARS AS MENTEE: 2
GRADE: Senior
HIGH SCHOOL: Hunter College High School
BORN: Queens, NY
LIVES: Queens, NY
PUBLICATIONS AND RECOGNITIONS: *The Toast,* Timothy McSweeney's Tendency; Scholastic Art & Writing: Silver Key (2), Gold Key (2), and Gold Key American Voices Nominee (2)

MENTEE'S ANECDOTE: *Robin doesn't know it yet but she'll be coming to college with me. After spending so much time together over the last two years, it is hard to imagine life without our weekly meetings. Robin has inspired and challenged me, and has helped me to feel comfortable taking risks in my writing. Thank you, Robin and Girls Write Now!*

ROBIN WILLIG

YEARS AS MENTOR: 2
OCCUPATION: Chief of Staff, Center for Reproductive Rights
BORN: Queens, NY
LIVES: Brooklyn, NY

MENTOR'S ANECDOTE: *Romaissaa and I are in our second year together and I can almost pinpoint exactly the moment when our relationship took off: when I realized that I didn't need to teach her anything, but rather to explore with her. She's such an extraordinary talent and thinker and I value her input on so many things. She has many rich rewards ahead of her, and I'm looking forward to seeing them come to life.*

HiJABi OR JiHADi?

ROMAISSAA BENZIZOUNE

This year I've been writing a monthly column about what it's like to be one of three hijabis in a New York City specialized public high school of about 1,200 students. I wrote this column after the Paris attacks in November 2015.

It's kind of awkward to "share" a religion with a band of killers who bomb capital cities and shoot up holiday parties in their free time.

It's not the frustrating awkwardness of falling on the school steps, or even the tragic awkwardness of wearing a denim-on-denim ensemble.

It's the kind of awkward where I actually ran away upon seeing a stack of newspapers on the sidewalk that described ISIS's attacks on the Stade de France. (To be fair, my phone had died and I was hopelessly lost; away from the *Washington Post* seemed as good a direction as any.)

Terrorism is a hard thing to outrun.

Hardly a moment has passed since then and already there is a new group of people to grieve for, even closer to home. A new collection of xenophobic Republican statements that I must make a point to debunk before the next horror hits.

You have to understand that my initial thought following these terror attacks was probably similar to yours: *Oh my God, these crazy fanatical Muslim terrorists.*

My second thought was more like one of those dreadful realizations you have after you wake up: *Wait, I am Muslim.*

How do I forget something like that for even a minute, you ask? I mean that's my whole *thing*, right? Like, hello, loud hijabi over here, victim of general American ignorance, self-appointed educator of both students and teachers (in a *gifted* school, no less), butt of all misconceptions, the fabulous star in her own sitcom life, etc.

Could it be possible that I, Hijabi in Plain Sight, am a secret Islamophobe?

I know that terrorism has no color or creed; that the word Islam itself means "peace"; that the Qur'an reads, "Whoever kills an innocent it is as if he has killed all mankind." And that ISIS has not only violated this basic tenet of Islam but dozens more. (What kind of Muslim bombs a mosque? You're not even supposed to wear your shoes in a mosque. I've seen someone get the stink-eye for reading the Qur'an too loudly.)

Despite all these facts, every time I hear the name of my own religion—and it's usually coming from the mouth of some politician who garbles the "s" into an omnipotent, multisyllabic "z"—I cringe. The Arabic meaning of the word bites at me like a personal mockery.

Peace. That's my religion. Literally. There are only so many times I can try and explain what the word *jihad* really means. There are only so many times I can try to explain the difference between a helpless refugee fleeing ISIS and an actual member of ISIS. Between beheading people and putting it up on YouTube and actually practicing Islam.

Like all Americans, I have processed the Islam/terrorist association. Unlike most Americans, however, I am at once the target audience and the monster to be feared.

This is an unpleasant state of being.

For the first few days after the Paris attacks, I kept myself in the dark. But there was no escaping the tragedy. When I tried to look up sites on which to illegally re-watch *The Mindy Project,* I found myself staring at the tiny black ribbon on Google's homepage. I tried to find humor in an episode of *Saturday Night Live* only to be a) met with a Paris-related intro, and b) reminded that Kristen Wiig was no longer part of the cast.

And when I went back to school the Monday after Paris, an exceptionally nice girl came up to me and hugged me.

I felt relief at first—*she understands*—followed by a twinge of annoyance.

Now, there are many reasons why I would like to be hugged. Surviving a weekend in rural Pennsylvania with no Wi-Fi. Consistently dropping the ball in gym class in front of a certain someone. Enduring the SAT (again) at a testing site where the sole hallway decoration was a laminated Tupac quote—something about dreams—peeling off the wall.

Note that international terrorism is not on that list.

The girl was being nice. But even sympathy propels me further and further away from normal, from the possibility that being American and being Muslim could someday overlap.

I am seventeen years old.

It is crushing to think about spending an entire life shapeshifting and explaining and overcompensating in a desperate attempt to prove that I'm okay. That I too am American. An entire life watching people watching me and wondering what they think, even though it is entirely possible that they don't care at all. My grief, my anxiety, my sense of alienation and obligation cannot be resolved with a brief "we stand with Paris" cold-open.

This column was supposed to be funny. It was supposed to be about gym class. But after the Paris attacks the plans changed. After San Bernardino they changed again.

What happens tomorrow?

PHOTOGRAPH

ROBIN WILLIG

This poem came from a writing prompt about a picture. "In this one you are . . ." It is about a young girl, a family member, who has grown distant. Working with young women reminds me how we all constantly evolve, no matter our age.

In this one you are still unformed
or maybe just unburdened.
Your head back, your hair wild and natural
before you came to think of the texture
as something to be fixed, treated.

Your cheeks are full, your eyes squinty with giggles,
Your mouth open.
I can almost feel the warmth of air as you let out
a single throaty laugh.

You are six.

Now, twenty-four.

What do you think when you see this,
propped next to a clear vase of pink marbles
on my windowsill?

That's not me, you will say

And I'll say nothing, but it's true. It's not you.

But it's the you I keep,
even though you despise it,
me,
everyone,
everything.

Your shoulders now hunched,
your eyes now low and dark.

I don't know how to find you
I don't know how to help you

I keep you on my sill and silently lure you back
Maybe you will alight when I'm not around
A robin returning home.

ALEXA BETANCES

YEARS AS MENTEE: 1
GRADE: Sophomore
HIGH SCHOOL:
Urban Assembly School
for Law & Justice
BORN: Moca, Dominican
Republic
LIVES: Queens, NY

MENTEE'S ANECDOTE: *Working with Jane has been a new experience. We've both learned a lot from each other and have developed a mentee and mentor bond.*

JANE R. PORTER

YEARS AS MENTOR: 1
OCCUPATION:
Freelance writer and
editor
BORN: Stamford, CT
LIVES: Brooklyn, NY

MENTOR'S ANECDOTE: *The poet Marianne Moore wrote, "The deepest feeling always shows itself in silence; not silence, but restraint." Alexa's writing reminds me of the value in such careful restraint. Working with her has made me discover how challenging and rewarding mining our emotions can be through writing, and how, often, less is more when it comes to capturing our deepest feelings.*

THE PHOTOGRAPH

ALEXA BETANCES

*Growing up without my father was something I always managed
to keep bottled in, until recently, when I found this photograph
of my father holding me in the hospital. The photograph led me
bring these feelings that were once tucked away to the surface.*

My mother lies on her hospital bed in the city of Moca in the Dominican
Republic. Weary and worn, she manages to raise her head to look at the
camera, the reflection of the bright flash on the soft, lemon-green-colored
walls in the background. There are two beds separated by a little white
table. My mother lies in one bed; my baby bag on the other. On the bed
beside her sits my father, one arm casually on the headboard, the other
arm cradling my baby body.

As I look at this photograph and my father's facial expression while
holding me, I don't see the big scary man who rarely shows emotion usually described in family stories. I see a different man—his tough exterior
gone. While my mother looks at the camera, my father looks down at
me, as if he is trying to grasp every detail of his firstborn. His eyes are so
relaxed—an expression so clear and vivid, still so unreadable.

What thoughts are running through his mind while he gazes down
at me? Is he wondering how my future will look? What my favorite food
would be? My interests, dislikes, friends? Will I prefer to wear skirts or
pants? Heels or sneakers? Will my hair be long or short? All the details
that create the person I am today. Did he know where this picture would
end up—stuffed deep in my drawer with the rest of the blurred memories

he left behind? Did he know he would only be present for three years of my life? Did he know I would be looking at this picture right now—almost sixteen years later, a sophomore in high school—wondering what went wrong? Would you have stopped it, Dad? Wished it away?

Most of my life, you were only a pile of old photographs and sudden, quick phone calls asking how I've been; then, with a nonchalant whisper, I'd say, "Good," knowing it would be different if you were here. The phone calls would have been face-to-face conversations, laughing and checking up on each other. Those old photographs would have been photographs of recent trips we took together—trips to the movies, to the beach, photographs of new experiences and memories being made all the time. They wouldn't be blurry because I was too young to remember them; they would be blurry because there would be too many of them to keep track.

Analyzing this photograph—my father's facial expression and the story behind it—used to be part of my daily routine. But over the years, this burden has turned into an object. A photograph that used to symbolize my father's inner thoughts is now as dull as a brick wall. The tears and empty feeling triggered by this image have turned into an unfamiliar feeling. It's not a careless feeling; instead, it has shaped my mindset. Something I have no control over should not be forgotten, but it also should not weigh me down. My grandma used to say, "Write it on a small piece of paper; fold it until it's too small to be folded again; hold it in your fist; blow on it, and that's it."

It disappears.

THE LOST PHOTOGRAPH

JANE R. PORTER

Alexa's piece, inspired by a photo taken after she was born, made me think back to the important photographs in my life and the people I've loved and lost. Picking up where her piece left off, I tried to focus on what remains when we lose someone we love.

It disappears. The memory. You don't write it down and it's gone. You don't capture it somehow—in film, in pixels, in words—and it evaporates. The day in September, when things for you changed forever, when everyone around you began the long, daily process of adjusting life to fit around the one they'd lost and strained to live without.

I would not understand it until seeing that pained look on your mother's face, your father's face. Your grandmother there, never believing she'd outlive her own child's child.

My friend gone. Still so alive in photographs. A grinning toddler in a summer dress, in a snow suit, in a tub. A college girl balancing a tequila glass full of milk and a giant chocolate chip cookie in each hand, smiling in my ratty college dorm. Smiling on the subway, my legs flung over yours. The two of us. Two grinning girls. And the lost photograph I think of often. Of us lying down, grown women making angels in the snow. The photograph exists somewhere. Lost, but not forgotten.

And your laughter, too, like a wind chime stirs, and stirs my memory. The image is lost, but your laughter is not. No cancer can eat that away. It does not disappear. Grows vivid and alive. It stirs when I feel a memory or moment slipping, when I am lost, when I need it most.

It's right there. Always.

LAURA ROSE CARDONA

YEARS AS MENTEE: 1
GRADE: Junior
HIGH SCHOOL:
Williamsburg Preparatory
High School
BORN: Brooklyn, NY
LIVES: Brooklyn, NY
**PUBLICATIONS AND
RECOGNITIONS:** Winner
of Dark Souls Story
Contest and First Place
in 2015 Flash Fiction
Blank Ink Contest

MENTEE'S ANECDOTE: *From the moment my mentor and I first were paired together, I knew this would be a very prosperous relationship. In the span of a few months, we have developed rich stories, while also enriching our individual novels. What I particularly enjoy is finding out that without any coordination whatsoever, we often find ourselves working with similar themes and characters. I think that coincidence alone stands as a testament to just how well Girls Write Now matches their mentees and mentors, as well as how much I truly enjoy working with my very own Kathleen Scheiner.*

KATHLEEN SCHEINER

YEARS AS MENTOR: 5
OCCUPATION:
Freelance writer
and editor
BORN: Biloxi, MS
LIVES: Brooklyn, NY

MENTOR'S ANECDOTE: *My mentee Laura and I meet weekly at Dun-Well Doughnuts in Brooklyn to work on our novels. But we also like listening to the customers around us, eavesdropping on their conversations and picking up information to use in other ways. It's our "character collecting." Our notebooks are fat with stories, but when we hear a particularly tasty tidbit, we have to write it down for later. We have so much material that Laura jokes our anthology pieces next year should just be about what we've overheard at the coffee shop.*

SNAKES IN MY BOOT

LAURA ROSE CARDONA

When thinking about what to write, I recalled the time when my mentor, Kathleen, noted that she found the fact of my house being entirely beige intriguing. Having never considered my personal feelings on the color, this piece was a journey for me in unraveling a world dominated by neutrality.

A big step of (r)evolution is knowing exactly what you're revolting against or escaping from. In my house, I am surrounded by the color beige. Everything is beige. The furniture is beige. The popcorn ceiling is beige. The roses have turned beige in their decaying wilt. Even the lighting the tungsten bulbs give off is a dull beige incandescence. It used to be a pristine shade. A gently neutral palette. Easy on the eyes, meant for relaxation and luxury. Now, it is anything but. For as I long as I can remember, my mother has used these colors in our home decor to prevent her chronic migraines. Vibrant colors send her head into seemingly ceaseless pains.

Unfortunately, I am the exact opposite. I've learned that in order to survive in my household, you have to muffle your colors. Cool down the warms, tone down the blues, hide the spectrum. My body has evolved into a prism, where all my hues are trapped within me, and who knew such natural beauties in the rainbow could be so painful? Ironic, considering the purpose of the neutral-colored house is to avoid pain. A false safe haven has been created, and the only question that I can ask is, How do I maintain my individuality in a house where everything is exactly alike? Where everything is beige?

This question lingers in my mind as I enter my apartment. A few meters away from me, the TV flickers almost inaudibly. The broadcast today is yet another report on an autistic child running from school, undetected. As the station suggests, this is supposed to be news, yet it is all too familiar. Running runs through my veins, my bloodline, my heritage. First it was my mother, who ran when she was a child. Then my father after her. Soon after, they convinced my sister, who ran on her own a number of times. After her birth came my brother, who's held his own share of abandonments. It seems like in order to belong to my family, you have to escape belonging. I don't wish to share the same fate as them, but I don't want to lose my spectrums to this muddling beige, either. How, then, can I escape escaping? And how can I possibly escape the color beige when that is the underlying skin tone of my entire family? How can you outrun something that runs through you?

Sitting in the IKEA foldout plastic chair that lays in front of my desk, I stare at the document on my computer screen. The dim illumination of the monitor allows for convenient and speedy typing. Yet the document still remains blankly white. Today, I intended to vent. To somehow allow the monochromatic tones of the black text and white digital sheet to release a plethora of colors. However, the fear of running cripples my fingers so that they, too, cannot run any longer. Writing is supposed to be my expression. The fantasy worlds that I create and tailor to my every need allow me to escape into a place of solace—a place where vibrant colors can thrive—but even my desk, a magnificent mahogany glaze, has been painted over in a dull beige. It pains me to look down at my own fingers, who are rebels simply trying to construct the foundation for my own mental warfare, dancing around the black keyboard that is encased in a chipping beige.

Because of this, I direct my attention to my nephew, hoping to distract myself. I listen in on a conversation taking place between him and his Sheriff Woody doll.

"There's a snake in my boot!" says Woody.

"Relax, Woody, there's no fucking snake in your boot," the five-year-old responds. I can't help but laugh. Slightly inappropriate, considering the fact that a child in kindergarten should in no way be as vulgar as he is; but still, it's a squeaky voice cursing out a talking doll. The laughter lasts far longer than the humor of the scene actually does. It spirals beyond my understanding, and far beyond my control. Almost like a deranged laughter erupting from the very crypt of my subconscious—yet I allow the shrill noise to continue, because at least insanity has colors, and if there's any place I belong to in this house, it's the madness. The uncontrollable laughs, the perpetually aggravated five-year-old, the paradoxes, and yes— the snakes in my boot.

HiPPiE HOUSE

KATHLEEN SCHEINER

This is a memory about a time when I unintentionally rebelled against my living situation and ended up evolving because of it. Looking back, I'm surprised by how something simple like a time change can transform everything.

I moved to Portland, Oregon, on July 4th—my own independence day, since it was the first time I had ever lived completely by myself, away from my family. I moved to a big house in Southeast Portland after traveling halfway across the United States, and ended up arriving right during the middle of the Rainbow Gathering, a big annual hippie festival. There were ten or so people camped in the house and its adjoining garage, an RV full of travelers in our driveway, and a broken-down van in the front yard that was a dead ringer for the Mystery Machine.

The washer and dryer were in my basement room, so even when I wanted to get away I was never truly alone, with people knocking on my door wanting to wash their clothes. It took me months to find a job in Portland, and then the only one I could find was for the third shift, from 8 P.M. to 8 A.M. It was a rocky transition going to living at night instead of during the day like most people.

I had such a bad stretch of insomnia during those first three days—no sleep at all—that I started to hear voices in the electronic whir of streetlights and in empty bus shelters. An old woman's voice yelling, "Get out of my house!" and a hairdresser gossiping about her grown daughter, saying, "I told her never to go back to him, blackening her eye like that." But then I made the jump, sleeping the days away and working at night.

I kept the same schedule on my days off, and those nights were magical—a different universe from the rest of the hippie house. Everybody slept while I was awake, and my cat and I prowled the house alone. I spent as much time in the bathroom as I wanted, taking hour-long baths and reading without anybody banging on the door. I made coffee at four in the morning and sat at the kitchen table for hours, writing in my journal, reading comics and books on color theory. Sometimes I'd go dump things in the backyard compost heap and hear the secret sounds of animals burrowing in the waste, see their eyes flashing in the darkness.

I'd watch daylight come up on the back steps, birds winging into the yard to snap up berries and grapes, and I admired the way they moved, like they knew me and we were having a secret meeting. When I first heard the early-morning stirrings of people waking up, I disappeared down into my basement room—spray-painted silver—and worked on my art projects or beautifying my room until I grew sleepy.

I had my own parallel universe in the hippie house, where I lived by myself with my own rules while sharing a space with more people than I ever had before in my life.

MARYCLARE CHINEDO

YEARS AS MENTEE: 1
GRADE: Sophomore
HIGH SCHOOL: Bronx Lighthouse Charter School
BORN: Bronx, NY
LIVES: Bronx, NY

MENTEE'S ANECDOTE: *"Okay, Maryclare! Tell me what works and what doesn't work." Or, "Okay, Maryclare! Time to read what you wrote." If we could go a session without Morayo saying one of the above to me, I would throw a party. She knows I don't like giving myself feedback and that I'm shy to read my work, but she ALWAYS tells me to do those things! Her intent isn't to annoy me (I hope), but to help me grow as a writer and an aspiring author.*

MORAYO FALEYIMU

YEARS AS MENTOR: 4
OCCUPATION: Senior Program Manager, Peer Health Exchange
BORN: Miami, FL
LIVES: Elizabeth, NJ

MENTOR'S ANECDOTE: *Maryclare's bold vision and imaginative spirit inspire me to take my characters out of their ho-hum experiences and plunge them into new worlds.*

GONE BUT NOT FORGOTTEN

MARYCLARE CHINEDO

The only time I got to see him was when my family and I traveled to Nigeria every once in a while. When he passed, I was sad because I felt like I didn't have enough time to show him my care. I wrote this for him. Hope you enjoy!

Tribute to my Grandpa /You showed us love

He was the main man, onye m ji k were di.
Papa, it is so painful to know that you are gone.
All the good plans we had for you have become a dream. You were a great man, a role model, kind-hearted, free-spirited, loving, with a contagious smile. You showed us love.

You told me stories that warmed my heart.
Remember the one about you climbing the palm tree?
Yea, I remember that too.
The one about you dedicating a day to help everyone in the village was a pretty good one too.
My absolute favorite is the story about how you made my mom feel welcomed into your home.
That one always puts a smile on my face!

It hurts me that I did not get a chance to clean you, wash you,
and change your soiled clothes, as I would have loved to,
but it is consoling knowing that you know that if not for distance,

I would have done that and even more.
I have so many questions but no answer.
One of the questions would have been, "Why now?"
Less than a year after our house burned down, God took you away from us.
I would have also asked God, "Why?"
But I was taught not to ask God why he does the things that he does.
I was hoping that the news would turn out to be a lie;
I asked God to wake you up when you heard the voices of your children who ran home to the sad news, but it did not happen.

I wish heaven had visiting hours.

You have left a void in us that no one can fill.
You have also left memories that are everlasting.
It is so hard to come home and not find you coming out to greet me with a heartwarming smile.
It is so hard not to hear you giggle and make jokes.
Coming home will no longer be the same.
You showed us love.

I promise you, I will tell our children's children about you, and how awesome you are!
I promise, I will live up to the promises I made to you before I left Nigeria.
I promise, I will use all the advice you gave me, to the best of my knowledge, in your honor.

However, I bless the Lord who made it possible for me to know you, one of his living angels.
Since it pleases him to take you away from us now, I pray that it will also please him that you see him face to face.
I pray that he will grant you rest in his bosom until we meet again.
We love you, but Jesus loves you most.
Rest in peace, Nwoke Obioma.
Until we meet again.
I love you, Papa!
Go in peace until we meet to part no more.

REMNANTS

MORAYO FALEYIMU

This is fiction masquerading as poetry: I wanted to submit a piece that examined the same topic as Maryclare's—loss—but from a different angle. In my tale, loss is experienced through the objects, not the people, that are left behind.

Every time you move, you leave something behind:
old, sticky fingerprints on the refrigerator door
a carpet stained red
your blue anorak crumpled under the stairs
notes from Margaret, passed during Earth Science class
you regret none of these—except for the anorak on certain days.
You tote the memories from house to house. As the years pass, they begin
to tumble, unannounced, out of their boxes and suitcases. They crowd the
potatoes from the pantry and replace the musty baby clothes in attic. Once
you found a memory, quivering, in your mother's teacup. It floated filmy
and unsubstantial. Before you could file it away, it burst—the thin skin of
milk in an overheated pot.

ALYSSA COLON

YEARS AS MENTEE: 1
GRADE: Senior
HIGH SCHOOL: Williamsburg Preparatory High School
BORN: Brooklyn, NY
LIVES: Staten Island, NY
PUBLICATIONS AND RECOGNITIONS: Scholastic Art & Writing Awards: Gold Key, Silver Key; first place in a poetry contest for a poem titled "Day One" that focuses on ending domestic abuse relationships between youths

MENTEE'S ANECDOTE: *In my one year in this program, I have been lucky enough to have had three mentors. My first mentor, Lacy, definitely pushed me out of my comfort zone and challenged my writing. She taught me strong eye contact, which enabled me to speak with confidence more than before. My second mentor, Emily (pictured above), taught me to really believe in my work and to be my own best critic. She's also taught me the art of being adorably quirky in the best way possible. My third mentor is teaching me how to strengthen my writing. I've gained a lifetime of experience.*

EMILY YOST

YEARS AS MENTOR: 1
OCCUPATION: Senior Program Coordinator, Girls Write Now
BORN: Fitchburg, MA
LIVES: Brooklyn, NY

MENTOR'S ANECDOTE: *Mentoring Alyssa has been a top highlight of my first year working with Girls Write Now. Alyssa is a poetic talent with a philosophy on life that is beyond her years. I'm honored to have had the opportunity to be a part of her writing process and will miss laughing together while sharing stories. We aren't supposed to have favorite mentees . . . but I can't deny that Alyssa is one of mine! She has sincerely been a shining star at Girls Write Now, and I have no doubt that she will continue to shine in all of her future endeavors.*

INSTITUTIONALIZED

ALYSSA COLON

My personal revolution is learning it's okay to be different. In being different, I found myself. I heard the quote, "I was born with a pen where my mouth should be," and found it to be an apt description. I'm learning to wield the madness in words and create art.

It's me
I'm paranoid
Why do I do this to myself
It's all in my head
None of those hurtful things
Have been silently said

No no no
I'm not crazy
Aww look at those pretty daisies
No
I saw her bladed eyes
Gosh
They're dark from all the dreams that had died

Can you stop pretending
Like you're not crazy
The mad hatter has died

And put his personality in your head
Just Shut Up
And sit down
Wear your metal and leather crown
My hands are nowhere to be found
Damn it
My mind is bound

Is this how it all ends
With the word insanity
Stamped on my head
Rip it off! Rip it off!
My eyes in a box
To the ground they will be sent
Mmm . . . the taste of metallic corn syrup
Feels good against my lips

SAMORI COVINGTON

YEARS AS MENTEE: 3
GRADE: Junior
HIGH SCHOOL: Millennium Brooklyn High School
BORN: Brooklyn, NY
LIVES: Brooklyn, NY

MENTEE'S ANECDOTE: *Brooke has opened my eyes to a ton of new things this year. I was completely out of my comfort zone with writing this anthology piece because I've never written journalism, let alone satire journalism, before, but she challenged me and I think it worked out perfectly. This writing piece is revolutionary for me because as a writer my writing genres are expanding.*

BROOKE BOREL

Years as Mentor: 3
Occupation: Freelance science journalist
Born: Topeka, KS
Lives: Brooklyn, NY
Publications and Recognitions: First book, *Infested: How the Bed Bug Infiltrated Our Bedrooms and Took Over the World,* published in April 2015

MENTOR'S ANECDOTE: *Samori has a sly sense of humor, and I always look forward to brainstorming new ideas or working through ongoing pieces with her. I'm primarily a writer in my own work, so taking on the role of editor and adviser is always an interesting and welcome stretch for me. It's so fun to try out new genres, too, and to watch how her writing—and my editing, for that matter—adapts to new challenges.*

BREAKiNG NEWS!

SAMORI COVINGTON

This piece was inspired by a New York Times *article describing hoax news about monsters in China—it's a satirical news item that pretends one of those monsters is real and living in the US. It was a revolution in my writing, because it played with a favorite genre in a new format.*

**MYSTERIOUS CREATURE FOUND IN CONNECTICUT FOREST IDENTIFIED
LOCAL TEEN SNAPS PICTURE AS MONSTER ESCAPES**

Croxx Falls: A popular local teen hangout has been harboring an unwelcoming party pooper.

Yesterday, a senior at Cross High School named Ivy Mayweather stumbled upon an unknown creature in Lindsay Woods. Mayweather was invited to attend a back-to-school party in the woods, three miles from the city, at around 8 P.M. But when she arrived there was no one there.

"I thought they stood me up," she says. The next thing she remembers is walking towards a cliff near where the party should have been and seeing something with pale skin sitting on the cliff's edge.

"I felt frightened but intrigued at the same time," she says. "At first I only got to see the backside of the monster, but when I went to take a picture with the flash on it turned around."

When Croix Falls officer Billy Bob arrived on the scene, he found feces scattered throughout the woods, along with small footprints. "I found it really strange because this has been the third incident reported, but I never bothered to come and check it out," Bob says.

The photographs that Mayweather was able to take were the first-ever of the creature.

According to Dr. Joe Ferdinand, a professor of monstrology at Yale University in New Haven, the feces were the largest piece of evidence used in this case to help classify the creature. When asked what, exactly, monstrology is, he replied, "It's the study of monsters, you silly goose."

Ferdinand compared the DNA of the unknown creature with the DNA of other animals and discovered that the monster was *Homo Squashian,* also called a nightcrawler. Ferdinand says that the discovery was life-changing, and that he plans to build a research center to track down the monster. "My only wish," he says, "is that I could have seen it in person."

Mayweather picked up some of the feces herself, having accidentally stepped in it, and had to surrender her favorite pair of shoes to evidence. She says, "I will never go to the woods again."

BLIND ITEMS!

BROOKE BOREL

I was inspired by Samurai's satirical news piece and decided to write some old-fashioned gossip column blind items—but with a sci-fi twist. Writing fiction always feels revolutionary to me, and makes me stretch as a writer, because I am primarily a journalist.

GALAXY NEWS BLIND ITEMS!

Which Martian Denizen Blew NASA's Water Budget On Space Rocks?

This alien astronaut, originally from the outer planets but hired by NASA as a researcher on Mars, has been seen transferring outrageous amounts of Earth dollars in exchange for rare space rocks in watering holes across the galaxy. Last week, an anonymous source claims they overheard the astronaut making frantic travel plans to Jupiter's red spot district. "He said the water on Mars was gonna dry up really soon because he'd dipped into the funds too many times," the source said.

Which AI Company Is Under Investigation For Sneaking Spy Cams In Its Helper Bots?

A recent leaked e-mail from the World Organization of Robot Law suggested that a popular artificial intelligence company may need to recall millions of helper bots because of a security breach. The email doesn't name the company, but does reference that a rogue employee—who has since apparently gone on the lam—snuck SpyCams into the right eyeball of the bots in order to collect private moments and sensitive data from users and their families.

Who is The Mayor's Mysterious Mutant Boyfriend?

Late last night, New York City's Mayor Martha 74 was seen slipping out of the back of the Clone Club, a popular mutant hangout on the Lower East Side Level Four. According to several sources, Mayor 74 was linking arms with a young centaur. The canoodling couple hopped into a waiting Air Taxi and flew off to parts unknown.

MEDELIN CUEVAS

YEARS AS MENTEE: 1
GRADE: Sophomore
HIGH SCHOOL: H.E.R.O. High
BORN: Santiago, Dominican Republic
LIVES: Bronx, NY

MENTEE'S ANECDOTE: *Before Girls Write Now was introduced to me, I was a very shy and skeptical person. I would always put myself down because I'm used to experiencing that type of behavior in school. When I went the Girls Write Now office, the atmosphere was so pleasant and cozy. This feeling I had felt so foreign (in a good way); my heart did what it most desired. I started to be very interactive without acting so awkward. For me this was an evolution, because I changed as a young, unique woman.*

REBECCA VOLPE

YEARS AS MENTOR: 1
OCCUPATION: English teacher, Bronx Community College
BORN: Bronx, NY
LIVES: Bronx, NY

MENTOR'S ANECDOTE: *Medelin shared some beautiful memoirs with me describing life in high school today and growing up as a child in the Dominican Republic. She painted vivid images of this time in her life in her writing, which I have enjoyed being a part of so much.*

I'M FINALLY HOME

MEDELIN CUEVAS

Everyone evolves every day—mentally, physically, or intellectually. Every time we have that moment of clarity, we tend to embrace that moment and keep it in our memory forever. The reason we do that is because we think we've changed as a person. Now that's a (r)evolution.

I remember the smell of palm trees and coconut shavings when I got off the plane in Santiago in the Dominican Republic. It was nine years earlier that my family had decided to create a new chapter in a new country. I never imagined the day I would go back to my people, where I belong.

As we walked out of the airport, I saw my Uncle Carlos (that's his middle name; his first name is very long and very difficult to pronounce). He still had the same white, crooked smile and the same motorcycle I used to ride on.

The first thing I did was hug him tight, leaving teardrops on his shirt.

"Te extrañé mucho," he said, making me cry even more.

After our long welcome home hugs, we climbed inside his friend's Jeep. It only had five seats, and we were six in total (including his new wife, Ana, who he mentioned a lot in his letters). As in any family tradition (or is it my family tradition?), the middle child must sit in the middle seat. But I kind of broke that rule because I wanted to see my house.

As we got ourselves comfy (well, tried), my uncle put an old mixtape he made for my mom, titled *"Mi gente está allá,"* in the stereo. The music started playing, and everyone was doing a little dance in the jammed seat—except for me. I was looking at the stars and remembering the times I had before leaving: running after the ducks in my backyard, wearing my grandmother's jewelry and heels to make myself look older, the early mornings when I would wake up before the rooster woke the rest of the family and go to the top of the little mountain near our house just to see my grandfather cut the coconuts off the trees.

Snapping myself back to reality, I noticed all the small, metal shacks that looked like parts from the Tin Man in "The Wizard of Oz." After a couple more metal houses, we finally came to a stop at the white concrete house that was decorated with beautiful tropical flowers. While my uncle was reminding the family about the family rules, I hopped out of the Jeep and admired the house for a few seconds. I smelled the fresh air and told myself, "I'm finally home, where I belong."

8 THOUGHTS ON WHY NORA DOESN'T LIKE THE CANARIES IN HER GARDEN

REBECCA VOLPE

I wrote this piece with a dear friend in mind. I was interested in exploring the way the world sees her and the way she navigates the world. She is strong and bold and exquisite but quiet.

1. She's tired of being compared to them, with her soft quick movements and fragile, high-pitched voiced.

2. They have no sharp lines or impressive angles, only round-
   ness and fluff.
3. They wake up too early. She does, too.
4. Their indecisive nature mirrors her own; branch to ground,
   ground to bench, bench to tree.
5. She's powerful.
6. She's small.
7. They're small. Small and frenetic and wearing the wrong
   outfit to the party.
8. The canaries arrived by mistake and stayed on. She was
   given no choice.

DENAJAH DEDRICK

YEARS AS MENTEE: 1
GRADE: Senior
HIGH SCHOOL:
The Young Women's
Leadership School
East Harlem
BORN: Bronx, NY
LIVES: Bronx, NY

MENTEE'S ANECDOTE: *When I first met Maryellen, I was nervous that we wouldn't connect well because we are both reserved. But during our first session, we had a stimulating discussion about ourselves and we opened up to one another. We were able to connect because we share similar life paths: we are both vegetarians and have had surgery. We learn from each other, and she helps me grow in the craft of writing. To help me with creativity, we structured our sessions so that when we begin we find writing prompts online, which gets me out of my comfort zone in writing.*

MARYELLEN TIGHE

YEARS AS MENTOR: 1
OCCUPATION:
Reporter, Debtwire
BORN: Council Bluffs, IA
LIVES: New York, NY

MENTOR'S ANECDOTE: *When Denajah and I started meeting I thought we would be discussing journalism and reporting. But our weekly meetings often delve into book recommendations, which has opened my eyes to a world of women writers that were not part of my high school experience. Denajah also has an appreciation of poetry and the rhythm of it, which I've learned from, and that now carries over into how I structure my creative writing.*

A LIFE EXPOSED

DENAJAH DEDRICK

My revolution derives from how my struggles will prepare me for a brighter future. This piece is a reflection of how my pain, hardships, and burdens have guided me toward a fulfilling relationship with God.

My life is fragmentary. It is an identifiable yet indescribable shadow that follows me to no end. I have chased the wind trying to find myself. Why do I always fall short in the endeavor to acquire what I want for myself in my profound visions for prosperity and success? Are my dreams not grand and noble? Am I not destined to achieve perfection—what I rendered as my fate? Perhaps I am blind to the promptings of God and how He is revealing Himself to me. Perhaps my life needs to be redefined so that I can see the world with different eyes. No, not perhaps—I am instilled with the potent conviction that it must be done. My comfort has derived from my glass house, and now that it's shattered my house must be rebuilt with cement. But how do I carry this out? How do I become more receptive to God's promises and fulfill His will instead of my own? How do I let go of me?

There is something so ineffably disheartening about dreams unachieved. High school was where all my dreams died. All my reserves were broken down, and I wore vulnerability and brokenness not only on my countenance but also on my sleeve. Going into high school, I thought I could work hard, and that work ethic was somehow crystallized into my nature as a talent and strength. I had graduated middle school as valedictorian.

When I entered high school I thought that I would reach the pinnacle of achievement and new heights—success that I had never dreamed possible. Instead, I was faced with a harsh reality. With more demanding work, I did not achieve the results that I had strived for. In my junior year I had scoliosis surgery and returned to school before I was emotionally ready; consequently, I submitted to mediocrity many times. Despite all my efforts to heal what was damaged, I was unable to move forward and progress where my grades were concerned because I was still emotionally and spiritually distressed.

My burdens continuously gained momentum each year that I moved up the high school ladder. My spirit was weakened because of waning confidence, overwhelming procrastination, and my inability to sustain friendships. Now, as a senior in high school, as I reflect on my decay in these past few years I want a radical change that bursts at the seams with life.

Should I graduate to vegan? Should I exchange my naturality for straight hair? Is it my destiny to be a journalist? How do I transcend my loneliness? When will I gain the competence to speak without fear? When will I work hard in school with unwavering tenacity? There are a litany of life decisions and plans that I don't know how to approach. Everything that transpired in high school is so stained and tarnished; I don't want my future in college and beyond to follow suit. I am tired of being stuck and broken. My heart yearns to be liberated from all the stumbling blocks and afflictions of yesterday. I have the potent conviction that my life will not change fortuitously.

I need God like I need my lungs because I need to live a life that is meaningful and has a profound purpose. My spiritual life has taken a drastic turn. I now have a deeper awareness of God, and through osmosis I am learning how my story ingeniously connects to His life plans for me. What does it mean to depend wholeheartedly on God? This is the ultimate question that I am confronted with each day, and it is revealed through my actions. Through despair, pain, affliction, or sadness, I must trust God and believe that He can gracefully give me the promises of rebirth and liberation that I need.

SCREECH OWL

MARYELLEN TIGHE

This piece was inspired by a hike. It's about freedom and recovery, and how sometimes doing what you've always done can be revolutionary.

"Whooo whooo," said the small owl.

The calls of other owls echoed around the valley. If the small owl turned its head it could hear the river flow by, out the window and down the hill, at the bottom of the valley.

The small owl stretched out its wings. The left came up strongly. The right moved awkwardly up to the wall of a small cage. It was supported by a rod, and bright-colored wrap. The wings stretched across the small cage. The owl moved its wings up and down. And up and down.

By day the owl dozed, and the people moved the owl's hurt wing to help it heal.

Now the owl was alert, looking from side to side.

"Whoo whoo."

And the owl waited.

One day the people took the splint off the small owl. And the small cage was opened and the owl walked out into a bigger cage.

That night the owl was farther away from the window. It could see the moon through the big windows, but it couldn't hear the river at the bottom of the valley.

The small owl flew from side to side of the medium-size cage. The small owl watched for the mice that sometimes ran across the floor of the room by the window with the moon.

"Whooo whooo."

And the owl waited.

One day the people took the owl out and they put it back into the small cage. And the small cage with the small owl was carried outside and put in a small car. A small car full of people that drove down the road.

When they stopped, the people and the small cage and the small owl piled out of the small car. The owl could hear that it was closer to the river at the bottom of the valley.

The people opened the small cage and the owl walked out into a giant cage. The giant cage had a tree and water and was open to the wind.

The small owl flew up to a tree branch and alighted. The people smiled and exchanged high fives.

And the small owl dozed in the giant cage.

"Whooo whooo."

Night came and the small owl watched for a mouse to walk across the floor of the giant cage.

The owl dozed during the day, when people came by, and hunted in its cage at night. Where it could hear the river at the bottom of the valley.

And the owl waited.

One afternoon a person left open the door that they usually entered to bring in water or food or new leaves.

And the small owl walked out of the cage. The people smiled and exchanged high fives.

And the small owl flew down to the river at the bottom of the valley.

JODI-ANN FEARON

YEARS AS MENTEE: 1
GRADE: Sophomore
HIGH SCHOOL:
Collegiate Institute for
Math & Science
BORN: Bronx, NY
LIVES: Bronx, NY
**PUBLICATIONS AND
RECOGNITIONS:**
Scholastic Art & Writing
Award: Silver Key

MENTEE'S ANECDOTE: *My mentor and I have come a long way since September, and we've both grown, not only as writers but as women. She's helped me cross new genres in my writing, and has taught me to loosen up and step out of my comfort zone. She's been there to remind me it's okay to make mistakes.*

JENNIFER ROWE

YEARS AS MENTOR: 1
OCCUPATION:
Teaching assistant
BORN: Miami, FL
LIVES: New York, NY

MENTOR'S ANECDOTE: *Working with Jodi-Ann has helped me to rekindle my creative side in writing. We always have a good time during our meetings writing silly and serious prompts. I was pleasantly surprised (and happy!) when she told me she'd received a Silver Key from the Scholastic Art & Writing Awards for her poem. It was her first time working with poetry and stepping out of her regular writing comfort.*

FRAY

JODI-ANN FEARON

This piece is very personal and I hold it close to my heart. My grandmother has Alzheimer's and it affects my and my family's everyday lives. I decided to attempt to write this poem in her scrambled, but lovely, mind.

Twisting and turning, nightmares churning from my insanity
I'm playing games with my mentality
My dark side and I, two forces in one
Someone—please, call the referee
It's getting harder to see
I mean breathe
Behind my clouded mind
It's hard to find clarity
Who are you? Where am I?
Friend help, I'm on the brink of losing me, the girl I once used to be
I can't sleep
When there's someone out after me
With my face, and my name
I'm not safe, I'm not brave
Give me space—no, come closer
Give my life some social order
And have a piece of my mind
See, underneath peace of mind

Cobwebs and flies unwind
To show the depths of my disorder
And not to mention,
my comprehension is at an all-time low
I want to leave this place but I don't know where to go
I don't know how much of this I can take anymore
When there's no cure
But there's an end
I need you now
Please hold my hand
Remember who I used to be
And cherish all the love in me
I love you, Jodi-Ann.

THINGS i WON'T APOLOGIZE FOR

JENNIFER ROWE

I wrote this poem during our Poetry Workshop after our guest speaker spoke about writing raw and honestly. I wanted to express my feelings on street harassment and its degradation towards women. This is my response to those men who find it okay to catcall.

I won't apologize for your ignorance and blatant disrespect
for me as a woman when I see you breaking neck

With your slithering eyes creeping and prowling as if I don't exist—
especially when a man says my skirt is asking for it

I won't apologize for these uneducated fools
who think it's okay to say and act as you do

I am not your baby girl or your sweet thing
I am not an object wrapped with a pretty bow and string

I won't apologize for your disgrace as a man
it seems you've forgotten how it is that you stand?

Remember a woman like me was carrying you on her back
and pushed you out through pain and love before that

I won't apologize for your clouded views and thoughts
and for all of the nasty aggression you were taught

I won't apologize for taking this peaceful walk down the street
and I especially won't apologize for being the phenomenal woman that is me

So next time you see me walking by with my head held high
and you try to give me that leering side-eye

Just know that I won't apologize
for being the woman that is Me.

JADA FITZPATRICK

YEARS AS MENTEE: 2
GRADE: Senior
HIGH SCHOOL:
Preparatory Academy
for Writers
BORN: Waterbury, CT
LIVES: Queens, NY
**PUBLICATIONS AND
RECOGNITIONS:** *New York
Times* College Scholarship,
Scholastic Art & Writing
Award: Honorable Mention

MENTEE'S ANECDOTE: *My senior year has resulted in the most invigorating moments ever. I won a* New York Times *Scholarship. This will allow me to have an internship at* The New York Times *during the summer, as well as a new laptop and scholarship money. Linda has been at my side through every step of the college application process, applying for scholarships, and even having relaxing downtime at museums and concerts. I am excited at the prospect of beginning a new chapter of my life in college and to have her by my side through all that is yet to come.*

LINDA KLEINBUB

YEARS AS MENTOR: 3
OCCUPATION:
Teaching artist trainee,
Community Word Project
BORN: Maspeth, NY
LIVES: Queens, NY
**PUBLICATIONS AND
RECOGNITIONS:** Recently,
The New York Observer &
Yahoo! Beauty

MENTOR'S ANECDOTE: *Jada continues to grow as both a writer and confident young woman. Her positive attitude always amazes me. She triumphantly overcame a turbulent year, which included a move that requires her to travel two hours each way to school. I love spending time with her. We enjoy taking in everything the city has to offer. A recent highlight this year has been reading* The Curious Incident of the Dog in the Nighttime *and then seeing the play. I know Jada will excel at college next fall. She has become more confident, and our time together has yielded a (r)evolution.*

FITZPATRICK

JADA FITZPATRICK

*This piece is inspired by those who continuously contemplate
their identities and histories.*

My last name is Fitzpatrick: Irish in origin and a product of European
imperialism and enslavement.
Meaning: "The one of noble birth."

The result: an African American with no knowledge of her lineage,
permanently detached from it due to the diaspora,
African blood spilled across the land, and absorbed into the world's soil.
The only remaining marks are images of shackled ancestors.

She said,
"My family could've been from the plantations of the red hills of Alabama."
She sees her distant cousin Niecey,
back bent over, her struggle simply Americana;
a spectacle to look back on but never reflect on.
"Move forward," society said, "that brutal part of your history is done."

Yes, Black history exists outside of slavery,
but who can live up to more than that
when you live in similar circumstances presently?

"The one of noble birth"; so full of irony,
we are all human beings,

but it seems like humans being themselves
have less to do with your character
and everything to do with your color.
That fact remains as transparent
as the Caribbean waters that brought us here.

Fitzpatrick—
sometimes burns in my ears
as ignorant beings question my blackness,
becoming willing to erase it completely.
"You don't look black. Are you mixed?"
my doctor once asked of me.
It's sort of blasphemy
to erase that vital part of me completely.
It'd be easy to claim I were Hispanic,
after all, I'm technically half Puerto Rican, but they're just like us.
It's easy to say I'm a quarter Indian and Irish
and list every facet of my ethnic background, but why beat around the bush?
Why deny my blackness?

Fitzpatrick—

The last name that might work to my advantage
because when employment calls, they'll be expecting an Irish woman,
not someone with melanin.
A facet of my identity that gets me through the doors
pushes me to prove my worth.

Fitzpatrick I hear loud and clear.

Fitzpatrick, Fitzpatrick the name I hold near.

Fitzpatrick, Fitzpatrick
"Yes massa, I'll be good"
Fitzpatrick—a name that holds so much history, still misunderstood.

GEMINI TWINS

LINDA KLEINBUB

*I was inspired to write about my experience working with Jada
for two years. She was reluctant to enter the Princeton Summer
Journalism Scholarship program, which she won, resulting in
an incredible ten-day experience at Princeton. This led her to
applying for and winning a* New York Times *Scholarship.*

Two strangers meet.
First impression:
Jada is petite, demure, soft-spoken.
I notice first her hair, bright, bold,
crimson red, curly, going somewhere.
Instantly we bond,
lefties, born in June, Gemini twins,
quick-thinking, multitasking women,
we inspire each other.

I teach her lessons learned,
"Don't be afraid to write something bad.
Revision is a process.
If you write nothing, there is nothing to revise."
Jada teaches me, "Determination—
to focus on your dreams,
not get distracted by the world around you."

On a chilly January afternoon
she speaks in a subtle, mousy voice,
says, "There's this Princeton
Summer Journalism Scholarship program
for high school juniors, I probably won't get into it . . ."

"Do you have to pay to enter?" I ask.

"No," she says, shaking her head.

"So what do you have to lose?"

She shrugs.

"I recently heard an interview with Tracy Morgan.

He was asked, 'How did you feel when you had to audition

for Lorne Michaels for *Saturday Night Live?*

That must have been the most terrifying thing you ever did.'

Tracy replied, 'No, I had nothing to lose.

I was broke and all I had to do

was make Lorne laugh.'"

Jada smiles, nods.

"We got this," I tell her.

"We'll send in your best work."

She smiles, we high-five.

We have a mission.

JADAIDA GLOVER

YEARS AS MENTEE: 1
GRADE: Junior
HIGH SCHOOL: High School for Medical Professions
BORN: Brooklyn, NY
LIVES: Brooklyn, NY
PUBLICATIONS AND RECOGNITIONS: Scholastic Art & Writing Award: Honorable Mention

MENTEE'S ANECDOTE: *Kate pushes me to challenge myself, whether it's in writing or academically. She has been a listening ear when I needed it, and a motivator when she saw it was necessary. Kate reminds me to never put myself in a box that others may create for me.*

KATE JACOBS

YEARS AS MENTOR: 4
OCCUPATION: Senior Editor, Roaring Brook Press/ Macmillan Children's Publishing Group
BORN: Grand Rapids, MI
LIVES: Brooklyn, NY

MENTOR'S ANECDOTE: *I like to tell Jadaida that she's a woman of mystery. When you first meet her, she's all smiles and friendliness—she's the social butterfly of the Girls Write Now Workshop!—but after she shared her body of poetry with me, I could tell that Jadaida had depths and insights beyond her bubbly personality. It's been my great privilege that she's willing to share this mysterious side of herself with me. When she discusses the inspiration behind her work, when she tells me what she's excited about and afraid of—that's when I know this woman is going to change the world.*

LETTERS FROM THE HEART

JADAIDA GLOVER

My favorite book of all time is The Color Purple. *The relationship between Celie and Shug amazes and confuses me. Shug has love but doesn't truly understand how to return it, while Celie has never been properly loved but understands it. This is my initial response to these two characters.*

Dear Celie

You probably won't get this letter but i needed to know
How did you know Shug was the one?
What made you save all of that beauty and all of that love for a woman
your husband still stuck on?
Cause when y'all first met
After you washed away the makeup
After the music stopped being played
And she stood before you naked and frail
She insulted you
How did you feel when the woman whose picture you idolized
Called you ugly?
Did your bones go weak?
Did your heart just break?
Celie you should have locked the dead bolt on your ribs
Cause love is not easy and i doubt Shug Avery is capable of returning it
Don't think I'm unappreciative

I understand she gave you your body back
And showed you that God is in everything you see
But Shug is selfish and thinks of me me me
Her loving you was an accident
And she still took advantage
Slept with different men and climbed in bed next to you with scattered and missing pieces
I can't watch this anymore
Cause Celie your love is too pure to be thrown back in your face
Like half-scattered notes
Signed
Lover girl

Dear lover girl

I love with open arms
Rose petal lips
And mahogany skin
What about my love for Celie upsets the ocean in your throat?
Her smile is like water
Skin like silk
I love her because of the moon in her mouth
I love her because of the stars in her eyes
And every time i see her i know God believes in second chances
Did you know she cried when she read your letter?
She retreated so deep into her soul you would've thought she belonged in the spirit world
When she drained herself i ran her a bath of orange mint jasmine and honey
And while she soaked away the venom in your words i braided my melody into her
Do you know she shook like she was having a seizure when i touched her?
I felt the atoms shift in her body
So under the cover of darkness i outlined the lips of my goddess and kissed each of her eyelids
And when she stopped shaking i placed a magnolia behind her ear

She smiled so bright the moon disappeared.
Never worry about my love for Celie
She is my color purple
Signed
Shug

WHEN i WAS BORN, I HAD RED HAiR

KATE JACOBS

This piece started as a rumination on The Color Purple *by Alice Walker, and became my reflection on colors in general and the color purple in particular.*

When I was born, I had red hair. Just a fuzz on the top of my head that didn't really start to grow out until I was over a year old, but everyone in my family agreed it was distinctly red.

When I was a teenager, I liked to wear green. I decided that I couldn't wear red, or even worse, pink—it would clash with my hair. Which was just as well. I was never a girly girl, never good at things like makeup or fashion or even flirting with boys. So I wore green, and blue, and black, and brown. Colors that wouldn't draw attention to my body, because I was too tall, too fat, too ugly.

When I became an adult, my hair turned brown. Or rather, all my life it had slowly been turning darker than the light red fuzz I was born with, but when I reached my twenties, I realized I could no longer say it was red. When I reached my thirties, I started wearing all the colors—orange and red and bright green, seafoam blue, even pink and red. Because who says I'm too tall and too fat? So I flirted with boys, and I painted my nails (when I had the time), and I decided that maybe, just maybe, I was pretty.

When I wore a purple dress, tailored to hug my wide hips, and a lilac cardigan, and heels (even though I'm so tall), people told me, that's your color. It matches the pink undertones of your skin and the auburn highlights of your hair. And I realized it was true. My color is purple.

SHAKEVA GRISWOULD

YEARS AS MENTEE: 2
GRADE: Senior
HIGH SCHOOL:
Marta Valle High School
BORN: Bronx, NY
LIVES: Bronx, NY
PUBLICATIONS AND RECOGNITIONS:
Scholastic Art & Writing Award: Honorable Mention; Internship at *YCteen Magazine*

MENTEE'S ANECDOTE: *This is my second year having Anna as my mentor, but it feels like I've known her for longer than that. Every time we meet for our pair sessions, we unwind and chat like old friends, then dive into writing. She always introduces me to new authors and poets who inspire me to write. She pushes me to step out of my comfort zone and encourages me when I need it. She wants me to be the best I can be, and with her help, I can be.*

ANNA J. WITIUK

YEARS AS MENTOR: 2
OCCUPATION:
Poetry Editor,
12th Street Journal
BORN: New York, NY
LIVES: Brooklyn, NY
PUBLICATIONS AND RECOGNITIONS:
Multimedia Video on 12thstreetonline.com

MENTOR'S ANECDOTE: *For the past two years I have been honored to know the incredibly perceptive and gracefully outspoken Shakeva. I have watched her poetry and writing expand into a powerhouse of wisdom and action. Our mentor-mentee connection has been a crucial part of my existence; our weekly meet-ups often engender in me a sigh of relief, because I am excited to just hunker down and learn the musicality of a word, inspect the life and death of a line break. Shakeva has taken on every foreign task with only sureness, and I can't wait to see what next she will forge.*

BROKEN

SHAKEVA GRISWOULD

"Broken" is a piece that represents my fight against police bru-
tality and the mistreatment of Black Americans. It is a piece
that wakes up the activist in all of us so that a greater change
can occur. Black lives matter and they always will.

Ain't enough time in the world to heal me but
they keep telling me to wait
Justice is on her way

Meanwhile another Sisterbrotheruncleauntadultteenchild is shot down in
the street
not even deserving of a blanket to cover their bodies
bodies stripped of humanity
and draped in blood

Every time I see those flashing lights I see my life flash before my eyes
and I wonder if this will be somebody's last day
my brother's last day
my father's
mine

I've been told to ignore the evil emanating from the earth and focus on
me alone
but it's hard to shine like a star

when your entire galaxy is being destroyed
So when I raise my fist high into the air
don't see it as a threat
I'm just pointing to where the stars have dropped from the sky.

DROP THAT

ANNA J. WITIUK

This poem came from discussions Shakeva and I had about natural rhythm and meter in certain poetic forms, like the human heartbeat heard in iambic pentameter. The poem is about the act of tearing off that which tethers and debilitates one's voice and soul, especially as a woman.

Thwip thwap thwip thwap the entourage of my heart goes How
bout that honey pie ? No more dingy in my soul—hole lettin
those monsters coast right on through No more of anythin quite
like the blues i.e. ravenous rage I craved that for too long that
addictive self-sacrifice So stubborn my evolution was I had to
scream more than twice *CHANGE you damn mule ! You
trepidatious madam !* Was it fear or just plain stiff-necked ?
Gimme back my lovin Gimme back my pride a wised-up woman
once wailed Wailed on it for days until her teeth just couldn't
handle no more treble and shattered Thwip thwap thwip thwap
Hear that echo up her lungs now Dingys dead Monsters gone
It all begins becomin more sound than sound linked to meanin
And hoo BABY I am through with that life life of just leanin.

GRACE HAN

YEARS AS MENTEE: 1
GRADE: Junior
HIGH SCHOOL: Queens High School for the Sciences
BORN: Queens, NY
LIVES: Queens, NY

MENTEE'S ANECDOTE: *Twenty-six and seventeen. I never thought these two worlds would collide—but they did! And out of it came laughs and conversations with my mentor, memories I would never trade for anything in the world. We talked about love, books, friends and family, and all the lows and highs of life. Through Christina, I have learned that self-awareness heals self-consciousness. She has inspired me to love and to chase after my own heart wholeheartedly. I thank Christina, my friends and family, teachers, and Girls Write Now for gracing this seventeen-year-old girl with such loving support. #teamgrastina*

CHRISTINA TESORO

YEARS AS MENTOR: 1
OCCUPATION:
Writer and sex educator
BORN: Queens, NY
LIVES: Queens, NY
PUBLICATIONS AND RECOGNITIONS: *The Toast, The Establishment, Cosmopolitan, The Learned Fangirl,* and *My Teen Diary*

MENTOR'S ANECDOTE: *I didn't know what to expect from being a writing mentor. We talked about stories—fairy tales and happily ever afters. But meeting with Grace week after week was so much more than talking about craft and writing. We talked about life—where we came from (Queens, our tight-knit families), and also where we want to go and who we want to be. I'll always be grateful for Grace and the opportunity to volunteer my time as a writing mentor through Girls Write Now. I've definitely learned from her as much as she's learned from me.*

16 GOING ON 17

GRACE HAN

One year. 12 months. 365 days. Smiling, crying, studying, dreaming. My life this past year revolved around life's greatest lesson—love. I learned from the people I have been graced with: family, friends, teachers, and my mentor, Christina. These are all of life's revelatory lessons I learned this year.

16 going on 17. Count it on a calendar: one year, 12 months, 365 days.

16 going on 17. One year weathered with seasons this 17-year-old girl had never seen before. Seasons she thought would never end; seasons she wished would never end. Seasons of confusion, of pain, of hurt; seasons of happiness, gratefulness, and hope.

The earth rotates around the sun in one year for one full revolution. I myself have completed one full revolution around this simply wondrous, at times a bit crazy, but completely eye-opening "funny place called life."

Time flies by in the blink of an eye. The harmonic hands on a clock instrumentally synchronize their song, *tick–tock*. The song beats a reminder that the only way to meet 2 o'clock A.M. again is to wait 24 hours to say to those familiar clock hands, "I know you, two o' clock"—another case of déjà vu.

The clock hands may land on the same numbers every day and every night, but time won't wait.

16 going on 17, realizing each second of every minute won't be returned back to me. It's not refundable; it's irreplaceable. But also realizing that that, in itself, is the beauty of life. The beauty of memories—left behind by the

things that disappear. Call it what you will—a handprint, a footprint, a scar—but those are the markers of life's remarks.

16 going on 17, seeing people come and go. Suddenly the distinction between waving hi and waving bye washes away. But the people who stay by my side are the people who interlock their fingers into mine after waving hi, just so we will never have to say good-bye.

16 going on 17, standing up for myself—the value in realizing that I have a voice no matter who tries to mute me. There will be people who try to stuff my mouth with a sock to assure themselves I'll only mumble, but I'll never give them that satisfaction. My voice is meant to be heard; my voice will be heard. And so I'll raise my hand high in class and look up when I'm walking on the streets to let them know that I am not an unheard voice.

16 going on 17, learning to love myself and my body—the very things God has given me that make me Grace Han. I may be missing a tooth, but that won't stop me from smiling ear-to-ear when I am laughing with my family and my friends.

16 going on 17, discovering my value and becoming aware of my self-worth. Discovering my love for the color pink and for Broadway musicals. Growing self-aware instead of being self-conscious. Knowing that I don't need to change to change others' views of me.

I am Grace. Bubbly and germaphobic. Korean and American. Sister and daughter. Friend and classmate. A lover and beloved. Crier and smiler.

16 going on 17, dancing through life and all the seasons that life has to offer. Through the bitter cold and sweltering heat, this 17-year-old girl is ready to embark on a new revolution. This time will be timeless, but it will write a tale as old as time—a tale of growing up, being loved, and loving. It will be my tale, my story—and this is only the beginning.

BiBLioGRaPHY OF 26

CHRISTINA TESORO

"To tell the truth is to become beautiful, to begin to love yourself, value yourself. And that's political, in its most profound way."—June Jordan

Self-compassion. Kindness toward the self. Not self-esteem, which is tied to ideas of worth. You are worthy—intrinsically, inherently, automatically. A radical declaration. Why?

The year of learning that yes, there is such a thing as second puberty. It hits at twenty-six. I am tired all the time. I feel growing pains. I experience an enormous, gnawing hunger. I am ravenous.

The year of learning that there are only twenty-four hours in a day, and some of them should be spent doing nothing.

But being.

The year of learning that I can be a woman who writes about love without being one of *those women who write about love*. In any case, there's nothing wrong with being one of *those women who write about love*.

"Do you want me to tell you something really subversive? Love is everything it's cracked up to be."[1]

Why shouldn't we write about love?

The year of learning how to say I love you. The year of learning how to mean it.[2]

The year of nights spent flat on my back crying in the dark of my room at 4 A.M., anxiety hour, with my heart a clenched fist in my chest *but I love you.*

The year of learning how to say meet me at the bridge.

The year of knowing I will walk away if you can't. I will walk away weeping, but I will walk.

1. Erica Jong; 2. Nayyriah Waheed

The year of learning that the way I love you could change your life. The year of letting you change mine. The year of learning that we have the potential to be wonderful—that is, to experience the wonder of each other, together—but sometimes, you have to choose.

Who do you want to be?

The year of learning that "somehow, in the midst of this confusion/ was the true dawning of myself."[3]

The year of learning that there is more courage in softness than in hard edges, more strength in empathy than in rage.

The year of learning that sometimes, love is not enough, despite what they say.

The year of learning that this is okay.

The year of my heart not broken—broken open.

There's a difference.

The year of the never-not-broken goddess.[4]

The year of daring greatly, boldness, courage.[5]

The year of *I love you, honey, but I love me more.*[6]

The year that Warsan Shire[7] described better: *the year of letting go, of understanding loss. grace. of the word 'no,' and also being able to say 'you are not kind.'*

The year of kindness.

The year of *good enough.*

The year of *worthy.*

The year of learning to love not Woman, but the thing that makes us women.[8] The year of learning what to call this common language between us.[9] It is called fierceness. It is called survival.

The year of grace, and learning that sixteen and twenty-six aren't so different, for all that they're worlds away.

The year of learning who I want to be.

The year of deciding to be her.

---

3. Dorothea Lasky; 4. Julie JC Peters; 5. Brené Brown; 6. Sandra Cisneros; 7. Warsan Shire;8. Maggie Nelson; 9. Adrienne Rich

SHIRLEYKA HECTOR

YEARS AS MENTEE: 3
GRADE: Senior
HIGH SCHOOL: International High School at Lafayette
BORN: Port-au-Prince, Haiti
LIVES: Brooklyn, NY

MENTEE'S ANECDOTE: *I feel like my two years with Shara went by so fast. However, those two years are unforgettable. We've shared many memorable moments. I'm going to miss Shara a lot once I graduate and go away to college, but we'll definitely catch up when I come back for breaks. I admire Shara's personality. She is so supportive and so sweet to me. I love Shara! I'm going to miss our weekly meetings at Union Square, especially our conversations.*

SHARA ZAVAL

YEARS AS MENTOR: 2
OCCUPATION: Publicist and editor, Faber & Faber
BORN: Boston, MA
LIVES: Brooklyn, NY
PUBLICATIONS AND RECOGNITIONS: Teenreads.com, ALM Publications

MENTOR'S ANECDOTE: *This year, Shirleyka won a Children's Defense Fund scholarship and I accompanied her to the gala. Throughout the evening, she'd run to our table to check in, but could rarely get in a full sentence before a judge, a donor, or even a celebrity would stop to congratulate her or remark on her moving acceptance speech. I couldn't help beaming, because hundreds of people were clearly recognizing Shirleyka as the all-star I've known she is for the past two years. She's graduating from high school and Girls Write Now; I'll miss her terribly, but I know that she'll only continue to do great things.*

JUSTICE FOR ALL— THE IRONIC SONG OF AMERICA

SHIRLEYKA HECTOR

This piece is the response to my classmate's question, "Why are we learning about racism? What does that have to do with me? Learning about racism only teaches hate."

"I just want to be free
Free like the sea
No chains; no shackles
No pain; unbreakable
I hear freedom
I see freed men
Happiness is ringing in my ears
Togetherness is the song that I hear
Justice for all
Will that take a miracle?
America, land of the free
That's why I shout Liberty!"

I was appalled by his statement, and said, "We're learning about racism because it is an issue that affects us all. I am Haitian. In the United States, I am considered an African American, and some opportunities will pass me by because of the color of my skin. We're learning about racism because white supremacy affects us all."

He responded, "Racism doesn't affect me. I don't care about that. Black people always get the attention. Black people get too much attention."

I was disgusted by his comments. Although it can be hard to change someone's mind, I tried to explain that when one's race has been exploited so many times over the years, it is normal to shout louder and louder, because it seems like one is not being heard.

We need to emphasize the value of black lives as much as the lives of other races. Protesting against institutional racism and the broken justice system is not wrong. In fact, it is a right given to us by the First Amendment. Protesting against police brutality and white supremacy is a must if we want a better future in the United States. I strongly support the Black Lives Matter movement because it is raising awareness about how black people are treated in the United States.

During the time of slavery, black people were traded like animals and were considered as three-fifths of a person. We were not considered full and capable human beings. During the civil rights movement, black people were bitten by ferocious dogs and were subjected to horrific treatment. Despite the civil rights movement, there is still discrimination and prejudice in the United States today. In 2016, we are still fighting for the same reasons.

The justice system is broken, and we have to fight to reform this unfair system. A lot of people are angry at black people because of our protests, and we are scrutinized as extremists when we throw our hands in the air. However, all we're trying to do is absorb the energy in the air, because it fills us with the power to revolt against injustice in this country. When it is our sweat that built America and we are still treated like crap, we need to shout louder than before, because anyone can see that we truly are not free in America. Clearly, there is still much progress to be made, and racism is as relevant today as it ever was.

We have to learn about racism in schools because it teaches us the importance of fighting against unfairness, and it builds tolerance so all races can live and work together and, eventually, truly be free.

THE HiGH LINE, NEW YORK CITY

SHARA ZAVAL

*I was inspired to write this poem after seeing one too many
cameras faced inward, instead of outward.*

In 1936, a beacon of public safety,
catapulting trains far above the streets
so they can chug along, undeterred
and leave the cars, cyclists, and people below in peace
instead of pieces.

In 1996, a monument to disrepair.
A snakeskin more than a mile long.
Wild ferns stumbling over decaying tracks;
the sole breath of life in a route long forgotten.

In 2016, a place for me, for you, for us
to glide above the avenues clogged with exhaust.
To slurp popsicles with expensive-sounding names
while admiring the art that teeters on railings
and climbs up stairways from Ganesvoort to 34th.
To spy into windows high above the world,
and to take photos.

To remember.

To remember the way your hair looked
when the wind caught it just right.

Eyelids painted like Egyptian cats
mouth contorted into a pout
so you look cute, innocent, sexy on that High Line.

For your friends, frenemies, enemies to remember
that you're fun, that you go places,
that you smile with impeccable makeup
and white, white teeth while you do so.

And if they squint hard enough,
they'll see that landmark fighting its way into the frame
The spire of the Empire State Building poking above your hat,
the glint of the Maritime Hotel
desperately competing
with the glare of your sunglasses.

The High Line, New York City.

EVELYN HINTON

YEARS AS MENTEE: 1
GRADE: Senior
HIGH SCHOOL:
Fannie Lou Hamer
High School
BORN: New York, NY
LIVES: Bronx, NY
**PUBLICATIONS AND
RECOGNITIONS:**
Scholastic Art &
Writing Award:
Honorable Mention

MENTEE'S ANECDOTE: *Because I'm interested in writing horror, I really liked all the disturbing and upsetting sights there were to see at the Morbid Anatomy Museum, such as the wax figures of babies being pulled out with forceps. I really liked it because I was able to go with Nicole. Most of my friends would have been grossed out by those disturbing sorts of things, and it was easier to like what I like when I was with someone who was comfortable having the same interests.*

NICOLE GERVASIO

YEARS AS MENTOR: 2
OCCUPATION:
PhD candidate in English,
Columbia University
BORN: Trenton, NJ
LIVES: New York, NY
**PUBLICATIONS AND
RECOGNITIONS:**
New York Council for
the Humanities Public
Humanities Fellowship;
Northeast Modern
Language Association's
Women's & Gender
Studies Caucus First
Place Essay Prize

MENTOR'S ANECDOTE: *Absorbing these gruesome objects—a life-sized serial killer, a hand pocked with lupus, a breech baby—piqued Evelyn's imagination to write a very elaborate scene. The adjacent library gave us more material to wonder over. I was trapped between disgust and awe of the embryonic animals in glass cylinders, whereas all the spare human teeth disturbed Evelyn. Our uncomfortable laughter and shameless curiosity brought us closer together, reminding me of a very important lesson we've both affirmed for each other this year: that often, surviving means finding hope and even whimsy in horror. We're all the more resilient for it.*

SYNAESTHETIC

EVELYN HINTON

When I saw Benton's painting at the Metropolitan Museum of Art, I liked how all the colors blended. I've taken art classes before. There's a certain way you paint things—different strokes. I also liked how it was one whole mural but it had different stories in each panel. I decided to focus on a story that highlighted that blending because of the mood I was in. Everything in the part of the painting I focused on was the opposite of what things really are, and when you looked, you could see things you wouldn't normally see. That's how I felt that day.

The beauty of the dark is not the light that it gives off but the sounds you hear.
The silence is loud but the light is brighter.
Giving those who don't normally see a vision.
Colors unimaginable to the blind eye.
The yellows, lime green, sky blue.
But something changes.
Overpowered by the light, the darkness soon fades.
Emotions take over.
Sadness walking around with a slight smile.
Not knowing what it had to offer, the blind eye quivers.

TWO WOMEN IN NEW YORK

NICOLE GERVASIO

*When Evelyn and I went to the Metropolitan Museum of Art,
a wall-to-wall mural tucked inside the modern art gallery capti-
vated Evelyn. Thomas Hart Benton's "America Today," from
1930–1931, depicts (r)evolutions in America's race, labor, and
gender politics up to the Great Depression. These ekphrastic
poems respond to Benton's story.*

I. MAY
In his arms
 she goes limp,
not with desire
   but like a puppet
whose strings have been cut
 mid-Charleston. Her ankles

quiver in her black pumps
 as her strap shimmies past
her shoulder, almost exposing
   her uncupped breast. Her downcast eyes
give nothing away; nothing in her hips,
 her heart, just his arms,

propping her up, lifting one hand
 of hers to the ballroom ceiling.
He gazes into her open palm
   as if a flame burns inside,
a message from God.
 "May, you love me," he prophesizes

and she smiles in spite
of herself, hearing her name.

II. JUNE

Upon arriving she expected
to grit her teeth on the fumes
dancing up from the sewer like spirits.
She expected gruff people,
all heels and dark glasses, shrill
whistles. She expected the work to be
tiresome and unrewarding, and really,
it was. But thanks to the suffering
she permits herself to enjoy the kiss
of cheap cotton sleeves on her shoulders,
a milkshake sweating out July
in her hand, all the fans dead
in this diner. Her elbows crossed on the table,
she looks up and thinks of all
she left behind—
fields of exhausted corn,
an unheated bungalow on the prairie,
Lew and his smirched moonshine.
The waiter slips her a wink, rubs
his brow in hello. She had not known
how malt tasted, or how some women
wear hats in summer,
much less that a whole world might
want to know her name was June.

JANNY HUANG

YEARS AS MENTEE: 1
GRADE: Junior
HIGH SCHOOL: Hunter College High School
BORN: New York, NY
LIVES: New York, NY

MENTEE'S ANECDOTE: *Before joining Girls Write Now and meeting Judy, I had never read my own words aloud in public. Girls Write Now allows me to explore genres beyond short stories and creative writing. Judy is very supportive and gives me courage whenever I am in doubt (which is most of the time!). She is both a mentor and a dear friend whom I can share anything with!*

JUDY ROLAND

YEARS AS MENTOR: 4
OCCUPATION: President, Roland Communications
BORN: Oceanside, NY
LIVES: New York, NY

MENTOR'S ANECDOTE: *Janny is a real star who combines writing talent with hard work. She is always prepared to work, always ready to try something different, and a joy to spend time with as both a mentee and a friend. I still don't understand her love for chemistry—and probably never will—but that's okay, we have lots of other things in common. Thanks to Girls Write Now for bringing us together!*

EQUILIBRIUM

JANNY HUANG

*This piece explores the notion of resisting change, a theme
present everywhere throughout history. In a way, this work
represents my past, trying to conform to "social norms."*

She lived alone. She was not a fan of someone else messing up her intricately placed furniture. No one to shift the perfectly framed photos askew.
No one to diminish the height of the grass she so neatly trimmed every
morning so each blade was between two to three inches at all times. No
one, especially, to take and use her silverware only to leave them in the
sink. No one to destroy all her hard work. Her only pet was a goldfish
named Nick, who was confined to the volume of his fish tank.

She needed no one. Yes, the only person who understood her vision
was herself. She knew where everything was and that was how it should be.

Waking up one morning at 6:59 A.M., she knew something was wrong.
There was a scent of imbalance as she took her first breath. She sat up in
her bed and looked around. Her slippers were exactly two inches away
from the left corner of her bed. Her glass of water was just the way she
liked it: three-eighths full. The transparent curtains were precisely three
inches apart, swaying in the slight breeze. Everything seemed to be in its
place—until she raised her head.

Her gray eyes locked on the deep blue orbs of a portrait across the
room. They were at an angle today, giving the painting a condescending
glare that brought chills to the woman. She rushed out of bed and grabbed
the polished frame, tilting it so that the sapphire dots were parallel to the

floor. Perfect. She took a step back and huffed satisfactorily at the sight, but something was still nagging at her.

Pivoting around on one foot, she turned her back to the portrait and looked at the mess that was her room. Her slippers, tilted too much to the right, were too far from the edge of the bed. The water level was slightly less than three-eighths full. The curtains were being pushed away from each other by the wind. How could she not have noticed this before? She needed to fix everything.

How could she let this happen? Was she really this incompetent, that she could not maintain everything just the way she liked it? Just like nature, she wanted everything to be at equilibrium, unchanging. She had to fix all disruptions to this state. It gave her a sense of purpose, made her feel wanted.

First things first. She had to shift the slippers so they were parallel to the mattress. Next, she needed to add drops of water to the glass so the meniscus was just right. Finally, the curtains needed to be pulled closer together. All of these modifications would make her room flawless.

After settling all these issues, the woman escaped to the living room. She grabbed the bottle of fish food and looked up to find an orange corpse floating on clear water. Nick's scales reflected the seven o'clock sunlight coming through the windows, blinding her for a moment. His glazed eyes stared into the clear glass in front of him.

She heard the drop before she knew it. All the food scattered on the floor and on her feet, falling into all the creases. She reached for her head and twisted her hair. Why was this happening? Why today? Nick was dead; she needed to replace him quickly, before she lost it. Another goldfish that looked *exactly* like him. He would be named Nick, too. No need to list which Nick he was, because he *was* Nick. She had to leave now. To the pet store, to find Nick.

She left the door and found the grass of her lawn all below two inches tall. Someone had cut it. Or stepped on it. Or ripped its tips off. She did not have the time for the grass to grow. Unfortunately for her, there was no immediate solution to this imperfection.

She ran to her car and slipped in. The leather seat screamed at the weight of her body.

Why was everything changing around her? Everything had to be permanently set in place. Nothing tweaked. She always corrected all these defects, mending them to perfection. There never were this many flaws in need of refinement on any day. Was it all in her head? Maybe she was the one who needed to change. Have an open mind. Embrace all the cracks and blemishes. Stop repairing every single mistake.

Forget it.

She just needed a break today. Sitting inside the car for the rest of the day, the woman fell asleep, hoping to find her home in perfect shape tomorrow.

* * *

The neighbors watched as the lady ran to her car and grinned contentedly.

"I guess our plan worked?"

"Yeah, she finally got some spice in her life."

PiNK DONUT

JUDY ROLAND

Janny and I wanted to evolve in our writing this year by taking risks, and freewrites are the perfect vehicle. This piece was prompted by part of a conversation I overheard between a mother and daughter at the bus stop.

It would have seemed like such an innocent request to any outsider who was listening, but her mother heard it differently.

Since she was an infant, Penelope had suffered from a rare nervous disorder that caused her to look, speak, and move like a robot. These symptoms were a sort of rigidity that would set in because her body lacked the enzyme commonly known as Mezotaze-20.

Her mother could tell when Penelope's medication was wearing off because her face and body would begin to stiffen. The longer they waited, the worse it would get, until she was a virtual statue.

The biggest problem was getting her to take the medication, which tasted like fermented broccoli. But in its pure state, the medication was bright pink—the color of Pepto-Bismol.

Penelope's mother finally thought to fold the medication into vanilla icing and, voilà, problem solved! She always had a batch handy, and used it to ice plain donuts.

"Mommy, can I have a pink donut" quickly turned into "Mooooommy, I waaaaant a piiiiiink dooooonuuuut."

Penelope's mother raced to the kitchen and returned in a flash with the donut. But not quite fast enough, as she saw her daughter's arms and legs were already stiff as wooden planks.

RAHAT HUDA

YEARS AS MENTEE: 1
GRADE: Junior
HIGH SCHOOL:
Stuyvesant High School
Born: Queens, NY
LIVES: Queens, NY
PUBLICATIONS AND
RECOGNITIONS: Scholastic
Art & Writing Award:
Gold Key

MENTEE'S ANECDOTE: *Before Katherine, published authors seemed otherworldly; becoming one seemed like an impossible mission. One day, I asked Katherine about the process of getting her book published. She told me how stressful it was to see if anyone would bid on her manuscript, and that the night before the final bids were due, she wasn't sure if the book would have the chance to get published at all. Our conversation helped me understand that even professional writers worry about the things I do. Katherine made me realize that my name could be on the cover of a novel one day.*

KATHERINE HILL

YEARS AS MENTOR: 1
OCCUPATION: Novelist
BORN: Washington, DC
LIVES: New York, NY
PUBLICATIONS AND
RECOGNITIONS:
Yaddo Fellowship

MENTOR'S ANECDOTE: *One afternoon Rahat and I met at PS1. She was in the bathroom when I arrived, wiping her foot with a damp towel in preparation for prayer. We used my iPhone to figure out which way was East, and then she went into the stairwell while I waited in the next gallery. I live in a fairly secular world, and I'm pretty sure that was first (and only) time I've helped anyone face Mecca. Not only was I proud I didn't screw it up, I was grateful to get a chance to experience Rahat's devotion firsthand.*

MY FATHER'S HOME IS MY MOTHER'S PRISON

RAHAT HUDA

Last summer, I was finally able to reunite with my motherland after ten years. This is an excerpt of a piece that was born out of a series of epiphanies I had about the true nature of my family while I was there.

"Your hair is disgusting. Doesn't your mom ever put oil in it? Maybe it would be less frizzy if she took care of it. Pass me the amla oil on the dresser."

I handed my paternal grandmother the small bottle and sat by her feet. I listened to her voice, the voice that taught me to read Qur'an when I was six. She told me how much harder she worked for her seven children than my mom did for us.

"Your mother just cooks and cleans all day. She doesn't pay attention to you. That's why your hair is like this. When I was younger, I would give my seven children baths in the lake and catch fish for dinner at the same time. Your mother is sick all the time from doing nothing." My dad listened, head down, fiddling with his mother's cane.

My dad started to become my father. Back home, he scolded us for not appreciating everything our mom did for us, but here he was a coward. He let his mother chip away at mine. My grandmother jabbed my mom with hateful words and snide comments. I remembered the stories she told me of her life when she first got married. My father had moved to America and left her at his parents' house. She was treated like one of the servants. They screamed at her and tortured her emotionally. Now, after having escaped their wrath for ten years, she was being forced to face the root of her depression.

After spending half of our trip with my dad's family, we were allowed to go to my mom's brother's house. We watched *Friends* with my cousins there. We talked for hours and hours. We snuck into the kitchen and ate Nutella from the jar. This was the Bangladesh I remembered from ten years ago.

But, of course, my father was angry that we spent so much time with my mother's family. Five days was too long. We should've been at my aunt's house taking care of my grandmother. That was why we came all this way, wasn't it?

My mom spent a lot of time in the guest room to avoid my grandmother's remarks on every aspect of her life—she was too dark, she didn't feed us, she didn't respect my father. I hid out with her, stroking her hair as she waited for the trip to be over. She didn't have family in America, but at least she had peace there.

I took long showers and studied to escape the harassment. I am my mother's daughter, so my father's family hated me just as much as they hated her. Why didn't I dress like this? Why didn't I act like that? Why was I dark like my mom? It didn't matter that my father was their eldest brother. It didn't matter that my father had put them through college. It didn't matter that my father sent them money when we didn't have enough to get by in America.

A few days before we left for Bhola, my dad was unusually moody. Why didn't we call our grandmother "Dadu"? Why didn't we help her shower? Why were we always in the room?

On the ship that took us to Bhola, my father briefly became my dad again. He spoke to my mom and joked around with us. I tried to enjoy my dad's company when he was in a good mood, afraid that it would end as quickly as it came. I was relieved to be away from my grandmother, and maybe it was my imagination, but my dad seemed to be as well. Maybe he was relieved that he didn't have to choose between his mother and us anymore.

When we finally got to Bhola, my sister and I decided to stay at my late maternal grandfather's tin-roofed house with my mom's family. This didn't go over well with my father. He wanted us to spend our entire trip with his family.

My father told us how much better the seated toilets at his house were compared to the flat toilets at my uncle's house. He told us he had air conditioning and the electricity never went off; he didn't realize that the Bangladesh I remembered, the Bangladesh I loved, had blackouts and hand fans.

After we got back to Dhaka, we continued staying at my aunt's house, where my grandmother was as cranky as ever.

My mom bought her three dresses she could wear at home.

"These are ugly. Take them back. What a waste of money," I heard my grandmother say to my father, in an audible voice so that my mom could hear her in the next room.

Later, my father went into the guest room and scolded my mom for not having better taste, for spending money recklessly, for never getting anything right. My mom apologized—she was sorry, she didn't know any better, she just wanted to do something nice. In that moment, I began hating my father. This hatred burned in my heart and made me nauseous, because I loved him, and because I didn't want to believe that he was a terrible husband and my mom's worst enemy when he was a great dad and my best friend.

My father sighed heavily as we took our seats on the plane. "You're never going to see your grandmother again," he said to me. I tried to seem heartbroken, but I wasn't. I wouldn't have to see her break my mother into pieces. I wouldn't have to be ashamed at my dad's cowardice. I was relieved. But I was also ashamed of myself—I hated the person my father loved the most.

ODD JOBS

KATHERINE HILL

Rahat and I love to freewrite after spending an hour or two at MoMA. This exercise, in response to Henri Rousseau's painting "The Dream," features the protagonist of my current novel, a football player who grows up in rural Virginia.

The summer before his senior season, Mitch worked the grounds crew at the college with Joe. Odd jobs were always coming his way there if he made himself available. An extra ten to catch a snake in a French professor's garden. An extra twenty to rescue the president's daughter's yellow cat from a giant oak. She looked like a tiny lion, that cat—huge muzzle, long shoulders—which might've accounted for her insanity. She didn't belong in Central Virginia; he could relate, because neither did he. When he arrived at her branch she didn't even fight him, just hooked her paws over his shoulder and exhaled as they descended together, back into captivity.

Not long after that, Joe found him in the break room, told him a girl in Madison needed some help with a couch. She had some kind of special status that allowed her to move in early, weeks ahead of the other girls. Why anyone would want come back to Virginia any sooner than absolutely necessary was beyond him, but he went down to Madison anyway to see what he could do. She was from New York, Joe said, a Northern girl, and Northern girls knew how to tip.

The couch was an absurd object, purple velvet with a curving back.

"It won't fit through the door," he said. "Don't you see?"

"That's what the movers said," she told him drowsily. "That's why they left it here." She seemed utterly unconcerned with reality, as though the solution to her problem were only a matter of finding a person willing to rethink the door.

They stood there together in the decadent grass. Her hair was long and black and she didn't resemble the cat at all but for some reason his mind went there anyway. These crazy females, he thought, always trying to do the impossible.

Then she did a strange thing: she went and reclined on the couch. For a moment he was afraid she was going to take off her clothes, like a woman in a painting. It wouldn't have been the first time a girl had thrown herself at him, but it would've been the first time it happened in broad daylight.

"Maybe I'll just keep it here," she said, not naked. "Nap in the open air."

"Folks'll call you a redneck," he said. "But suit yourself."

Her face was a question.

"Redneck," he clarified. "Kind of person who keeps couches outdoors."

She lifted her head, seemed to feel her own neck, and smiled. "Guess I'm a redneck then."

"Hate to break it to you, but you aren't."

"What am I?" she asked, suddenly, as though she'd just shaken off a bad dream.

The question took him by surprise. "You're a college girl," he sputtered, hoping he hadn't jeopardized his tip.

"Oh," she moaned. She was on her couch and the world was so hard. "Why can't I be both?"

KIANA JACKSON

YEARS AS MENTEE: 1
GRADE: Junior
HIGH SCHOOL: New Explorations into Science Technology and Math (Nest+M)
BORN: New York, NY
LIVES: New York, NY

MENTEE'S ANECDOTE: *My first year in Girls Write Now has been enlightening. I felt free to write what's on my mind and express it through different genres. My (r)evolution was when my mentor and I started talking and writing about "Who can tell the story?" Can an African American write about the experiences of a Caucasian and vice versa? At first I thought no one has the right to tell someone else's story. The more we talked about it, I decided it is okay to interpret someone else's experience as long as you acknowledge that it is an outside point of view.*

DEBORAH HEILIGMAN

YEARS AS MENTOR: 1
OCCUPATION: Author of children and young adult books
BORN: Allentown, PA
LIVES: New York, NY
PUBLICATIONS AND RECOGNITIONS: *Intentions, The Boy Who Loved Math: The Improbable Life of Paul Erdos, Charles and Emma: The Darwins' Leap of Faith.*

MENTOR'S ANECDOTE: *Kiana and I have been talking about diversity (and lack of diversity) in children's and young adult books, and of the misrepresentation of experience. Are writers "allowed" to tell the story of someone from a different background and experience? In our weekly meetings, Kiana and I have been writing from this prompt: "Who can tell the story?" I have found that writing from another person's viewpoint expands my world. These discussions and writing exercises are helping me grow as a writer and a human being. I am grateful for this (r)evolution.*

Recognitions: Sydney Taylor Award from the Association of Jewish Librarians; *New York Times* Notable Book; Cook Prize from Bank Street College of Education; the Anne Izard Award; Orbis Pictus honor from the National Council of Teachers of English; National Book Award Finalist; YALSA Excellence in Nonfiction Award Winner; Printz Finalist; *LA Times* Book Prize finalist

EVERLASTING RIDE

KIANA JACKSON

This piece was inspired by a Helen Levitt photograph from 1978. There's a couple sitting together on the subway. The guy's arm is wrapped around the woman and they're looking at each other adoringly. I'm writing from the perspective of the man, whom I perceive to be Cuban and middle-aged.

Ever since Mary moved to the Midwest for graduate school, I had been stuck in muggy Boston, Massachusetts all alone. Paranoid. Concerned. Worried that she would find someone she liked better than me. I would be cast away, and our three years of being together would be nothing but a distant dream. But now here she was with me, and I was taking her out on a spectacular date. I had been taking extra shifts at work in order to save up the money.

We got onto the T and headed to Marinara, a fancy Italian restaurant that had just opened up in the heart of the city. Money was a challenge, because even though I had been saving up, I was on probation at work for being late too many consecutive days. I still wanted to show Mary a good time, so I called up my brother in Chicago and asked him to spot me fifty dollars. I promised to pay him back once I was off probation and receiving my full salary again.

I met Mary one day three years ago when I bumped into her and made her drop all of her groceries. I offered to buy her all new food, but she kindly declined. I insisted. I had never met a woman who smiled at me as genuinely as she did. Her eyes sparkled and her dimples emerged as her smile grew wider. Her hair was up in a messy bun with a strand of hair hanging in front of her face. Whenever she looked at me, she had to flick the hair away from her eyes. Then she would quickly look away and grin.

We started to hang out more often, and I began to fall more deeply in love with her. When she moved away to go to graduate school I was worried our relationship would wither away. But now here she was, and I was taking her to an Italian restaurant to get her favorite food—pasta with marinara sauce.

She thought we were just going on a walk through the park downtown. I wanted to surprise her. I was scared she would be mad about the amount of money I was spending, since she knew I sometimes struggled with keeping up with rent payments. But what was the worst thing that could happen?

We were almost at our stop when the train screeched to a stop in the tunnel.

"Martin, how's work?" Mary asked.

I hesitated at first, but then said, quietly, "It's fine, but I kind of am on probation for being late."

"Martin! Seriously! You know how much I hate lateness." Mary turned away from me.

When we lived together, Mary was always annoyed that she had to wake me up in the mornings because I overslept. As I touched her arm, she turned to look at me with a fierce glare in her eyes. She opened her mouth to say something, but stopped and took a deep breath instead.

To avoid further arguing, I decide to stop talking for a while. When I thought I was in the clear, that she had calmed down, I hugged her, because I did not want her to get worked up about my whole "being late" issue. I whispered, "I love you," in her ear and she giggled. Then her eyebrows raised at me and she stood up—it was our stop. I followed her off the train, covered her eyes, and guided her toward the restaurant.

"Martin Van Goodwin! Why are you covering my eyes? I thought we were going to the park," Mary shouted.

"Nope! We're going somewhere special," I said with a slight chuckle.

"Martin!" Mary protested.

"Okay, okay. Open your eyes," I said.

Her mouth fell open and her eyes widened in awe. I could see the look of doubt in her eyes, because she knew how expensive the place was. But

I smiled and kissed her forehead. Excited, Mary turned around and kissed me passionately. I love her so much. Gosh, I never knew how much you could love someone. It really is crazy. I guess maybe I underestimated how powerful love can really be.

After that lovely night, we headed back to my apartment to watch some movies before Mary had to leave to catch her flight. I hope she will move back here when she has gotten her degree in child psychology. Then we will grow old together; maybe have a kid or two. I could see us taking our children on the T for the first time to the aquarium.

We are soul mates. I can feel it. To me our future together looks bright. Who knows what will happen. I could be wrong and I could be right. We will see where this ride takes us.

MY ViEW

DEBORAH HEILIGMAN

This piece was inspired by a Helen Levitt photograph from the 1940s. A little girl is looking out her window, an angry expression on her face. Her tiny brother, barely visible, is looking out, too. The girl has brown skin and long, loose curls that hang past her shoulders.

"Come away from there," Grandma yells at me. "I want to fix your hair."

I don't answer. I'm too busy looking out the window. Why is Mama kissing that man? I've been waiting for her to come home since last night. She promised she'd be back, and I did just what she told me to: I got Jimmy dinner, even wiped his grubby face before and after. I read him a book, made sure he wouldn't wet the bed, got him to sleep, and most of all didn't bother Grandma with any of it.

But Grandma woke me up hollering this morning because she saw Mama's neat-as-a-pin, not-been-slept-in bed and knew she never came home last night.

I don't know why it's my fault, but Grandma's taking it out on me. She got herself a bee in the bonnet to do my hair, calling at me all morning from her chair. Lucky for me she can't chase me down, not with her bad legs, because no way in a million Saturdays am I going to let her touch my head. Once was enough. She about killed me last time with that steel brush on my half-white-girl curls. Daddy said the police would show up for my screaming. He got her laughing and laughing, like he always did, her son, the light of her life. She handed him the brush and I was saved. But now Daddy's gone for good and there's not much laughing around here any more. Not much taking care of my hair, either. Mama can't deal with hair like mine, not with her own head covered in that baby-fine yellow silk of hers.

"When is that woman coming home?" Grandma yells now.

I can't tell her that Mama is standing in front of our building, kissing some man right there in broad daylight with everyone to see. Even Jimmy is trying to get a look, because all the neighborhood boys are hooting and wolf-whistling because Mama has been kissing that man for so long.

"By and by," I say to Grandma, imitating her so she likes me. "She'll be home soon, ma'am."

I am caught between the two of them, as always. Grandma pushing me from behind, Mama pulling me from in front. Why can't they let me be me?

"Well, she better!" says Grandma. "I need her to help me with my bath."

Oh no. I know where this is going. No way am I going to get that old lady into the tub.

"Won't you, Mama?" I yell out the window. "Won't you come on in already?"

I yell that last part really loud and it's like every noise in the neighborhood stops, every motion freezes, because Mama pulls away from that man and we all see who it is. Jimmy gasps and I almost fall out the window. The man she's been kissing all this time, that man is my daddy.

And my daddy, he's dead.

SARANE JAMES

YEARS AS MENTEE: 1
GRADE: Freshman
HIGH SCHOOL: Bronx High School of Science
BORN: Bronx, NY
LIVES: Bronx, NY
PUBLICATIONS AND RECOGNITIONS: Scholastic Art & Writing Award: Silver Key

MENTEE'S ANECDOTE: *Even before I met my mentor Margo, I loved Manhattan. Despite living in The Bronx, Manhattan's concrete jungle of hopes and accomplishments felt like a distant dream to me. Margo has given me so many more excuses to explore the city, and even acted like my personal tour guide. She has helped me find so many little gems in Manhattan that I would have never seen without her, and each one adds to me in its own unique way.*

MARGO SHICKMANTER

YEARS AS MENTOR: 1
OCCUPATION: Editorial Assistant, Penguin Random House
BORN: Lenox, MA
LIVES: New York, NY

MENTOR'S ANECDOTE: *In college I studied creative nonfiction and poetry writing. When I was paired with Sarane (who was only writing fiction at the time), I think we were both a little nervous. I have watched Sarane take on new genres with enthusiasm and curiosity, and she has challenged me to do the same. Working together has been a revolution in that alongside her I have written my first fictional pieces ever, one of which is included here. I can only hope that the self-confidence Sarane exhibits in the world and in her writing keeps rubbing off on me!*

I'M NOT A NIGGA

SARANE JAMES

Spending three years in a middle school attended by mostly black and Hispanic children meant that the word "nigger" was just as commonplace as "the" or "I." I tend to let people know very quickly that I will not let them apply it to me.

"Aay, mah nigga, what's up?"
Silence.
"I said, what's up?"
Oh, I'm sorry, were you talking to me?
'Cause last I checked, I'm not a nigga.
Yes, my skin is brown. Yes, I consider myself black.
Those are not the only reasons why I'm not a nigga.
I preach equality and practice self-respect.
Therefore, I'm not a nigga.
Forget planes,
Somewhere there's a rocket ship
That shoots for the stars and lands on the moon.
That rocket is me, and I'm not a nigga.
You can change the spelling and
skew the pronunciation,
But that won't change the meaning.
Nigger is a word associated with slavery,
Being three-quarters human,
But I'm free as a bird
And more human than I can sometimes bear.

I refuse to forget my heritage or give up on my legacy
So that I can be "hip" and "street" and "on your level."
I refuse to let you call me "Your Nigga," because
"I'm.
Not.
A Nigga."

RADICAL EMPATHY

MARGO SHICKMANTER

I often feel guilty when I put myself first. Generosity is an incredible quality, but our culture can sometimes take advantage of the specifically female capacity for empathy, turning what should be a positive emotion into a self-destructive force. This dystopian flash fiction takes that idea to the extreme.

"Five minutes of your time, ma'am?" The wind was sharp on my face and I had been walking with my head down. When I raised my eyes, the volunteer had stepped directly into my path with her clipboard and bright red vest. She was petite, but there was a sharpness about her—white-blond hair, small eyes, chapped hands.

"Just five minutes, ma'am. Think of the soldiers. They're out there for us." Her words came out fast, a familiar tumbling. The soldiers. The men. It was interchangeable at this point, really. There were no men who were not soldiers. The city was filled with women. Women like me, going out to eat, being served by women, sitting with women. The biggest danger to be had here was the slight dusting of snow on the sidewalk. We lived safely because the men were fighting for us.

She pointed to the sign on the red donation tent. I understood the anger I felt towards those signs was just a symptom of my own selfishness. I could not walk by one and not feel like I was undeserving, like I had taken something from someone else and refused to give it back, even though the war had started before I was even born.

The photo on the sign was new. Sometimes when they did not change, it could feel like the men were watching you. I was told this was an old feeling, the being watched, but it was as alien to me as the men on the signs. This soldier was shirtless, and part of the skin on his torso and face was burnt off and scarred in pink bunches. His bare biceps ended in stumps. The volunteer searched my face for a reaction. She sighed. "Where are you headed today, ma'am?"

I knew Claire would understand if I was late. Her wheelchair usually slowed her down on public transport anyways.

"I . . ."

"I can assure you, we've got state-of-the-art replacements, and we're working with the newest technologies."

That's what they had said about my knee, but it was cheap and it throbbed whenever I tried to get back into running. The voices in my head—my mother's voice, my teacher's voice: *What's a little throbbing when you haven't seen a day of fighting in your life? Could you survive that kind of trauma? Look at you, living in the lap of luxury. Headed to lunch.*

The woman's mouth had turned down, her beady eyes squinting with irritation. She gestured again towards the sign. I imagined how futile the man staring out from it must feel now. How afraid he must be, unable to draw his own weapon.

"Is it for him?" I asked.

I felt her touch my back lightly as she steered me towards the tent clinic.

"Of course, ma'am." She was excited now, almost jogging. "You know we only ask for what we need. And we always show you where it will end up. Even a finger would be an enormous gift!"

MARIEL JAQUEZ

YEARS AS MENTEE: 1
GRADE: Junior
HIGH SCHOOL: New York Institute of Technology
BORN: New York, NY
LIVES: New York, NY

MENTEE'S ANECDOTE: *My mentor has opened me up to many new opportunities—she is always positive in how she frames her feedback on my work. She challenges me as a writer. My favorite thing is getting coffee at Starbucks and discussing ideas about feminism and aeronautics, and pulling apart poetry.*

REBECCA GILL

YEARS AS MENTOR: 1
OCCUPATION: Producer
BORN: Adelaide, Australia
LIVES: Queens, NY

MENTOR'S ANECDOTE: *Even though Mariel is my mentee, I have learned just as much from her as she has learned from me. Just in our casual chats before or after meetings, I learn about the city, what it is like growing up here—and how to chill out! Mariel is extremely ambitious, highly organized, and quietly confident, and in many ways, I have had to rise to the challenge so I can be a step ahead of her. Our time together is always some of the most fun and collaborative times of my week!*

THE END OF THE WORLD

MARIEL JAQUEZ

My personal revolution is that I am beginning to become an advocate for topics that I feel strongly about, and continuing to gain confidence by doing so. My character in this flash fiction piece, Marie Ann Joseph, embodies the part of me that strives for that.

The end of the world did not turn out the way I thought it would.

NOVEMBER 12TH, 3024

A rather recent ultimatum to humanity, the population on Earth is growing faster each second, like approaching comets. The government is greedy and presumptuous, only caring about establishing the new world order.

Since I can remember, I have been taught to never question the elites. It is obvious, though, that there is something suspicious going on behind those in charge. I have seen stock markets crash, protests and the destruction of stores, a ton of people die suddenly (some say they got a virus), violent wars, and an alarming rise in environmental issues. In times like these it is important that everyone protects not only themselves but their loved ones as well. Well, I am so hungry that I am daydreaming about mac and cheese as I write this, so I will be back later!

NOVEMBER 15TH

There has been such a commotion going on in this home lately. "She is genuinely nice! She doesn't care about our ethnicity, so why do we have to care about the fact that her family is Asian?" Matthew reiterates. My mom replies with the same thing, "Dear, we are not discriminating against her race. The government's main prey is currently the people in China and their descendants. They are known to have a broad population, and you know that they do not like that. Now stop arguing with me."

So we should cut out everyone in our lives who is Chinese? Does not seem very fair to me.

I have to get up soon for the big event tomorrow. Good night!

NOVEMBER 16TH

His birthday party went great! The pasta did not let us down. Although Matthew only invited four close friends, I am very happy with the way it turned out. I will keep you updated on anything else.

NOVEMBER 17TH

Matthew does not seem too good . . . It could not have been the pasta, though, because we all ate that. I mean, he did decide to have a chocolate brownie in addition to his birthday cake that only he tried. He says he feels lightheaded and has thrown up six times already since last night. But going to the hospital is only allowed for the government members and their families. Dear God, please let him be okay.

NOVEMBER 19TH

The light has gone out of my life. We thought Matthew would get better soon, but we were naive. He was sweating from all over—forehead, neck, arms . . . He was bathed in his own perspiration. It was yesterday that his body gave up.

My job was to keep my family safe from anything and everything, healthy. I have failed as a sister, daughter, friend, cousin, and individual. Our society will not be able to fully function if the government keeps doing ruthless things to get the population under 500,000,000. I refuse to continue living this way. This nation has stayed quiet for far too long, and it is about time that a new leader arises.

—Marie Anne Joseph

NEW YORK REVOLUTION

REBECCA GILL

My piece is about the personal revolution that had to happen (and is still happening) for me since moving to New York from Australia. My mentee always inspires my work—because she has such a different perspective, and always makes me see her city in a new light.

My therapist says.

I never thought I would say those words.

But then again, I never thought I would get to write "New York" as my home state on application forms.

Ever since leaving the small town in Australia where I grew up, I have felt like my life has been evolving, changing, growing.

But coming to New York. That was—still is—the revolution.

The big shake-up.

Like falling out of a branch on a Gum Tree and having to climb my way back up, ragged nails clawing on the gummy bark.

Okay. So it is not like I endured some personal life tragedy. I didn't even squeeze a baby out of my body (the commonplace cause of soul-shaking and personal revolution). I didn't lose a limb. I didn't get into a car accident.

No. I moved to a different country. I had done that before—five times, to be exact.

But New York was always the glimmering beacon of career audacity. *If you can make it there, you can make it anywhere.* That's what Alicia Keyes said.

A city full of people who do not belong.

A city full of ambition. Of people chasing dreams. Goal setting.

Of people who measure happiness in terms of whether they are accomplishing, achieving.

No wonder we all need therapists! Our support network is other dreamers and overachievers. Or the chronically busy.

I thought having a therapist would be like a glamorous badge of honor. In *Sex and The City*, Carrie has this stylish therapist on the Upper East Side with whitewashed walls who she visits wearing fabulously flirty summer dresses. In the waiting room, Bon Jovi asks her on a date. Other therapists in lesser shows and films had wood-paneled rooms and vases and leather couches you could lie on.

But my therapist is not like that. My therapist, like most things in my life, lives inside my computer. On the Internet. Isn't technology amazing? She actually has quite a nice office—from what I can see of it. But I can sense, almost for certain, that it is not on the Upper East Side. And that Bon Jovi is not one of her clients.

Anyway. So now I can say that I live in New York, and that I have a therapist. And as it turns out, like most things in life, both of those truths are not all they are cracked up to be. But that is where the revolution part comes in.

The first time I talked to my therapist, I called her from what looked like a cupboard. She looked mildly concerned.

"It's not a cupboard," I said, aware that it was 2 P.M. on a Tuesday and I was cloaked in pitch black, save the fluorescent glow from my Mac-Book lighting up my face.

"It's okay if it is," she said.

"It's not, though."

I told her the real situation. She looked mildly convinced

My therapist asked me to tell her about myself.

How much do you work? A lot.

Do you have family in New York? No.

Do you have friends in New York? Does your business partner count?

What do you do for fun? Work.

But what do you do for fun? Silence.

Okay, she said. Here's what we need to do. You need to get out and have fun, and you need to make some friends.

Great, I said, taking notes.

To do this—you're going to create a bucket list. Not like a death one. One for 2016. You know you live in arguably the most amazing city in the world, with exciting things happening every minute?

Yes, I know that.

I was happy—because it seemed that with all this list-making, I could spreadsheet my way to happiness.

Next step. You are going make friends. You need to go to a "MeetUp" event. You can meet friends in so many places. At the gym: after class, you go up to someone and say, "That was a great class, huh! Wow, I really couldn't get that stretch—you're so good at it. Do you want to get coffee?"

I couldn't believe it.

I was getting advice on how to pick up friends at Zumba class.

This was not at all what I thought my life would be like in New York. This was not at all what I thought my therapist would give me advice on.

Who knows what I thought she would give me advice on . . . but something more sophisticated and urbane than making friends in Zumba class. My mum makes new friends in Zumba class in the suburbs of Adelaide, where I grew up.

Anyway, the metrics are thus: By the end of 2016, I need to have ticked off sixteen "fun" things on my bucket list. And I need two (2) new friends. Revolution begins now.

ZARIAH JENKINS

YEARS AS MENTEE: 1
GRADE: Sophomore
HIGH SCHOOL: Midwood High School
BORN: Brooklyn, NY
LIVES: Brooklyn, NY
PUBLICATIONS AND RECOGNITIONS: Writer for Women's eNews

MENTEE'S ANECDOTE: *When I first joined Girls Write Now, I was afraid. I was afraid that my writing was not good enough or that my mentor and I would not see eye to eye. Later, I realized I had no reason to worry. Girls Write Now has had a big impact on my life. I am no longer afraid to show my writing to the world. I can show anyone a story of mine without being afraid of what they might think. Girls Write Now has helped me develop a louder voice, and helped me realize that my voice deserves to be heard.*

RACHELE RYAN

YEARS AS MENTOR: 1
OCCUPATION: Executive Assistant, CDR Studio Architects, PC
BORN: Honolulu, HI
LIVES: Brooklyn, NY

MENTOR'S ANECDOTE: *Working with Zariah has been an amazing experience for me. Each week I look forward to our meeting. Like me, she can be shy, but when it comes to writing, she always has something to say. I am envious of her imagination. It is inspiring to work somebody who is still so excited about their writing, who is constantly discovering new things, and who above all has fun with it.*

WOULD I SEE THINGS DIFFERENTLY IF i COULD SEE MYSELF?

ZARIAH JENKINS

Imagine what it would be like not to see your reflection. People are always comparing themselves to others and putting themselves down because of what they see in the mirror. I tried to imagine a world without mirrors to see if this changed how we see ourselves.

Before today, I never got to see what I looked like. For years, my appearance was based off of other people's descriptions of me. Some said I was tall, some said I was short. I never got a clear description of what I looked like until today.

Living without seeing my reflection is not as easy as you think. It bothers me. It bothers me that people can see what I look like, but I can't see it too. Sometimes I dream of stepping out of my own body and going into someone else's, to see how people see me.

Except it felt like I have done that. There is this person in my dreams who is exactly like me. She does not have a name, but I consider her my sister. I know it sounds crazy. At least it is not real.

I get excited when it rains because I can get a peek of my reflection in the puddles. But it barely rains here. My whole life has been dedicated to what I think I look like. It is something that is always on my mind. Can you imagine a society where mirrors, phones with cameras, and reflective glass no longer exist? Well, welcome to my world. I live in a society where you are not allowed to see your reflection until you are sixteen. Sixteen is the age you are considered *mature* enough to handle seeing your true identity. And it has been this way for over a century.

Even before today I had an idea of what I looked like. I always knew I was tall. When my friends were not able to reach something, I could. My long legs were never able to rest comfortably in the backseat of my mother's car. I always liked my height, even though I could not see it. In its natural state I was never able to see the texture of my hair, not even the length, unless it was straightened. However, I knew my hair was dark brown and curly. Whenever I brushed it little strands of my hair would get stuck in the brush. And whenever my mom did my hair she would talk about my luscious curls and how healthy it was. "If only you could see how beautiful you look right now," she would say as she parted my hair into two separate sections.

When it came to my eyes, I had no idea what color they were. But what I did know is that I had terrible eyesight and needed glasses. I hated my glasses, even though I could not see how they looked on me. I hated the feeling of having something on my face. My face was smooth like silk, and I rarely got pimples. Not touching my face is the secret recipe to keeping it that way, although that is hard, since I am so obsessed with finding out who I am.

Almost every family has a mirror room. It stays locked up until one of the kids turns sixteen, and then it is locked again.

Right now, I am standing in the mirror room. The mirror is covered by some satin cloth. Anxiously, I rip the cloth off the mirror.

The person I have seen in the mirror looks oddly familiar. I know I am not crazy, because I have seen this person before. We have the same brown eyes and the same smooth chocolate skin, and our hair is the same length. On the right side of my cheek there is a beauty mark in the same exact place as my sister's. I always used to compliment my sister's smile. She had a beautiful smile, and I used to hope that one day, when I saw my reflection, I would have a smile like hers. Smiling into the mirror, I start to laugh. I don't just look like my sister. I am her.

With thousands of mixed emotions and crazy thoughts running through my mind, I rush downstairs to my mom.

"I have a twin! All this time I looked like—"

In confusion, my mom cuts me off. "Honey, you are an only child."

I look deeply into my mother's eyes, hoping that this is all a story, but I know my mother would never lie to me. To be 100 percent sure, I run to the mirror and ask my reflection, "Who are you?" But when I get no response, I realize I never really had a twin. And I never really needed a mirror, because I have been seeing myself all along.

BLIGHT

RACHELE RYAN

I tried to write something that worked on two of my weaknesses: (1) getting to the action quickly, and (2) not overexplaining the story.

We walked home under a goldenrod moon. The meeting had gone well, and Christine held my hand. It was September, that last warm month. Our street was dense with trees, and the moths hovered between the branches, their wings pumping audibly as they grappled with the air.

I squeezed her hand. "I'll go to as many of these as you like."

She nodded.

"I want to help," I said. "In any way I can."

"Jack?"

"Yes?"

She smiled at me, but I saw that she was tired. "Please stop."

We reached our twig-and-leaf-strewn lawn. The porch light cast itself across everything. Here were the scattered objects: a rake and shovel, a yard glove, the parked car on the street.

"How about some coffee," she said.

I nodded.

She stopped at the door and looked out at the sky. "I'll bring it outside. It's such a warm night."

I sat in one of the chairs. Christine moved behind me in the kitchen. There were sounds of the kettle on the stove, the clink of cups.

When she came back she was holding a letter.

"They're coming Friday," she said.

"Who?"

"They're going to take down the oak. There's blight."

We had had neighbors complain. There were signs: a soft decay, a white powder that appeared. They were wary of contamination. Someone had called for an inspection.

I reached for her, but she moved away.

"Don't," she said. She began to fold the letter, in half, then again, until she could no longer work it. She sighed. We listened to the gentle movements of nighttime traffic, of the wind through the leaves.

"So you don't care?" She had turned to me. Her eyes were drawn.

"What?"

"You love that tree. It doesn't upset you that it has to go?"

She was crying now. The rivulets on her cheeks shone brilliantly in the porch light.

"We'll be fine, Chrissy."

She shook her head. "Fuck these stupid meetings. There's no point anymore."

"Don't be like that. You were in such good spirits."

"Don't you think, after everything, that I can at least talk however the hell I want?"

We sat in silence. I looked up at the giant oak, the branches that extended over our house, reaching out, out.

"It's only one tree," I said after a while.

"Only one tree," she repeated. She looked down at her chest, encased in the soft silk of her blouse. She placed a hand on her left breast, the one with the growth. She swore the skin was darker there.

"It's only a tree," she said again.

"Only."

"And the rest will be fine?" Her eyes were not looking at what grew in the yard but at my face.

From inside I heard the noise of the kettle shrill. For a brief instant we both tried to ignore it, but the sound was soon unbearable. Christine untangled herself and stood, unbalanced.

"Milk?" she asked me. She knew the answer, and went inside.

MARIAM KAMATE

YEARS AS MENTEE: 2
GRADE: Senior
HIGH SCHOOL: A. Philip Randolph High School
Born: New York, NY
LIVES: New York, NY
PUBLICATIONS AND RECOGNITIONS: Scholastic Art & Writing Award: Silver Key

MENTEE'S ANECDOTE: *I have learned that my mentor is quite inspiring. She too has been put down by people, but she did not let it get to her. Instead she worked hard to prove them wrong. I feel comfortable talking to my mentor because she is a great listener and she gives me a lot of advice. She challenged me to share my writing, and to read in front of a lot of people since I am pretty shy and I mumble. Now I'm ready to share my poems with the world.*

BROOKE OBIE

YEARS AS MENTOR: 1
OCCUPATION: Senior Digital Editor, Guideposts.org
BORN: Kokomo, IN
LIVES: New York, NY
PUBLICATIONS AND RECOGNITIONS: Published on EBONY.com, Guideposts.org

MENTOR'S ANECDOTE: *In my Girls Write Now interview, I was asked if I had a preference to mentor a girl in a certain genre. I said, "Any genre but poetry!" I thought I wouldn't be much help. Of course, Mariam and I were paired together, and she is an awesome poet. I was nervous at first, but reading her poetry encouraged me to read more poetry so I could better help her. Watching her grow in her writing and confidence inspired me to open myself back up to poetry, and now I have written a tribute poem just for her.*

A TIME TO HEAL

MARIAM KAMATE

This piece is part of my life story, of what I have gone through and where I am going. Though life could get better or worse, I have learned that I am brave and I am a survivor. I can do anything.

Where I am from, in Bamako, Mali, they say something bad always happens when it is too hot outside, but that day I did not listen. I was twelve years old, and I wanted to play with my friend across the street. I saw her and her little cousins standing in the shade of a tree, and I went to join them. As I got closer, I noticed an older boy near them, taunting them.

"I told you if I ever saw you outside, I'd beat you up!" I heard him yell at my friend in our language, Bambara, and I could see my friend had tears in her eyes. I ran to her and stood between her and the bully. "Leave them alone!" I told him.

Before I knew it, he swung his fist at my face and we began to wrestle on the ground.

"Stop, please!" he began to beg when I started to win the fight.

"Will you leave them alone?" I asked him, holding him in place.

"I promise!" Satisfied, I got off of him and smoothed down my long taffé skirt and my braided hair. I turned to ask my friend if she was okay, but she just said, "Look out!"

I turned back around just as the bully launched a rock at my head. It hit me right in the mouth, and an unending flow of blood gushed from my lips. It would take several stitches to close the wound, and I was left with an ugly scar on my lips that remains there today.

I was fourteen when I moved to America. I had a hard time keeping up and understanding English, since my classmates would laugh whenever I tried to speak it. We spoke French in school and Bambara at home in Mali. English was never a language I'd needed back home.

Still, I really wanted to do well in my new school. I worked hard to prove to those students how smart I was. I was speaking English in six months, and earned an A average in my first year in America.

Writing became my escape. When I write, I see my characters come alive. I feel in control. It makes me feel like a goddess. It is where I can create a world of my own, where I can be hopeful, joyful, and free; anything can happen when I am holding the pen.

Soon, writing evolved into my lifeline when my classmates went from simply teasing me to all-out bullying. Every time I looked in the mirror at the scar on my lip, it reminded me of what happens when you stand up to bullies. So I said nothing.

When they would taunt me, mock my accent, call me ugly and fat and weird, I would write poetry. "To my dear, depressed, sleepy friends," was the name of my favorite poem I wrote for others whose depression from bullying caused them to be just as exhausted as I was. But writing was not enough.

I could not focus in class. When they would laugh at me, I sometimes quietly cried, and my teachers never seemed to notice any of it. So I started skipping class. Soon, my A average dropped significantly.

The morning I decided to stop skipping school, I looked in the mirror and saw my scar, like I do every day. But this time, I saw something different. I saw the time I stood up for my friend. I saw myself as courageous. I saw myself as a survivor. And everything changed.

Bullies had no right to mess with my education. I realized I should not care about what they think of me, because I was here for myself, not them.

I went to the back of my favorite notebook and wrote down every word the bullies had ever said about me: stupid, fat, ugly. The names they called me over the years filled the entire page. Over the top of those words, I wrote in capital letters, "HEAL."

I took every ounce of power out of those hateful words and gave the power back to myself and began to heal the wounds. Then I wrote another poem:

I didn't give up, it only made me get stronger.
You'll no longer be in my way
You'll no longer be the reason I won't show up.
If I fail, it must be because of me and not you.

I began to share my poems online and got amazing feedback. People were able to relate to the struggles I was going through and to find some encouragement in my words.

Suddenly, my writing was not just for my own healing anymore. By sharing my pain, others felt like they were not alone, that someone out there thinks their life matters.

Writing taught me that loving yourself and making peace with your soul leads you to love others better. I learned to love the world—even the bullies in it.

Writing not only gave me a new sense of self and an opportunity to help others, it also earned me my first major award. It was truly an honor when I received a Silver Key for my poetry in 2015 from the Scholastic Art & Writing Awards.

Writing even led me to pursue a degree in nursing, once I realized that my goal for myself and all people is healing. I want to help people be well, physically and mentally. I believe everybody has the right to be happy. And through my writing and my future career as a nurse, I can help heal the world.

MARIAM'S (R)EVOLUTION

BROOKE OBIE

Working with Mariam this year, I have seen amazing growth in her as a writer and poet and person. Reading Mariam's poetry reminded me of how much I love poems, and that when someone as extraordinary as Mariam comes along, a poetic tribute is the least one should offer.

They think they killed you.
But I saw you yesterday
And read Assata to you,
Your face lighting up.
You reminded me: poetry is
Love.

They think they killed you,
But I saw you yesterday
Sitting tall and knowing
You've got the gift.
Penning words in journals,
Healing yourself.

They think they killed you;
But I saw you yesterday
Going on about the dramas you love.
No longer shrinking into yourself, I saw you
Wide-smiling, all cheeks
Speaking with three tongues.

They think they killed you:
But I saw you yesterday
Standing in the subway,
Reciting your poems to me, to us.
Knowing you have a right
To speak and be heard.

They think they killed you—
But I saw you yesterday
Admiring your own eyes
Curling your own lip with bravery
Anointing your own coils as perfect
Telling your own self you're worthy:

Black skin worthy
Kinky hair worthy

Tall child worthy
Curvy girl worthy
Sparkling eyes worthy
Kind heart worthy
Speak your mind worthy
Have no fear worthy
Deeply loved worthy
Safe from harm worthy.

They think they killed you.
But I saw you yesterday
And read Assata to you,
Your face lighting up.
You reminded me: poetry is
Love.

They think they killed you,
But I saw you yesterday
Sitting tall and knowing
You've got the gift.
Penning words in journals
Healing yourself.

They think they killed you;
But I saw you yesterday
Going on about the dramas you love.
No longer shrinking into yourself, I saw you
Wide-smiling, all cheeks
Speaking with three tongues.

They think they killed you:
But I saw you yesterday
Standing in the Subway,
Reciting your poems to me, to us.
Knowing you have a right
To be heard.

They think they killed you–
But I saw you yesterday
Admiring your own eyes
Curling your own lip with bravery
Anointing your own coils as perfect
Knowing your own self is worthy:

Black skin worthy
Kinky hair worthy
Tall child worthy
Curvy girl worthy
Sparkling eyes worthy
Kind heart worthy
Speak your mind worthy
Have no fear worthy
Deeply loved worthy
Safe from harm worthy,

Girl, they think they killed you!
But I saw you yesterday—
Alive.

KIRBY-ESTAR LAGUERRE

YEARS AS MENTEE: 3
GRADE: Senior
HIGH SCHOOL:
Leon Goldstein High
School for the Sciences
Born: Brooklyn, NY
LIVES: Brooklyn, NY
Publications and
RECOGNITIONS:
Scholastic Art &
Writing Award:
Honorable Mention

MENTEE'S ANECDOTE: *Sunday mornings at the Hungry Ghost café are serene times for Avra and myself. From laughing about unnecessary drama to serious college discussions to just talking about our week, there is never a dull moment during our sessions. These past three years have been extremely memorable, and I cannot believe that our time is about to end. I am beyond grateful to have found who I am as a writer and a young woman with the help of Avra and Girls Write Now. Though this chapter may be over, I will continue to write. About "her," about "him," about "it." About it all.*

AVRA WING

YEARS AS MENTOR: 3
OCCUPATION:
Writer/Writing
Workshop Leader
BORN: New York, NY
LIVES: Brooklyn, NY

MENTOR'S ANECDOTE: *How proud am I of Kirby? So, so proud. Because of her hard work, smarts, talent, and maturity, she snagged a full scholarship to college. I never doubted for a moment she would wind up at a great school. It has been a delight getting to know her these past three years and to see her develop into a strong, self-assured, and serious, as well as seriously funny, woman. What a world of knowledge about teenage life she has given me! I will miss her, but I cannot wait to see what she accomplishes next.*

WHY WON'T YOU STOP!?

KIRBY-ESTAR LAGUERRE

I struggled for quite some time with what I wanted to write about. I could not pick just one thing to be "revolutionized." So, I did not. I picked everything (or mostly everything) that annoys me and compiled it in true Kirby fashion—into a rant list.

Unfortunately, the past eighteen years of my life have been filled with endless frustrations—specifically, things I wish people would *not* do and things I wish people would *not* say. Here are some of the most notorious:

1) Don't ever say to me these two hackneyed lines: "These are the best years of your life," and "One day you'll laugh at this." My cousins told me that high school would be the best four years of my life. But if the best four years of my life happened before I turned eighteen years old and the average life span is seventy-nine years (one hundred and one years for me, if I'm blessed with my great grandmother's genes), what will the other sixty-one to eighty-three years of my life be like? Especially since high school wasn't all that great. Rumors. Heartache. Popularity contests. Fakers. That is supposed to be the highlight of my life? I desperately hope not. My cousins also told me that one day I would laugh at all of that. Oddly enough, I do not think I will ever find the fact that my best friend dated the guy I was in love with amusing.

2) Don't have your TV, movie, or fiction characters say "NOOOOOO!" as if dragging out the letter "o" could keep something bad from happening. If life were truly that easy, I would be saying "NOOOOOO" all over the place. "NOOOOOO" when my AP Chemistry teacher wants to give

us a test on gas laws and "NOOOOOO" when Kanye West goes on yet again another Twitter rant. But, of course, this has not yet been made possible in my time, and I am left leaving short response questions blank and reading tweets about Kanye's ego. So, news flash: saying "NOOOOOO" is in no way helping your characters' "critical" (though in my eyes overly dramatic and totally unrealistic) situation.

3) Don't portray every person who finds out that they have cancer as sad and miserable. My friend Elise did not cry, did not dramatically sob, and certainly did not ask, "How long do I have left?" like the characters you see in movies or read about in books do. Instead, when Dr. Harlow told her that she had been diagnosed with breast cancer, these were her exact words: "Will I still be able to have chicken wings for dinner?"

4) Stop making me look for a "Prince Charming" (a.k.a. the amazing man who makes it his mission to rescue the damsel in distress. According to Urban Dictionary, "he is handsome and romantic and makes all girls swoon."). I don't want one.

5) Stop telling me, "Love isn't always enough." Love should always be enough. If what I feel for someone is authentic, passionate, consuming, and simply beautiful in its rawness, it should work.

6) Stop calling me an "Oreo." I am not shaped like a circle. I do not have cream filling, and the word "Oreo" is not stamped across my torso. Speaking correctly does not equate to being white.

7) Stop asking me "Are you okay?" if all you want to hear is "I'm fine." We both know that anything more than those two words is too much for you to handle.

8) Don't text me an "I miss you" when I am finally starting to move on.

9) Don't tell me I am not allowed to feel that way.

10) Stop saying that I am "pretty for a black girl."

11) Stop comparing me to her. And her. And her.

12) Don't underestimate me.

I am begging you.
Please don't.
Please stop.

REVOLUTIONARY FIRE FOR THE YEAR OF THE RED MONKEY: A FOUND POEM

AVRA WING

After reading a horoscope for the Year of the Fire Monkey, I realized that it fit nicely with the theme of (r)evolution, specifically personal revolution. Obviously, the entry was badly translated from Chinese into English, but the meaning comes through, and the mistakes make the language delightful!

This is the Year of Red Monkey fire, an internal energy period.
If you have been oppressed in a crowd of people, events, emotions,
now get moving in the right direction. Monkey is not banality
and mindset poverty. In the Year of the Monkey, the stars dictate

the rules of the game, give signs to find your own spirit, courage
to walk upstream and be launched in the sparkling whirlpool.
Sing the madness of the brave.

From success point of view, actions not bringing immediate goals
may be useful in the future. It is like saving a drowning child
and in a few years know that she has come to be president
(maybe not the country but a large company)
and helps you in turn.

In school you may be reasoning problems while your friend
solves them in five minutes and has time to comment
with classmates the latest news. Meanwhile your math genius
sweats and dies on a blank page. In 2016, under the auspices of fire,
you will work a bit harder.

In love you will have to choose between custom of freedom
and feelings explosion. You may prefer to bite a piece of your heart
to escape loving traps, or decide captivity is not so bad. Monkey 2016
brings creative love that compels us toward building up and away
from scandal. This is a gift from Venus, the divine devious.
Even due to domain fire element, expect no forest fires. Most people
will be warm and simple on the bottom of their hearts.

Finally, even if everything goes wrong and through the window
always a storm cloud—not to lose faith. Eventually, Sun will appear.
In the end everything comes to natural balance.
Do not shame regarding circumstances lead you by reins,
do not let anyone take you by reins. Let your actions or omissions
be your own free choice!

Live the Year of Monkey 2016 with brightness, color, and joy;
otherwise, the stars will not notice your presence on Earth
and do not give you their blessings.

JENNIFER LEE

YEARS AS MENTEE: 3
GRADE: Senior
HIGH SCHOOL:
Hunter College
High School
BORN: New Haven, CT
LIVES: Queens, NY

MENTEE'S ANECDOTE: *Having been Alex's mentee for the past three years has meant so much to me. In the beginning we were awkward, and never knew quite what to do (How about a prompt? Or would you rather talk?), but now it seems that whenever we sit down together, words flow fluidly between us. I do not quite know where I would be now as a person if I had not met Alex; in so many ways, beyond just writing, she has led me to a deeper understanding of myself and the kinds of things I want to do in the world.*

ALEX BERG

YEARS AS MENTOR: 6
OCCUPATION:
Video Producer,
The Huffington Post
BORN: Philadelphia, PA
LIVES: Brooklyn, NY
**PUBLICATIONS AND
RECOGNITIONS:** Guest
on The Nightly Show
with Larry Wilmore
discussing female
sexuality; campaign
trail coverage of the primaries

MENTOR'S ANECDOTE: *Over the last three years, it has been gratifying to see Jennifer's writing evolve and watch her grow as a person. We manage to write on occasion during our meetings, but our relationship has become much more than just a literary one. Jennifer has a fearlessness about challenging the status quo in her work, which is in line with this year's theme of (r)evolution.*

MOTHER

JENNIFER LEE

I used to think I wanted to be an author; now I think I want to study literature, or go into translation. The possibilities before me are immense, and being a senior, I look forward to pursuing the fields of study I am passionate about in the coming years.

"My mother crossed an ocean for more power."

This is what I say on the angry days, when I think of my mother crossing the Pacific to come study in America, stripping me of the language of my ancestors and bringing me to a country I cannot call my own. But then I remember who that power was for, and I think I am being little too heartless. I say instead: "My mother crossed an ocean for me."

This is how I first remember my mother: I am four, and she is visiting my classroom for parent observation day. The teacher calls my mother "Mrs. Lee." My mother does not correct her. I want to take her by the shoulders and shake her, ask, Why don't you tell her that your last name is Kim, K-I-M, 김 in Hangul, 金 in Hanja? Instead, I learn not to correct the teacher; never speak up in the classroom, the teacher is always right.

We move to the city in second grade; in third, my mother packs up to leave. "It's all your fault," she tells my father. "It's all your fault," she tells my father. It's all your fault; It's all your fault; 다 너탓이야, I hate you and I hate you and I hate you. She has been alternating between spending a month in the city and a month in New Hampshire, back and forth, back and forth, studying for her PhD. This time, she says she wants to leave forever, and I want to draw the words back into her mouth, grab them from the air, apologize for her a thousand times and tell my father She didn't mean it She doesn't mean it She never means what she says She never says what she means.

My mother is in New Hampshire when my father is arrested; silence blankets our family like snow; winter has never been quieter. I imagine she wants to tell my father I trusted you to look after our kids; 어떻게 이럴 수 있어; how could you do something like this, but she says nothing when he comes home. That year she finally finishes her dissertation; she comes back home to stay when I am in fifth grade.

Once, my sister said to my mother, "I don't want to be a housewife when I grow up. I'm going to get a job. I'm going to be better than you." My mother said nothing; she ladled sweet potato curry into my sister's bowl. I wanted to take her by she shoulders and shake her, ask, *Why don't you tell her that you do have a job, that the only reason why you work from home is because you have to take her to school every day, that with a PhD from Dartmouth in computer science you could be getting a real job outside of the house, that if Milkman was right in saying that 'Wanna fly, you got to give up the shit that weighs you down,'[10] then we are the ones weighing you down?* I say nothing; my sister begins eating; I think, *Maybe my mother wants my sister to do better, too.*

I am on the 7 train, talking to a girl I just met at a writing workshop. She is Chinese; she moved to America two years ago. She stares out the window as she says, "When I lived in China, I knew what I wanted to be: a doctor. But now I'm here, and don't know; I'm lost. Sometimes I regret coming to this country." Her bangs hug her glasses, and I imagine she could be a younger version of my mother; I realize I have never seen photos of my mother from before she married, that I do not know what she looked like before I was born. I wonder if this is how my mother feels in America: lost. I wonder what she wanted to be in high school. I wonder if she regrets coming to this country. I wonder what she looked like in high school. I wonder if she regrets my being born.

My sister and I are eating curry again for dinner when my mother says, "If I leave, know that it was your fault." I wonder what she means by leave—leave as in leave the city, leave as in leave the country, or leave as in die, as in, There is nothing for me here, but there is nothing for me

---

10. Morrison, Toni. Song of Solomon. 1977. New York: Random House, 2004. Print.

elsewhere, either. She goes on to say, "너 때문에 참고 있다"—that is, I am putting up because of you, or I am enduring because of you. I wonder what it is she is putting up with—my father, or the loneliness of working at home, or maybe the unbearable weight of not being heard.

As much as I may say that my mother crossed the Pacific for more power, I think maybe I am just lying to myself. I do not know why my mother came to this country, or what she was running from; all I know is that what she found was not what she was looking for. I try to remind myself of that when I think of what it would be like to return to Korea— that my imagined homeland, too, may be nothing but a utopia: "u-" as in "no," and "-topi" as in "place."

HUFFPOST: SIX THINGS WHITE FEMINISTS CAN DO IN RESPONSE TO SANDRA BLAND AND POLICEBRUTALITY AGAINST WOMEN OF COLOR

ALEX BERG

Our nation has become more conscious of police brutality against people of color thanks to the Black Lives Matter movement. As a white feminist, we need to have more conversations about how we're complicit in these systems—an "evolution" of our views that could be part of a "revolution."

Dear fellow white feminists,

We need to talk about Sandra Bland.

More specifically, we need to talk about why we *are not* talking about Sandra Bland.

Bland was a twenty-eight-year-old black woman who died in a Texas county jail after she was arrested during a traffic stop for allegedly failing to signal a lane change. During the stop, officer Brian Encinia attempted to physically remove Bland from her vehicle and threatened to "light her up" with a taser because she refused to put out her cigarette. Three days later, on July 13th, Bland was found dead in her cell. Officials have ruled her death as suicide by hanging. However, her family and others have contested this claim, as Bland had recently moved to Texas to begin a new job at her alma mater, Prairie View A&M University. She was "someone who was extremely spontaneous, spunky, outgoing, truly filled with life and joy," according to one of her four sisters on CNN.

Bland's death did not happen in a vacuum—it is part of a pattern of brutality against cis and trans women of color. Her death comes in the wake of the killings of Tanisha Anderson and Natasha McKenna, black women who perished while in police custody and prison, respectively. Her death comes a month after a white police officer pinned down a fifteen-year-old black girl at a pool party in McKinney, Texas. It punctuates the eleven transgender women—many women of color—who have been murdered in the past seven months. Her death comes almost exactly a year after Eric Garner, Mike Brown, and Tamir Rice, two unarmed black men and a black child, were killed by police. And, now it precedes Ralkina Jones, a thirty-seven-year-old black woman who was found dead at a Cleveland jail on Sunday.

Black, Latina, indigenous, cis, and trans women of color are under assault in America. But white and "mainstream" feminists have yet to take up the brutality against them as a feminist issue.

From the blatantly racist white Suffragettes to Taylor Swift shutting down Nicki Minaj over her VMA critique, we white feminists have marginalized, trivialized, and erased women of color in the movement throughout the ages. We have rightfully taken up reproductive justice, same-sex marriage, and closing the wage gap, but we have made these issues our priority even as the safety of women of color has reached a state of emergency. Just last week, we filled our feeds with support for Planned Parenthood over misleading videos on fetal tissue research—why didn't #SandraBland consume our feeds the week before?

We forget that feminists of color have be fighting with us and for us, so we buy into a false narrative of scarcity in activism. We fear that we will lose resources if we re-center the mainstream feminist movement on the needs of women of color. We are scared of giving up the economic and social benefits of our privilege. Or maybe we don't even know where to begin.

Yet there are many changes we can make as white feminists to take up police brutality against Sandra Bland and other cis and trans women of color. And, many of these changes are accessible and cost-free. Here are six things we can do—though hardly exhaustive or new—that can be a jumping off point.

1. TALK, TALK, TALK

Too often the work of racial justice in feminism—and moving feminism forward—falls on the shoulders of feminists of color. We need to have conversations about race among white feminists *before* the Patricia Arquettes of the world incite us to address our biases. Let us talk about our privilege and how we act on that privilege. Let's talk about how there is no monolithic experience of being a woman. Let's talk about how Sandra Bland's identities intersected as a woman and as a person of color to make her more likely to experience state-sanctioned violence. Then, let's discuss how other identities—queer, class, citizenship, different abilities, religion—impact a woman's experience of her gender.

2. EDUCATE OURSELVES AND EACH OTHER

Feminists, intellectuals and activists of color have done boundless work on racial justice, feminism, and police brutality—and we can access much of it from the comfort of our laptops and e-readers. Start reading websites like Black Girl Dangerous, For Harriet, and the Crunk Feminist Collective every morning. Follow Twitter accounts like Black Lives Matter, its creators, Patrisse Cullors, Alicia Garza, and Opal Tometi, and writers like Mikki Kendall and Jamilah Lemieux. Parse through the hashtags #BlackLivesMatter, #SayHerName, #SolidarityIsForWhiteWomen, and #GirlsLikeUs. Pick up a book like Ta-Nehisi Coates's *Between the World and Me*, Michelle Alexander's *The New Jim Crow*, or Janet Mock's *Redefining Realness*. Do not stop at these websites, accounts and books—there are so many more. Which leads us to . . .

3. SIGNAL BOOST

As you read articles and tweets, repost! And lend books to your family and friends. Reposting and sharing have two benefits: we can elevate and spread the work of women and activists of color, giving credit where it is due, *and* we can introduce our social media circles to ideas around brutality and privilege that they might not see otherwise. As white feminists, we have access to people of privilege in our social circles that others may not be able to reach. When we boost the work of women of color, we are digitally bringing these issues to those followers. Thanks to Facebook, my high school track coach in Pennsylvania has an opportunity to learn about intersectional identities—and it's as easy as a click of the mouse.

4. SPEAK OUT AND SHOW UP

When we witness racism in public, we have to speak out. When we see microaggressions in the office, we have to speak out. When we hear a biased joke in the comfort of our own homes, we have to speak out. Then, we have to show up. The #BlackLivesMatter movement and other organizations have protests and gatherings around the country on a regular basis. They are often posted on Facebook. It takes a couple of hours to attend these events, and we can provide numbers and support with our presence.

5. STEP BACK

There are times to speak out, and there are times to remain silent. We need to listen to women of color. And when we ourselves are called out, we have to step back and meditate on our actions and discomfort. When we are taking up the conversation, we have to step back to give women of color the space to speak. Once we show up at a demonstration, we need to support women of color without co-opting their movement. That is when we should take cues from black leadership and remain peaceful. We should avoid any actions to make protesters of color more vulnerable, such as being violent, throwing debris, or agitating police officers.

6. DONATE

In addition to time, we can donate money or other resources to organizations that are bringing justice for Sandra Bland and other women of color killed by police brutality. A few organizations include the Dream Defenders, Dignity & Power Now, and the Sylvia Rivera Law Project. Again, like education, there are so many amazing organizations, Kickstarters, and activists. Find them and donate to them, too.

MUHUA LI

YEARS AS MENTEE: 2
GRADE: Senior
HIGH SCHOOL: Flushing International High School
BORN: Henan, China
LIVES: Queens, NY

MENTEE'S ANECDOTE: *This is my second year in Girls Write Now with my mentor, Alanna. This year with her is a little different from last year. Because we already know each other well, this year we just spent all of our time writing. When we practice writing together, we can always find new common characteristics between us, and we like to share personal experiences with each other. My mentor is like my friend instead of a teacher, I enjoy myself when we meet.*

ALANNA SCHUBACH

YEARS AS MENTOR: 2
OCCUPATION: Freelance writer and teacher
BORN: Oceanside, NY
LIVES: Queens, NY
PUBLICATIONS AND RECOGNITIONS:
2015 Fellow in Fiction with the New York Foundation for the Arts

MENTOR'S ANECDOTE: *Meeting with Muhua for the second year in a row has been exciting; in the fall, she will go off to college, and I feel privileged to have gotten to know her better during this time. She is as intelligent, imaginative, and funny as ever, and she is definitely going to do something special with her life. I am sure we will keep in touch, and continue sharing our writing and our thoughts with each other.*

MY LiFE WiTH MY DAD

MUHUA LI

I wrote this piece because it shows how I evolved and tried to maintain the relationship between my dad and me. It represents the changes we made together, and how we came to understand each other better gradually.

After my mom and I came to the US to meet my dad, my mom went out of the state for work, and the daily life between me and my dad has become that I hide my maturity and show off my naivety and childishness. Because I found out that my dad feels happier to see the childish me instead of seeing the mature me. I like to portray myself as a girl who likes to steal food from the kitchen, like a thief, and I also like to pretend that I accidentally left some evidence for him to realize my "crime." For example, I will leave some sauce on my lips, or make my footsteps sound really loud. I enjoy playing the role of a little daughter, and I like when I can show off my naivety. As a young lady who is turning eighteen this summer, I need to find someone and show my mischievousness and coquetry. And I believe that my dad likes to see that I am still his daughter, and I will always be the little girl who followed him all around.

My dad is a dull guy—his dullness is the same from ten years ago. I remember in my childhood, when my friends snuggled in their dads' arms, I was so jealous because my dad never allowed me to hug him. And his reason for that was a cold sentence: "That is too hot, leave me alone." Since I was young, I've had the recognition that my dad can hardly understand and accept my love for him.

Once, my dad cooked a table full of delicious food for me, and we had dinner together that night. I remember those delicious foods were so attractive, not only because I loved the food but also because they were made by my dad. At that moment, I felt that all my loving cells had gathered to my brain. I was moved to say, "Daddy, I wish I can still eat the food you cook for me after thirty years." I swear to god that I was trying to use a metaphor to show that I want my dad to stay healthy and still stay with me after thirty years. I knew he couldn't show his heart to me directly, but at least he should say something like, "We will always be together, don't worry." However, my dad, the affection murderer, once again killed all my feeling in one sentence: "What? You still want me work for you after thirty years?"

And there it is. I was totally shocked, and I didn't know how to explain myself to my dad. We just finished that meal embarrassedly. My dad always has the magic to ruin all the love in a moment. Sometimes I really want to figure out how he chased my mom.

My dad's dullness is kind of well-known. Sometimes my mom and I, us two women, will come together and criticize my dad's dullness. But even though he is not romantic at all, he still shows his love to us in his own way.

Once I watched a movie about school violence. There was a little boy who got slapped on his face by his classmate. When the little boy told his parents about it, his parents didn't trust him—they thought it was just a joke between friends. I felt so sad for the kid, and felt very disappointed by his parents. Then I called my dad and asked him what he would do if someone slapped my face. And he didn't give me an answer; instead, he immediately asked me if I had been slapped by someone. I heard his worries through his voice, and that was so warm and nice for me.

In that moment, I thought that even though my dad is a dull and quiet man, he is a good dad for me—a great dad.

THREE GENERATIONS OF SEX POSITIVITY

ALANNA SCHUBACH

This is an excerpt from a longer essay published in the Washington Post *about my revolutionary grandmother and mother, and how they influenced me.*

When my grandmother died last summer at ninety-seven, my family asked me to write the eulogy. The only challenge was which stories to highlight from her long life: Her stint during World War II as a Navy Wave, driving ambulances and delivering ship plans? The time she chased down a pickpocket on the subway, or befriended a biker gang during a solo trip to Las Vegas? Her piercing intellect, how her idea of a fun read was *Thus Spake Zarathustra*?

Though I managed to patch together a tribute that communicated the sheer abundance of her ninety-seven years, and hinted at her progressiveness, I was struck by what I *couldn't* include, perhaps one of her greatest gifts: her sex positivity.

Born in 1917, three years before suffrage, my grandmother came of age in an era not exactly known for giving women's sexuality much consideration. And yet, mysteriously, she somehow learned that she, as much as any man, deserved to experience pleasure.

And did she ever. My grandmother taught by example that sex was not only fun and fulfilling, but one of the engines that powers healthy relationships. "How's the chemistry?" she'd ask me each time I started seeing someone new. Her marriage to my grandfather was a great romance; my mother recalls that well into their sixties, he'd often give my grandma a playful pat on the rear as she walked by. After decades of partnership, they were still excited to be near each other. Every night, over the many long years after his death, she sprayed his cologne on her pillow before going to sleep.

Thankfully, my parents kept their own sex life private—but they didn't withhold any information. My mother provided me with a frank and shame-free education about sexuality, and answered honestly when I had questions.

And in my case, coming of age in a sex positive environment made me take sex *more* seriously than I otherwise might have. I learned it should be pleasurable and fun, but also a way for two people who appreciated and respected one another to connect—which meant I didn't want to have it with just anyone. That would have struck me as wasteful.

Even my first kiss became a kind of holy idea: when it was clear it was going to happen one summer evening, during a backyard game of Spin the Bottle, I pulled my friend Erikk aside and told him I wanted it to be with someone I cared about rather than subject to random chance. He obliged, and we kissed in the narrow space between the house and a row of hedges. I was elated that I had experienced this rite of passage on my own terms.

In retrospect, what I was doing on a small scale was advocating for myself. And this is not a skill that is innate: I had to be taught.

JANE LIU

YEARS AS MENTEE: 1
GRADE: Senior
HIGH SCHOOL: Millennium Brooklyn High School
BORN: New York, NY
LIVES: Brooklyn, NY
PUBLICATIONS AND RECOGNITIONS: Scholastic Art & Writing Awards: Gold Key, Silver Key, Honorable Mention; Stage of Life essay writing contest winner; jaBlog! contributor

MENTEE'S ANECDOTE: *Bright lights, streaking cars, first meetings. Welcome to Times Square. At the corner, below glowing storefronts and numerous billboards, I struggled to hold my bag steady as I waved my hands, fairly stumbling over my words. Maeve understood then, as she does now. "Like antidepressants!" she exclaimed. "Taken to extremes," I agreed, my mind already dissecting this new example, admiring it from all angles, and finding it a perfect fit. "You really think this could be worth publishing?" I asked. "Totally." This was like getting struck by lightning; I went home and madly drafted another scene, then another. I'm still writing.*

MAEVE HIGGINS

YEARS AS MENTOR: 1
OCCUPATION: Writer and comedian
BORN: Cork, Ireland
LIVES: New York, NY
PUBLICATIONS AND RECOGNITIONS:
Off You Go, Hachette UK, 2015

MENTOR'S ANECDOTE: *I do not know what or who I was expecting, but it certainly was not Jane. She dazzled me with talk of her novel, her poetry, her love of books. I immediately loved her curiosity and smarts, and her brilliant imagination. We got to work, editing, rewriting, applying for scholarships, trying to find an agent. We have been working since, and it is a lot! Watching Jane's growing confidence and dedication to her craft has been fantastic for me, and helps me to be braver in my own work every day.*

BUTTERFLY WINGS

JANE LIU

I have always been fascinated with butterflies: their ephemeral incandescence and natural metamorphosis astounds me. Across cultures and regions, butterflies are symbols of hope and change. In New York City, there are few butterflies of the sort captured by glossy magazines, but the many revolutions emblazoned across monochromatic newsprint serve in their stead.

When
A revolution begins,
No gunshot marks the start
It begins with soundless wings
Sugarspun wings that bear a coming hurricane
Holding aloft a body close to death
Eggs are laid and discarded by the starved founders
Days later, perhaps one egg cracks
The inching body munches on young leaves
While an eagerly watching audience, gap-toothed
And knee-skinned, shudders in raw anticipation.

When
A revolution gains momentum,
No one believes that it can survive, not even
You, the caretaker and the scientist
You tuck the curled thumb-sized flesh

Into a soft white prison first
A loose netted pavilion, or a cold glass conservatory
To keep it safe and sheltered
You control the temperature and fetch sustenance
You bring pills and water because you're scared
It looks so delicate; it is delicate.

When
A revolution finds itself caged, you feel sorry
The revolution is supposed to be wild and free
Did you take it home and welcome it into your life?
No. You stole it and lied, saying
It couldn't have survived without you
You know it'll leave
You want to pet it; you can't
Because the chrysalis is shaking slightly with the breeze
It can be a hurricane, and a tide, and a quake.
It is all that, and more.

When
A revolution breathes in those first
Struggling breaths, it is so easily defeated
Those breaths are butterfly scales
You can't touch, you can't approach the glass
The revolution is fragile and delicate
The organism has
All of the colors and none of the substance.

When
A revolution's growth shudders
Like an infant's soft skull, the exoskeleton of the revolution
Has to knit together; needs a nurturer
And a protector and a fighter until
The chrysalis splits open, and the revolution
Leaves its former home, the casing, to shrivel and dry.

When
A revolution finds its footing
On slender hairy legs
It isn't just for you any longer
It's for a world, for the cruel universe of people
Who would not be this gentle.

When
A revolution lifts the thin membranes,
Of its forewing and its hindwing
They have not frayed or torn
The veins are narrow and sure
The cells sprouting from the base in
Striped black and orange are glistening
With mucus and new life
That's when the revolution takes flight.

When
A revolution launches itself into the air
It swallows up the sun and
Stars and earth and all the space
In between; the empty spaces and the
Full spaces; the places that wound and
The ones that throb
A revolution captures all
In a vibrant net of lines and curves
That flow from the base of a sweeping wing,
And the cycle begins anew.

DOING SOMETHING VS. DOING NOTHING

MAEVE HIGGINS

This is an extract from an op-ed I wrote for The New York Times. Lucky for me, we had a workshop in op-ed writing just as I was finishing up the piece! Jane read an early draft and had some helpful insight and advice. Win-win!

Somehow in September, on the comedian Todd Barry's podcast, we started talking about money. I'm not sure why but I told him that I had $1,300 in my bank account. I guess I was showing off, because that is the most money I have had since I moved to America from Ireland last year. Todd seemed rattled, like maybe that was not a lot. He asked what I would do if I somehow got more money, and I got flustered and said that I would probably give it to Syrian refugees. Then I felt embarrassed. Todd said I should do a fundraiser and I hurriedly agreed so we could stop talking about it already.

What was I thinking? I'm not even a good or proactive person! I'm a lazy person prone to melancholy. That very afternoon I didn't go to a free Pilates class because I couldn't find one of my shoes. "Even if I find the shoe and go to the class," I reasoned, wondering if maybe it was under the bed, "the body will age and disintegrate." My back was bothering me, which is why I didn't feel like crawling under the bed to look for the shoe, and also why I needed to take a Pilates class. You see? It's difficult for lazy and sad people to get things done, because our natural inclination is not to.

So, I'm putting on a show. How to do that is unclear at first. Stand-up comedy is a solitary profession. We are lone wolves, stalking the land at night, hunting for approval from strangers who've been drinking. To get a group of us together to perform, I'll need to ask for favors. It's a delicate thing—people are busy, it's the holidays, I'm asking them to donate their time. And then there is the irrefutable fact that what is happening in Syria is the opposite of comedy. I'm not hopeful, but I send out the call. Replies come in throughout the day, the same three words over and over: "Count me in." Perhaps they've been feeling tiny like me, powerless against the horror of wrecked boats and lost lives.

So, where does that leave us? The show is all set. I am doing something. If I'm bone honest I'm doing it for me, to alleviate my own pain. I'm beginning to understand that everything I do is about me, but at the same time I am part of something bigger, so really it becomes not about me at all. I see how calamitous things are for the people of Syria and I can't truthfully say that there is nothing I can do. The realization that I'm not helpless is uncomfortable. Yes, I'm in the world and part of the human race, responsible for more than just myself and my missing shoe. And yes, the shoe was under the bed. Just yesterday I used a coat hanger to fish it out.

ZAHRAA LOPEZ

YEARS AS MENTEE: 1
GRADE: Senior
HIGH SCHOOL: Cristo Rey
New York High School
BORN: Bronx, NY
LIVES: Bronx, NY
**PUBLICATIONS AND
RECOGNITIONS:**
Scholastic Art &
Writing Award:
Honorable Mention

MENTEE'S ANECDOTE: *Catherine is the older sister I always wanted. I honestly don't know what I would do without her. She listens to my corny jokes, boy drama, and complaints. She truly understands me, and I am so lucky to have her. I feel like I have known her for my whole life. I am really scared to go away to college, but I know it will be easier with Catherine by my side. I love her so much.*

CATHERINE LECLAIR

YEARS AS MENTOR: 2
OCCUPATION:
Senior Strategist,
Gawker Media
BORN: Bangor, ME
LIVES: Brooklyn, NY
**PUBLICATIONS AND
RECOGNITIONS:** Published
in McSweeney's Internet
Tendency, panelist at
the ASJA annual writers
conference

MENTOR'S ANECDOTE: *On the first day Zahraa and I met, she immediately greeted me with a huge, warm hug. In her writing she is so honest and genuine, glowing and ripe with a love of life. Each moment—no matter how small—that I spend with Zahraa she is filled with a palpable joy, and she's taught me to be a more joyful person because of that. The way Zahraa lives her life—with gratitude, an intentional presence, and fun-loving determination—will continue to inspire me long after she has headed off to college. I love her!*

KEEPING FAITH

ZAHRAA LOPEZ

Seeing my mother go through her own revolution by helping her complete college inspired me to go through my own revolution by applying to college this year.

My mother was always a warrior. She was born battling the tough streets of Bed Stuy, strong and ready to conquer the world. Quick to have her guard up and seldom trusted people. She never believed in her self-worth and she had no idea that she'd be a savior some day.

When she had us she decided she no longer wanted to linger on her past. She wanted to build a future that her babies would be proud of, an empire that would grow with us. But she didn't think she'd be able to do it on her own. The man she thought she loved grew distant, and her empire was falling. But she never lost hope. Her faith was as strong as her grip on God, refusing to let go. Two years ago she decided to go back and get something that could never be taken away from her: an education. She struggled through many sleepless nights, and I was always beside her, doing 2 A.M. grammar checks without my own homework done. But seeing her walk across the stage to get her diploma made everything worth it. That piece of paper was the key to freedom—Momma, you earned it. Tears fell down my face and I was so proud, like I was the parent and she was the child.

A year later the tables turned. Now I was staying up late to edit my college applications, and through it all my mother was my biggest motivation. Soon I'll be walking across the stage to get my diploma. I am afraid of the future. But I know my mother's perseverance will continue to inspire me. When I feel like giving up I will think of her: a single mother with the weight of the world on her shoulders. When I have children one day, I hope I can be half the woman she is. Half as strong, half as kind, half as determined.

If she can do it, so can I.

TRUST FALL

CATHERINE LECLAIR

All of the incredibly strong women I know have taught me that being independent doesn't mean going through life without help. Learning how to lean on my friends and family this past year showed me how essential vulnerability is for growth.

I am lucky that I've been able to live under the illusion that I am largely in control of my life. No grandparents have died, no great scandals or tragedies have scarred my relationships. When I interview I get offered the job, and when I sign up for a marathon I always cross the finish line. This correlation between hard work and success has been so drilled into my existence that it has seemed nearly impossible to imagine that I can't create the results I'm looking for.

But this year I am dumped. And my writing is rejected by editor after editor after editor. And then one warm summer night I am attacked from behind in my safe Brooklyn neighborhood, grabbed by my hair so hard that the next day no amount of Advil can quell the soreness in my neck. And it is only then, as I am flushing my hair, which has fallen out in chunks, down the toilet the next morning, that I finally begin to admit to myself that I might not actually be at the helm of this ship.

Finally, it was my turn to learn what it is that people do when they feel like they're getting punched in the gut by life: I had to let myself fall and be caught by the people who love me. No amount of can-do attitude could win back my boyfriend, make my writing get noticed, or ensure that I would never be in the wrong place at the wrong time again. So instead I lived out my own personal sad romantic comedy montage. I let myself be hugged and held close by my friends, went dancing and stayed out late, and talked long into the night over sloshing mugs of wine. I called my mom and wrote letters to my sister, and ate cake for breakfast. I relaxed into their embraces and tried to let my heart be open and believed that solace is found in people, not in solitude, because being a fortress sounds boring.

I am not a rock. I am not an island. I will be dumped and rejected and hurt again. I will, for a time, grow cynical and doubtful of the ability of the people I love to fix the situations that befall me, or that I get myself into. But whether I believe in them or not, whether I deserve it or not, they will work their magic on me anyway. And that type of love might be stronger than willpower was all along.

MARIAMA LOUCOUMBAR

YEARS AS MENTEE: 1
GRADE: Junior
HIGH SCHOOL:
International Community
High School
BORN: Dakar, Senegal
LIVES: Bronx, NY

MENTEE'S ANECDOTE: *My favorite memory was when we made metaphors using folded paper, like the fortune-teller game. We combined ideas with images to get silly or interesting metaphors to write poems with (like sadness is an icy moon). I loved it.*

SUSAN SIMONDS

YEARS AS MENTOR: 1
OCCUPATION:
Office coordinator
BORN: Milford, CT
LIVES: New York, NY

MENTOR'S ANECDOTE: *I remember teaching Mariama about poetry, and how she was already writing with concrete images and descriptive language. I really enjoyed one session where we revised a fiction piece of hers into a poem, it was so fun to show her how much of a poet she already was.*

AFRICA

MARIAMA LOUCOUMBAR

I wrote the poem "Africa" right after I watched Kendrick Lamar's presentation about Africa and how he is proud to be an African American. It made me realize how proud I was also to be African.

Africa made me.
Africa raised me.
Africa showed me the great horizon.
Africa made me feel the hot weather during December days and June nights.
I am standing on American land but all I see when I blink is the Africa that gave me a name.
The Africa that sings songs with its wind when baby me cried.
The Africa that built the stubborn me,
The independent me,
The joyful me.
The me that won't give up.
The me that will one day make a great difference and show the hidden Africa,
The beautiful Africa that media doesn't show and books don't talk about.
The palm trees,
The beautiful sand beaches,
The diversity of smiles.
Africa made me.
Africa raised me.
Africa loved me long before anyone else.
Africa makes me proud.

SECRET

SUSAN SIMONDS

"Secret" was inspired by a poem by Mariama in which she announced her love of reading and writing. Her poem motivated me to explore my own relationship with writing.

Glass was only an atom of separation
but she held it like a fragile bone
arms locked ahead, gravity teasing
nine point eight meters per second

per second glance, she was not afraid
of the fall, or the shatter
or the fragments announcing the pity
of a secret like a hazy night sky

she wanted only to share the maze
of ache she learned to release
and watch the dust of her shield
run ringlets round her in the wind

CHRISTINA LOW

YEARS AS MENTEE: 1
GRADE: Sophomore
HIGH SCHOOL:
Queens High School
for the Sciences at
York College
BORN: New York, NY
LIVES: Queens, NY

MENTEE'S ANECDOTE: *This year Shannon has opened me up to many new perspectives, both in my writing and life. She inspires me to be more confident in myself and to not be afraid to try new things, always seeing the glass half full. I am very thankful to have met such a caring and helpful mentor.*

SHANNON CARLIN

YEARS AS MENTOR: 1
OCCUPATION:
Freelance entertainment
reporter
BORN: Ronkonkoma, NY
LIVES: Brooklyn, NY
**PUBLICATIONS AND
RECOGNITIONS:**
*Refinery29, Bustle,
Bust Magazine*

MENTOR'S ANECDOTE: *When Christina and I meet on Friday afternoon she starts by telling me about her week, which she will often admit was not great. It is then I remember what it is like to be a teenager and how tough those years can be. In our time together I hope Christina gets a chance to relax and just write because when she does it is so thoughtful, with beautifully philosophical takes on her own life that feel universal. I almost feel selfish that it is me who gets to watch this young poet find her voice. Now you will get a chance to see it, too.*

SOCIAL ANXIETY

CHRISTINA LOW

This piece was inspired by my own personal experience dealing with social anxiety and my recent attempts to improve and get better. I am hoping others will relate to this. Here is my story.

Mouth agape and wide
No words escaping
Only the air around me,
stinging with insecurity

The locked, cold steel bars of my mind
Trapped, frozen, paralyzed
As if struck by lightning
Waiting to be unlocked

Cinder blocks piled on top of me,
deflating my lungs
Millions of thoughts scratching at the surface of my brain
Desperate to escape
But they are forever trapped
Racing against time
Racing against myself.

The ruminating starts
Infusing my cheeks like a boiling hot fire

I get lost in the beating of my heart,
a deafening drum.

"Why am I like this?"
"Just go and say it!"
"Go and speak your mind!"
"Be a rebel!"

But what if someone laughs
Thinks you're uneducated
I want to run away
Far away, just me and the birds
who have wings to fly somewhere happy

But I look back and my wings are clipped
Feathers falling, turning into ash
Disappearing the moment they hit the ground
Like me.

No.
I take off the invisibility cloak with all my might.
I let my smile shine through,
like the sun after an entire morning of snow.
I melt away the darkness.
I raise my hand and say a few words
that others might find effortlessly, like it's nothing
But to me, it feels like everything.

JENNiFER LAWRENCE WAS REMOVED FROM *HUNGER GAMES* POSTERS iN ISRAEL, BUT THIS iS NOTHiNg NEW

SHANNON CARLIN

My mentee Christina wrote a short story about girls in a dystopian world where one test could make or break their future. Later, I read an article about Katniss Everdeen–free movie posters in Israel and was reminded that Christina's story of women being held back wasn't fiction at all.

Hunger Games fans that live in Israel may have noticed something a little off about their *Mockingjay: Part 2* posters. Namely, that Jennifer Lawrence wasn't on them in the more Orthodox neighborhoods of Jerusalem and Bnei Brak; she was replaced with the image of a fiery mockingjay instead.

While this version of the final movie's poster may not do much to highlight Katniss Everdeen's role as the leader of a dystopian uprising, it's just one example of how some of the ultra-Orthodox in Israel, also known *asharedim*, have tried to make women disappear from public view.

In 2011 the *Los Angeles Times* reported that the ever-expanding ultra-Orthodox community, which practices a stricter form of Judaism, was "seeking to expand religious-based segregation into the public realm" and believed displaying photos of women in public was "indecent."

That same year, the mayor of Jerusalem, Nir Barkat, ordered the police to crack down on those who deface billboards with women on them. At that time, it was reported that billboards and advertisements featuring women had become "a rare sight in Israel's capital" because they were "habitually defaced and torn down within hours by strictly-Orthodox activists." A campaign looking to attract organ donors even chose to use only men in their advertisements after ones with women led vandals to light buses featuring the ads on fire. Many companies started to self-censor themselves, using only male models so that they wouldn't lose money.

But the real cost is much worse to the women of the community; as the New Israel Fund (NIF) wrote in an e-mail quoted in *The Guardian*, "When the advertisers eliminate images of women, they reinforce a worldview in which women must be hidden, where women can't have any meaningful role outside of the home."

This most recent poster battle in Israel is not about Jennifer Lawrence— it is about the growing discrimination women in the country face every day. The ultra-Orthodox community claims they are eliminating posters featuring women to "protect women's honor and dignity." But others say this is an example of religious extremism overpowering basic freedoms.

"The pattern is one of creeping encroachment," Anat Saragusti, the then-director of Agenda, an Israeli group that works on minority-rights issues, told the *LA Times* in 2011. "They try a little, see if it works, and then push the envelope a bit more every time until things reach a critical mass and are irreversible. That is when people wake up. But by that point, it is often too late."

The problem in the country, which has been described using the Hebrew phrase *"hadarat nashim,"* or "the exclusion of women," is much bigger than censored movie posters, and it is growing worse each year. Women are becoming invisible in public places. It makes you wish Israel had its own Katniss Everdeen to take on the ultra-Orthodox community. Of course, it's much harder to wage a rebellion if your photo is not allowed to appear on any of the posters.

WINKIE MA

YEARS AS MENTEE: 2
GRADE: Junior
HIGH SCHOOL:
Stuyvesant High School
BORN: Brooklyn, NY
LIVES: Brooklyn, NY
**PUBLICATIONS AND
RECOGNITIONS:**
Scholastic Art &
Writing Award:
Honorable Mentions

MENTEE'S ANECDOTE: *Before I met Stephanie, I tried to stick to the formula as much as possible. I wrote with the same ideas, feelings, and formatting that I had been using to write with my whole life. I was too afraid to step out of convention. However, under Stephanie's guidance, I started to ask more questions and think more deeply. My stories flourished in depth and detail. Our sessions went beyond just learning to write. I learned to challenge myself—to try something new each time. In doing so, I have evolved as a writer, and I have evolved as a person.*

STEPHANIE GOLDEN

YEARS AS MENTOR: 2
OCCUPATION:
Freelance author
and journalist
BORN: Brooklyn, NY
LIVES: Brooklyn, NY

MENTOR'S ANECDOTE: *I am the grandchild of immigrants, and Winkie is the child of immigrants. As we work on her pieces, I watch her thinking through perennial immigrant issue—conflicts between parents and children, between keeping the old culture and embracing the new—much as I saw them in my own friends and family, and as they are echoed in immigrant literature. It is such an American story, repeating over generations: both reassuring, because it's normal, and frustrating, because there is no single answer telling you what is right. But it is a struggle that helps us evolve.*

THREE REFLECTIONS

WINKIE MA

I wrote this piece for the Dystopian Fiction Workshop. It is flash fiction—only 500 words. As I wrote, I was thinking of power, but in a strange turn of events, the story went the other way.

Bella has been counting the days. It is day four. She's in the dormitory bathroom, staring at the mirror, cocking her head to the side. She looks different. Her orange hair, normally vibrant and pulsing with liveliness, is a shade darker. She lifts a shaky hand to her face. Her cold fingers trace the fading freckles across her cheeks. The matron said this is what those gray pills are for—it's part of growing up. All the other girls' faces have been blank and paper-like the past few days. One to two weeks is all it takes, her friend Jenelle reassured her. Then they'll be out of this godforsaken place and rewarded with a secure job in the government. Bella casts another lingering look in the mirror before heading back to the dormitory.

Day nine. Bella ducks into the factory bathroom. I am a mess, she thinks, gazing at herself in the mirror. The nightly pills are undeniably in full effect. Her hair is darker, limply clinging to her gaunt face. Even beneath layers of soot, she can make out the paleness of her skin. Bella leans in closer to the mirror, noticing how the pills have drained the emerald glimmer from her eyes. The other girls are changing, too. Each day a few girls are taken away by men in gray suits. And each day Bella wonders just how they are being rewarded. One night Bella considers spitting out the pill, but Jenelle convinces her not to. She reassures her that once it is all over they will be fine. But Bella can see the lethargy in Jenelle's blank eyes, can hear the doubt wavering in her voice. Even Jenelle doesn't really trust the pills.

At last it is day fourteen. Bella is alone. Jenelle, the other girls . . . they're all *gone*. Waves of fear crash over her as she stares at her reflection after dinner in the dormitory mirror. Her hair is pitch-black, her skin fairer than snow. Her freckles are gone. The pills have replaced her irises with black holes. She is like a ghost, ready to vanish at any moment.

Bella turns around and nearly jumps: the matron is there, holding out the gray capsule. With her heart pounding and the pill inside her mouth, Bella thinks, *It's my last chance to spit it out. I can do it.*

But it's too late. She's powerless. She swallows the pill.

Later that night Bella lies on her bed, hands folded on top of her stomach. She stares straight at the ceiling and doesn't sleep. Instead, she waits.

CONEY ISLAND: PLAYGROUND OF THE UNCONSCIOUS

STEPHANIE GOLDEN

I wrote this piece after Winkie and I visited the Brooklyn Museum. Her response to the contrast between Coney Island today and its past as shown in the exhibit, plus my own memories, got me thinking about the (r)evolution in girls' lives since I was her age.

I only visited Coney Island once as a child. But in my memory it's magical: the huge carousel horses in the Steeplechase amusement park, with waving manes and real tails (a horse-crazy kid could pretend her mount was alive); the polished wooden slides, so tall I was afraid to go down them; the Steeplechase ride, whose mechanical horses coursed along a long outdoor track (I longed to go but was too timid); the Tilt-a-Whirl, which made me sick.

By the time I returned as an adult, the Steeplechase had been torn down, the streets were shabby and seedy, the remaining rides were nothing special (and I got sick on the Wonder Wheel). The magic was gone.

So I went to the Brooklyn Museum's Coney Island exhibit looking to find it again. Old photos of the Steeplechase made me wish my kid-self had had more guts. The horses with real tails were there, but seemed small now. Mostly I found a Coney I never saw as a child: a site of the transgressive. The exhibit was a blowout of libido, grotesque freaks of nature, and fearful images bursting from the collective unconscious.

That Coney offered real freaks (deformed and disabled people who made a living displaying themselves) and imagined monsters. In the exhibit's movie clips, courting couples rode the roller coaster, crashed into each other in bumper cars, and disappeared into the dark Tunnel of Love, where women let their fences down, and men climbed over.

It was a modern Carnival, reincarnating the old seasonal festivals of Europe that featured disruptive inversions of social norms: people dressed as animals and as the opposite sex, fools exalted as mock-kings, clergy drinking and singing obscene songs in church. Carnival gave people a chance to let off steam, to give rein to unsocialized, anarchic impulses. So did Coney Island, as is clear from the names of two major attractions: Luna Park (ruled by the moon, a place to be a lunatic for a while) and Dreamland.

Luna and Dreamland were gone by the fifties, though the rides were still wild. I still regret my own timidity. But other young girls did have the guts.

Bonnie: I got scared on the Cyclone, but I went again and again. I loved one carousel. It was really fast and big. On the Ferris wheel I went in the swinging cars.

Arline: Boys would treat me to a ride on the Parachute. Only the brave would opt to go on that ride—and I was brave enough. It was very scary. You'd be strapped onto a small seat and slowly be pulled up to the top, and suddenly the world seemed to drop out and you went down very quickly. There'd be a big bounce at the end. It was a real thrill.

Think of girls growing up in the fifties, taught to be ladies, warned to be respectable, hemmed in by restrictions. Some loved scary rides—some loved horses.

SHANILLE MARTIN

YEARS AS MENTEE: 3
GRADE: Senior
HIGH SCHOOL: Academy for Young Writers
BORN: Kingston, Jamaica
LIVES: Brooklyn, NY
PUBLICATIONS AND RECOGNITIONS: Publication in *Newsweek* and winner of a poetry contest at school

MENTEE'S ANECDOTE: *My (r)evolution with my mentor developed gradually. I used to constantly jump from story to story, never sticking to one. I was never able to finish something because once I reached writer's block, I would quickly give up. Amanda helped me grow out of that, and I became passionate about and committed to the projects I work on. I have grown from being unable to finishing short stories to writing a book over 200 pages long. Our relationship has evolved in a big way; she is more than a mentor to me, she is a role model, and someone I can strive to be.*

AMANDA KRUPMAN

YEARS AS MENTOR: 3
OCCUPATION: Communications Manager, The Center for Popular Democracy
BORN: Cleveland, OH
LIVES: Brooklyn, NY
PUBLICATIONS AND RECOGNITIONS: Recently, "Misunderstandings," *Bloom Literary Journal*

MENTOR'S ANECDOTE: *Shanille graduates high school this year, prompting a necessary (r)evolution. So I spent this year being keenly aware of change. Changes Shanille has undergone—in her writing, in her presentation of herself to the world, and I suspect, in her own self-image. Changes in my life–with family, my professional life, and my writing. And the unavoidable change: as Shanille heads to college, we will no longer be a Girls Write Now pair. It is an emotional moment for me as a mentor: I will miss our sessions, but I am excited for her journey, and know we will continue to connect along the way.*

THE DRIFTERS: A NOVEL (EXCERPT)

SHANILLE MARTIN

I am a person who loves change, and in just a few months I will be leaving high school for college. My character in the story has to face a really big change: being on her own. Like her, I am too growing and learning about the world in new ways.

"Where you headed kid?" the woman asked.

"How much is the ticket for New York City?"

"Fifty," she said.

I handed her the money. "How long will the bus be?"

"It will come in a few minutes."

I sat on the bench next to an elderly woman who was using the few teeth she had left to ravage a red apple. I named her Nancy, because as a child I assumed all elderly women were named Nancy. She had lived an audacious life. She'd spent her younger years as a showgirl in Vegas; then, when she was twenty-five, she'd met her future husband, John Pines. They'd traveled the world together, but when Nancy decided she wanted kids, they'd realized she couldn't. John had stayed with her, though. They'd remained married for forty years, until John passed away from a heart attack. Nancy had then decided to travel back to New York in hopes of living that journey once again before she too passed away.

"Would you like an apple, dear?" the woman said, sticking out the fruit.

I nodded and took it from her. "Thank you, Nancy."

"Nancy? That was my sister's name. I'm Grace. What's your name?"

"I'm Stella."

The old lady slid over on the bench next to me. Her shiny, silver hair blew back in the wind. I could tell she was beautiful when she was my age: all the guys who passed us who were graying took a second look at her.

"What does New York City hold for you?" she asked.

I shrugged. "The unknown. What does it hold for you, Grace?"

"The unknown."

Grace sat next to me on the bus. She took my thin, pale hands into her wrinkled own and smiled. We talked for what felt like forever.

"I couldn't have children, Stella. But there was a little boy I knew once. I loved him like a son. He's only eight and already has a world of problems on his shoulder, but he was a foster kid, so I understand," she said. "His name was Ryland. The system moved him off to California for a change of scenery."

I did not know why she told me of this kid; what significance did an eight-year-old boy have to me? Yet Grace always knew something I did not. She always did. When she stopped talking, I told her how she smelled like lilac and other sweet things.

It did not take her long to knock out. Her head fell onto my shoulders, and she stayed like that for the hours it took the bus to get to New York. I looked out at New York City's renowned skyscrapers and the fast-paced people. Then it hit me. Where the hell was I going? I was really wandering into the unknown; the few things I knew about New York were all from pamphlets that came to my house. *Come to New York City this summer, folks. You will not regret your stay. Trust us, we're certified.*

Yet Grace didn't seem worried. She was confident that the unknown was all she thought it would be.

"Well, Stella, this is where I bid you farewell. Someone awaits my presence," Grace said when we stepped off the bus and into the cool September breeze. Her blue eyes were filled with so much wonder and light. I hadn't seen eyes like that for a long time.

I hugged her good-bye. "I hope the unknown is all you want it to be."

"Your life is only as good as you make it. Before you know it, you'll be old and gray like me, so live while you still have your youth. YOLO, as you teens say."

I laughed and watched her walk off into the crowd. I began strolling through the bright city, and the more I saw, the more I realized what I had been missing. The life I had been waiting for was out there somewhere, and I needed to find it. This was the first step. Running away was the first step.

FOREST BATHING (EXCERPT)

AMANDA KRUPMAN

Shanille's excerpt from her novel (!) really appeals to me, as it's liminal, a moment in transition. Her protagonist, on the precipice of an adventure, talks to a woman while waiting for a bus. My excerpt is also about transition—on traveling while grieving.

Walk with me, he said.
    I already do a lot of walking.
    He said, *But you do it alone. It's better with someone else.*
    I wanted to believe him, so I said, *Okay, I will, I'll walk with you.*
    So we walked. Into places we'd known separately, and out with new words and phrases and paragraphs we immediately wanted to forget. After I proved to him and myself that he was wrong, that I was better on my own, I took the walking more seriously and walked away. Away to Japan, and there I walked for five days through the forest on the Kii peninsula, through the Wakayama prefecture, along an ancient pilgrimage route called the Kumano Kodo.
    When Thoreau took to the woods, he wanted to suck out the marrow and live deliberately. I wanted to spit up and fall apart with no one watching, to trust the efficacious grace of dirt, and bugs, and upturned roots to work as an emetic. I'm not a religious person; I don't believe in purification rituals; I just believe in quiet and dirt and walking it off.

KARINA MARTINEZ

YEARS AS MENTEE: 3
GRADE: Junior
HIGH SCHOOL: The Bronx
High School of Science
BORN: New York, NY
LIVES: Bronx, NY

MENTEE'S ANECDOTE: *This being my third year as a mentee, I did not quite know what to expect. Things have changed, but with Rachel I quickly realized that change is not always a bad thing. I mean, we all have to evolve at some point, don't we? I can honestly say that the time I've spent getting to know Rachel has allowed me to open up. Sometimes we talked so much that we forgot to write at our meetings. I appreciate her always being there to give me an extra push, whether it be in my writing or in my life.*

RACHEL COHEN

YEARS AS MENTOR: 3
OCCUPATION:
Sports reporter,
Associated Press
BORN: Concord, MA
LIVES: New York, NY

MENTOR'S ANECDOTE: *It is Karina's third year as a mentee and my third as a mentor, but our first together. So we both know what to expect (though the CHAPTERS deadline did sneak up on us!). That may make our experiences more evolution than revolution, but in honor of Karina's science expertise, I am going to go all Darwin and say that adaptation to changing environments can create beauty. I admire how she holds herself to the highest of standards, and I hope to offer reminders of both perspective and perseverance.*

LEGENDS

KARINA MARTINEZ

This year I learned that despite feeling that I was constantly drowning, I have the ability to rise up and evolve as a person. I learned that I have the ability to become a legend. I learned that we all do.

He says he can't breathe,
That the world he's in is underwater and no one
has taught him how to swim.
Doesn't matter how many hands are stretched out to him,
Doesn't matter how many people offer up a breath,
Doesn't matter that he keeps kicking his legs,
He just can't seem to get his head above water.
I suppose he's just meant to drown for an eternity,
A fate so cruel you'd think it was set by the gods.
Like Atlas bearing the weight of the world on his shoulders,
The sting of water in his lungs will never fade.
His punishment could serve as a warning to others.
His pain could be a necessary evil,
Like ravens pecking at the eyes,
Lips never tasting water,
And the tears and sweat of the world pressing down
forcing one to kneel to those they despise.
Makes a pomegranate look appealing,
Wine a curious endeavor,

For the world's greatest wonders never come without a consequence.
I wish I could tell him to hold his breath,
That breathing is a luxury not needed,
But as he closes his eyes and dies for the thousandth time,
I know it won't matter.
People like him, they live in pain.
A tale to tell a child,
A story to be passed to others.
So when he dies again tomorrow,
His name escaping the lips of many,
At least he'll be dying a legend.

#FREEMOXiE

RACHEL COHEN

For a weekly meeting, Karina suggested we attend the Girls Write Now "Cringe Fest," where she read her first-ever short story, written when she was about ten. Everyone loved it—especially the part about the quicksand—but we all had one question: What happened to Moxie, the main character's dog?

I was a completely different dog before I met the Criminal. I used to let my owner, Trevor, drag me around by the leash. Sat when he commanded. Begged for food. I was so soft.

Lot of good that did me. "Take my dog, not me, take the dog!" That's what Trevor sniveled when we first encountered the Criminal. I realized at that moment I needed to take responsibility for myself. And what better role model for that, it turned out, than the Criminal.

The cops used the term "kidnap" for what happened next, but I prefer to call it "borrowing as collateral." While pretending to snooze, I observed the Criminal. I loved how he tells it like it is. How he stands up for himself. How successful he's been at his profession.

And when Trevor was rescued and forgot to come back for me, sure, it hurt. But soon I realized how lucky I was. The Criminal enlisted me to help him when he—well, the cops called it "shoplifting," I prefer the term "sharing economy." I distracted a store security guard by pretending to be a lost dog while the Criminal stuffed designer cell phone cases into the pockets of his cargo pants. Oh, the adrenaline rush! The satisfaction of feeling valued, essential! I had never experienced that in my cuddly suburban existence.

We would hide out by the quicksand near the mall, and whenever a car would get stuck in it, we—well, the cops called it "stole," I prefer "rescued"—all the valuables in it.

Alas, we got overconfident. One evening, the Criminal stopped to take a selfie for our Facebook page, and his foot got caught in the quicksand. The cops, incorrectly assuming I was stolen, returned me to Trevor. Fortunately, the acting skills I learned with the Criminal are serving me well. I'm just biding my time for three to five years.

KAMILAH MAXWELL-BOWDEN

YEARS AS MENTEE: 2
GRADE: Junior
HIGH SCHOOL: Vanguard High School
BORN: Brooklyn, NY
LIVES: Brooklyn, NY
PUBLICATIONS AND RECOGNITIONS: Scholastic Art & Writing Award: Honorable Mention

MENTEE'S ANECDOTE: *My personal revolution with my writing began when I decided to write for myself and no one else. If other people liked it then that was great; as long as I could be as accurate as possible in my portrayal of emotions, disorders, and human nature then I was fine. I also decided to go against my religion and support the LGBTQ movement with my writing. My mentor Gillian has been a great help in opening up my mind to new solutions and new ways of saying what I want to say, and she has been very supportive, which is always good.*

GILLIAN REAGAN

YEARS AS MENTOR: 4
OCCUPATION: Managing Editor, States at POLITICO
BORN: Worcester, MA
LIVES: Brooklyn, NY

MENTOR'S ANECDOTE: *I've always been a nonfiction writer, comfortable with journalism and memoir. Despite working with Girls Write Now for years, amongst so much creativity and inspiration, I have not strayed far from those categories. This year, Kamilah opened me up to new territory. She has an incredible imagination, and entire worlds in her head. I branched out and found new ways to tell stories. Although I do give her grammar and technical writing suggestions, my most important job as a mentor is to advocate for her voice, help her listen to it more often, and encourage her to tell more of those brilliant stories.*

DELTA (EXCERPT)

KAMILAH MAXWELL-BOWDEN

In the near future, a mysterious disease takes out 90 percent of the world's children. The remaining 10 percent get esper-like abilities. To cure them, the government creates Rehabilitation Camps to study the children. The story is narrated by Stephanie, a survivor who has been put in an isolated camp called Delta.

On the evening of the third day, they allow us to stand on deck and watch as the ship goes through the archway of the wall surrounding the island, passing various stalagmites, and stops at the docks. There are men and women in black lining the docks and our path into the camp, armed with assault rifles. I clutch the straps of the twins' bag as I walk past them. There wasn't this much security when I was younger. I have to remind myself that it is still the same island, but with a few added structures. No one knows it now—though I am sure we all guessed it—but soon this place that is supposed to cure us will be our prison. It's maximum security, the only way out being death—and it will be a literal hell on earth. After all, the camps are made to be our cages, and graves, if necessary.

We all gather around the center of the island, surrounding a thick wooden post, glancing at the guards, who are all wearing camouflage pants, combat boots, and black jackets with the word **TRUANT** written in red on the back. There's the framework for a building off in the distance, and somewhere dogs are barking. When all 200 of us are on the island and the ships are preparing to leave, a tall, broad-shouldered man with graying blond hair and hard brown eyes walks in front of us, a megaphone in hand.

"My name is Commander Albright," he says, his voice loud and hard. I am instantly reminded of a drill sergeant, and judging by his getup, it wouldn't be a stretch to say he was part of the army. "I am your camp controller, the head controller. President Coffer has charged me with the task of keeping you little freaks away from the rest of civilization and rehabilitated. Now some of you will die, and the rest of you will be changed forever. One thing is for sure: you will not leave these camps the same, and definitely not with your abilities."

I do not like the way he says "abilities," and neither does anyone else, because they all burst into chatter and cries of dissent.

"Shut up," Commander Albright barks, and we do, too frightened to do anything else. "Good."

Attendance is taken, groups are made. All the girls are sent to the north side of the island, while all the boys are sent south. Then we are put in cabins and given black uniforms to change into. I thank God that Nan, Kristen, and the twins are in the same cabin as I am. The cabins, I know, are new. Two years ago there was one cabin shared by three kids and one bathroom; now there are thirty cabins for boys and thirty for girls, each with two floors, two bathrooms, eight windows, and eighteen pairs of bunk beds to a floor. This place will be cramped.

They do not give us time to settle in. Instead we are told to leave our bags on our beds and are led to the Infirmary, where we are all given checkups. I stand in the hall with the other kids—all shifting from foot to foot, nervous and scared. Maggie and Maddie go in together. I expect them to send one twin back, but they do not. Nan goes in before me, and then, twenty minutes later, my name is called.

"Stephanie Abigail Rose-Meadows," says a female doctor with red glasses. I study her—her lips are bright red and her dark hair is tied back in a tight ponytail. She is pretty and has on black heels that peek out from beneath her long white lab coat. She watches me as I walk up to her, gaze cool and calculating.

In her office, the room is brighter than I expected. It looks like any other doctor's office: there's a scale, a bed with paper on it for some reason, a desk, and a bunch of charts. She tells me her name is Keriann Bishop and that I am to call her *Doctor* Bishop. She looks down at her clipboard and points her ballpoint pen at the bed and says, "Sit."

I do as I am told as she gives me a checkup—I breathe when she tells me to and cough when she tells me to. If I didn't know any better, it would feel like just another checkup at the doctor's. Then she takes me into the next room and I am made to sit still on a hard, cold, metal stool while Dr. Bishop sticks wire brain monitors on my forehead. She draws blood from my right forearm, and asks me how I am feeling.

THE TRAIN

GILLIAN REAGAN

When I was a little girl, my nightmares and the monsters in them felt real to me, as real as this piece of paper. Inspired by my mentee's ability to turn nightmares into a reality on the page, I wrote a short piece on my own experience. These are the first paragraphs.

I feel it in my intestines first—the rumbling as the train approaches. It ripples up to my ribs, my chest, my throat.

When I hear the first whistle, I close my eyes and watch the black.

I see trinkets dance off my bureau. My cassette player shatters on the floor. There goes my jewelry box with the twirling ballerina on her toe, spilling beads and plastic bracelets. Pound Puppy sheets fly out the window now. The plywood separating my side of the room from my brother's shoots toward the stars like an alien saucer. I grip the sides of my mattress, not sure if I'm holding myself down or bracing for what's coming. The whole apartment rattles. The train is almost here now. I see ghosts. They swam out from a black abyss through the train windows. They float with broad white wingspans, slow and steady, toward my bedroom window.

Sometimes they are beasts, wolves maybe, with hunchbacks and scraggly hair, slobbering mouths full of shark teeth. They gallop toward me. Their rotting swamp breath fills the room. I want to scream. Sometimes I do but it sounds like TV static, like I'm screaming through blankets, suffocating. Nobody hears me. The train is right outside my window now. I grit my teeth. Everything turns black.

When I hear the train's whistle in the distance, I open my eyes to the room, still in place. I listen for my brother breathing in his bed across the room, over the plywood still separating us. I can't see him, but I hear the flood and flow of air in his lungs. His small body breathes and so does mine. I finally fall asleep.

MUSE MCCORMACK

YEARS AS MENTEE: 2
GRADE: Senior
HIGH SCHOOL: Essex
Street Academy
BORN: Brooklyn, NY
LIVES: Brooklyn, NY
**PUBLICATIONS AND
RECOGNITIONS:**
Scholastic Art &
Writing Award: Gold Key

MENTEE'S ANECDOTE: *We read funny words/ And don't know what they mean, but/ we giggle and laugh. Walking with pencils/ from all over the world, but/ we write from our hearts. There's not just one tale/ one story to be told for/ we made too many.*

ELSBETH PANCRAZI

YEARS AS MENTOR: 1
OCCUPATION: Manager
of Institutional Funding,
Brooklyn Botanic Garden
BORN: Englewood, NJ
LIVES: Brooklyn, NY
**PUBLICATIONS AND
RECOGNITIONS:**
Recognized with
fellowships from
Poets House and
Caldera Arts

MENTOR'S ANECDOTE: *(a diary poem): It is delightful to become acquainted with the colored books of fairy tales, steal titles from* The Pillow Book, *and receive a list of Terry Pratchett novels in order of importance. Pulling together the poems we've written this year into a thick, solid stack of paper—this too brings delight. Like Frank O'Hara says in "St. Paul and All That," "I read what you read"—delight.*

GO WHERE YOU ARE WANTED

MUSE MCCORMACK

This poem is from a collection that Elsbeth and I have been working on most of the year. It is told from the perspective of a stepmother who, until now, has been perceived as an "evil" stepmother. The piece revolts against this archetype and asks how she evolved to become "evil."

When I first found you
because that's what it was
like discovering a stream
of light
through a bush
in a forest
a small white bundle
in the tangled dark
of a dead heart
You were perfect
and even though beginnings
aren't important
not in this case at least
I will say it
because it needs to be said
because I was lonesome
lonesome in the company of men
and woods

not yet my own
thick with shadow
old
but new to me
you weren't mine
but I longed for you
and your smallness
I wanted it to fit
in my arms
in my heart
my love wasn't forced
but it was circumstantial
so I loved you more
too much
a mother
should never love so much
but how could I help it
and even in your infancy
you were your own
I had no claim
no matter how I tried
you rejected me
turning from flesh
that wasn't yours
it still hurt
beaten by the dead
but I had no one
no one else
I was born soft
a sapling
yet to grow
bark in this new forest
If I could have
I would have given you
a grand gesture
flung my arms

out across the seas
the billowing sheet
of land and water
waves and winds
bringing back your happiness
from where it lay
away from me
like spices for a queen
burning oranges and reds
yellows
no more blues
burning
burning joy for you
but soon
you were mine
in all but blood
and love
responsibility
the fairy tale babe
swept away
like the dust from the house
crust from your eyes
tears from your cheeks
cries from your mouth
dirt from your skin
snot from your nose
shit from your ass
you from me
and again
and again
every day
till I was hard
hard and tired
and another
on the way
I didn't hate you

but that was all
just not hate
I had given up on love
I was too full
of everything else
grasping strings of emotion
frantic
frantic not to lose it all
frantic to stay
stay
alive
but too late
too late
I realized
it was gone
I had lost it
somewhere in the soap suds
and youth
you
you
were mine
mine to take care of
in all ways
mine
but love
how can you love anything
when it knows its existence
its own existence
is in some outside place
when it knows it has become a possession
a burden
an obligation
even if it didn't start like that
The beautiful babe was grown
and made aware of beauty
its own

and the one before me
I was a shadow blocking out the view
of the face
of the one you really wanted to see
My own child cried
so I left you
defeated
tired
hardened
unsure
if I could ever give to my own
what I had tried to give to you
but
not angry
just despondent
worse than hate
just
nothing
because unrequited
only lasts for so long
you never knew though
that I had to turn away
because you
had never even looked
at me
I resisted so long
those words
if you care
Step daughter

CASSANDRA LONGED TO FULLY COMPREHEND

ELSBETH PANCRAZI

With my background in poetry and Muse's interest in fairy tales, we came up with the idea to each write a collection of poems about a classic fairy tale or myth, taking a 360-degree view of the story, a complete "revolution" in perspective and form. It has been an amazing project!

The woman striding purposefully down the sidewalk who turns on her heel and continues purposefully in the opposite direction.

Denial is not a river in Egypt.

The general lack of attention to shadows, particularly long ones.

(On the apartment building opposite her own, a railing's shadow zigzags as it hits each stair on the way down.)

Whether others awoke in the night to hear the trucks salting the streets before the storm.

Out of sight, out of mind (vs. Absence makes the heart grow fonder).

Who invented these cycles (minutes, days, years, dynasties) when we're positioned too close to read the patterns?

Taking it one day at a time.

"Concerning the events of last week . . ."

The movements of sheep on the hillside sponging the dew from the air.

LAUREN MELENDEZ

YEARS AS MENTEE: 3
GRADE: Senior
HIGH SCHOOL:
Marta Valle High School
BORN: New York, NY
LIVES: Brooklyn, NY

MENTEE'S ANECDOTE: *This year with my mentor has been a good one. We share the same sense of humor and have great taste in musicals. She has helped me express myself through my writing and has shown me that you can write about anything, even if it's about a Cookie's Birthday party! The best experience we had together was when we were walking to the train and I spotted a Trump Bill. We both started taking pictures and sent them to our friends. We both revolt and evolve with our writing, and that is what makes us a great team.*

SASHA WOLFF

YEARS AS MENTOR: 1
OCCUPATION: Student
BORN: Chicago, IL
LIVES: New York, NY

MENTOR'S ANECDOTE: *I tend to be a serious, goal-oriented person, especially when it comes to writing. Lauren is so full of life, and open in a way that really shows. Whether she is pointing out a puppy's little head peeping out of a bag under a table in Starbucks or explaining Supernatural to me, she is teaching me about how to be a positive force. This is so corny, but working with Lauren has helped me turn off my brain and turn on my heart more. She's taught me to be more alive in the world instead of just processing it.*

FAILED EXPERIMENT

LAUREN MELENDEZ

This piece is a spinoff of a poem I wrote with my mentor. It was inspired by the movie Deadpool, *which I saw recently. It talks about how some people evolve and try to keep their heads up.*

I remember when my parents loved me—when they would sing me to bed, when they would give me soup when I was sick. But now everything is different. They sold me out. People experimented on me, and now I'm like this. An emotionless mutant with these abilities. They thought I was dead, that I wouldn't come back, but guess what? I did. And the rage could have taken over but it didn't. I heard a cry in my old room. I ran up to see a baby boy in a crib.

A baby brother? I thought. They moved on. But I didn't care. He was my joy. His eyes were a bright green. He was beautiful. I loved him—how could I say no to this bundle of joy? Because of him, my rage was kept under control. He was somebody whom they couldn't mess up, unlike me. I became the stronger person, able to forgive but never forget.

This led to them neglecting me while praising my little brother. I wasn't the star in their eyes anymore. I was nothing more than a failed experiment. I grew apart from people. They looked at me differently, like I was a lesser human being. It struck me, and came down on me like a hammer, that I had to keep my head up in my hoodie and keep on walking. Everyone kept moving on like nothing had happened, but everything was different for me.

THE HEADLESS HORSEMAN

SASHA WOLFF

I started this story in November after watching the Sleepy Hollow *film adaptation with Johnny Depp. I've always loved that movie, as well as* The Legend of Sleepy Hollow *by Washington Irving. I started thinking about what it'd be like if the Headless Horseman was a real, everyday person.*

I moved in with the Headless Horseman June of this year. I wouldn't call it love, but he treats me well. Listens. Cuddles. Offers to chop off heads I don't like. Like everyone, we have our rules. He has to rinse off his axe before bed, I have to sleep on his chest like he likes. Clean axe, girl on chest. It's a good living arrangement.

Maybe you're wondering how our little love affair began. The thing about the Headless Horseman is that his father taught him to cut off heads, including ladies', and he thought about them off more than on. Then he met me. The Headless Horseman likes his axe, and he likes killing, but he likes me best of all. He said my head was the first head he wanted to stay put.

I remember that night well, better than I let on. I was nine years old. I didn't know it at the time, but he'd come to kill me.

It was late. I was sitting up in bed, reading. I was reading a library book. It was *Le Morte d'Arthur*. I liked it for the battle scenes mostly, but also for the beautiful feasts and strange castles in the forest. The writing was nice and pleasant and made me feel like even though I was reading one book, I'd read all the books. This could even be my last book.

He came in through my bedroom window. I turned a wrinkled page and there he was, hooded, black-cloaked. A year older! He was exactly how I'd pictured him. Cute. Nice shoulders. His axe glinted in the moonlight.

I laid down my book. I would have preferred to keep reading, but it didn't seem polite to be reading in the company of my executor. My parents raised me well.

The Headless Horseboy stood there for a bit. I thought he was staring at me. Either that or my *Sweeney Todd* poster. One of the two. Although, in actuality, I found I didn't mind where he looked. He was headless.

Then he pulled a white handkerchief out of his cloak pocket and polished his axe, almost lovingly. I watched as he made the metal all shiny. Then he turned my way. This time, I had no doubt he was looking at me.

"I'm the Headless Horseboy," he said.

"Okay," I said.

"I'm here to behead you."

"That's fine."

He took a step toward me. This was the closest I'd ever been to a boy. His voice was edged with a smile. "Aren't you afraid?" he asked.

"Sorry. I'm tired."

By this time, he had reached my bed. He was a dark, ghostly thing. I watched his movements, so much calmer and easier than mine. He reached over and picked up the slim, battered blue volume on my bed. He studied the book's cover. "A love triangle?" he asked.

I said the title out loud. "They're French," I explained.

JULIA MERCADO

YEARS AS MENTEE: 3
GRADE: Senior
HIGH SCHOOL: Manhattan Village Academy
BORN: Brooklyn, NY
LIVES: Queens, NY
PUBLICATIONS AND RECOGNITIONS:
Scholastic Art & Writing Awards: Gold Key, Honorable Mention

MENTEE'S ANECDOTE: *The Soul Mentor and Mentee were back again this year as we plowed through college applications, submission deadlines, and a massive amount of schoolwork. This has definitely been the best year for my writing so far. Lauren has pushed me to get out of my comfort zone and to try new things. I always wanted to do poetry but felt like nothing I wrote made sense. "As long as it makes sense to you," she said. She's been a powerful influence. I'm really going to miss my Soul Mentor.*

LAUREN HESSE

YEARS AS MENTOR: 3
OCCUPATION:
Digital Marketing Manager, Penguin Random House
BORN: Albany, NY
LIVES: Brooklyn, NY

MENTOR'S ANECDOTE: *When Julia and I started writing together, we instantly clicked. This year we spent a lot of time in our favorite coffee shop, editing together. One Sunday, I really challenged Julia, causing us to question her entire piece. Admittedly I was a bit worried I had gone too far, but as we walked to the subway and I told her how proud I was of how she'd handled the edits and critiques, she smiled and said, "I know it's what you're here for. I'm in." I feel so lucky that our relationship has evolved to be so trusting and solid.*

WHERE THESE SHOES HAVE BEEN

JULIA MERCADO

Race and ethnicity are such powerful constructs across the globe. As a pale Latina, it seems as if I don't fit in with any category. Am I a type of minority? Am I privileged by my light skin? Here are some scenarios; tell me where you fit.

The darkness casts a shadow over him. You can make out the slight lines in his puffed jacket and the features on his face. The neon sign next to him shines a light on the rest of the street. His presence is overwhelming. You look away and look back to see him watching you carefully. You're bundled up in your winter coat, freshly put together from head to toe. He sneers at your high-top shoes, the bright Converse emblem shining against the neon sign. His eyes won't leave you until you walk away down the street. You feel you're not welcome here—as if you're intruding on private property. You can sense the anxiety in his eyes. He's worried you might not be so friendly. You are unlike each other. To him, you're at opposite ends of the spectrum. He doesn't know that you're closer to him than what he believes.

A man smiles at you as you sit on the bench, as you wait for the cheapest way home to arrive. His dog and children run after him as they pack into the minivan with automated doors. The dog kicks dirt up onto your high-tops. You do your best to make them clean again, wiping the dirt off.

"*Pero nena,* you need to be careful, I don't have the money to be buying you new ones." Your mother turns to your aunt and mumbles, "Especially after the price I paid for lunch."

Your aunt nods in agreement. You have to look away in embarrassment because the child hopping into the van is staring. She doesn't recognize the hard Spanish "r."

That same rolling trill hits your ear as you wait for the train to hit your stop. Beside you are two girls gossiping in the same tongue as your mother's. You notice a group of hipsters by the door. Next to you, a man is hunched over a book, oblivious to the stops passing by him. Slowly, the train pulls up onto Bedford Avenue and everyone by the door floods out as the automated announcement tells you the next stop is Lorimer.

"I can't believe the L is going to go out for three years! I wouldn't know where else to live!" a woman says as she trails behind her friend to get out onto the platform.

As you get off at your stop, the *bochincheras* are right behind you. They are turning to go out onto the street as you head for the stairs to grab another train. The man stayed on the train in his seat, trapped in a storyline. He's got a long way to go till the end. You pull out your phone and see that you got a text with a picture of rolled ice cream covered in strawberries, whipped cream and chocolate drizzle. The crisp marshmallow on top is what entices you.

"It's in Chinatown, we should go!" your friend says.

She always finds sweet spots.

You smell the rancid scent of the fish market and your stomach turns. After ice cream, you make your way out to get a real meal. Your friend knows the way; she comes here all the time.

You and your friends have travelled for quite a while—from the Heights, the Bronx, and Queens—and the four of you are exhausted from your journeys. Yet still, you want to make the most of your time together. All of you groan as the trek for food never seems to end.

One of your friends pleads for some *plátanos*, while your mouth waters over a sign reading "Fresh California Rolls."

The navigator claims that you'll be in the clear soon.

Another friend bumps you as she talks about cheesecake. She apologizes as she steps on your shoe. You wave it away nonchalantly—it's happened to you plenty of times. The smudges of dirt can vouch for that.

She looks down at her shoes and points. "Twins!"

She gasps and looks at your other friend. "Her too!"

The navigator turns around.

"Everyone has high-tops. Look at mine."

You all have tennis shoes, scuffed with time, each bearing skid marks of where you've been.

The concrete's the same color.

RULES FOR BEING A MODERN WOMAN IN NEW YORK CITY

LAUREN HESSE

I've always wanted to write satire but struggled with the form. I was inspired in our Spoken Word Poetry Workshop to try again. All of the lines in "Rules for A Modern Woman in New York City" are 'rules' that were told to me (none of which I wish to follow).

Don't take up space on the subway.

Don't give an exacerbated sigh like that; the man next to you can spread his knees and widen his elbows to play games on his phone for the commute. He earned it.

Don't wedge your way into the elevator; it is unnecessary and will inconvenience others.

Don't speak too aggressively in your meeting; you don't want to come off as scrappy to the executives.

Don't order a burger at your business lunch; salads are much more ladylike.

Don't have more than one glass of chilled white wine at your company happy hour.

Don't get off the subway unless you have your keys in your hand, ready to race into your front door.

Don't leave your house at night, but always be accessible to friends and male suitors.

Don't take the subway alone.

Don't take an Uber alone.

Don't hail a cab alone.

Don't bring up feminism, intersectionality, or privilege on the first date.

Don't correct him if he's wrong.

Don't forget to laugh at his jokes, even if he didn't land the punch line.

Don't text him first.

Don't text him back too soon.

Don't text him at all.

Don't lust, but be the perfect object to be lusted after.

Don't. Eat. Your. Feelings.

Don't forget to go to the gym.

Don't work out too much, your muscles will get too big.

Don't chop your hair into that bob you've been wanting.

Don't get bangs.

Don't dye your hair darker—blondes have more fun.

Don't stay blond, you won't be taken seriously if you do.

Don't wear that dress—it's too short.

Don't wear *that* dress—it doesn't show your figure.

Don't wear anything cut like that—it just doesn't work for you.

Don't eat too much sushi—you'll get mercury poisoning.

Don't eat sugar.

Don't eat carbs.

Don't walk like that.

Don't walk like that, either.

Just Don't.

BRITTNEY NANTON

YEARS AS MENTEE: 2
GRADE: Junior
HIGH SCHOOL: Landmark High School
BORN: New York, NY
LIVES: New York, NY

MENTEE'S ANECDOTE: *Working with Amy has been a wonderful experience. Our relationship continues to strengthen more and more every time we meet, and I am proud to have her in my life, as a mentor and also as a friend. I think she has really helped me to grow and to feel more comfortable talking about certain hard topics in my writing. I'm really glad to have her in my life, and I can't wait to have more fun experiences with her.*

AMY FLYNTZ

YEARS AS MENTOR: 4
OCCUPATION: Founder, Amy Flyntz Copywriting, LLC
BORN: Bridgeport, CT
LIVES: New York, NY

MENTOR'S ANECDOTE: *Mentoring Brittney has been an enormous source of joy and inspiration for me. I am repeatedly struck by how self-possessed she is at her age; she is a force of intelligence, wit, compassion, and talent. I've loved talking with Brittney extensively about current events as they pertain to politics, race, and gender. Through her writing, Brittney has begun to focus on the issues she is most passionate about. I can't wait to watch her continue to take on the world, because I know the world will be better as she does.*

BREAKING NEWS

BRITTNEY NANTON

This poem was inspired by the many news articles I see almost daily about young African Americans being murdered by the police. I feel like this best relates to a revolution, because Americans are starting to see how unjust our society really is.

friday afternoon, the school was in a bit of a haze
you could hear the whispering of teachers,
and you could feel the glaze of their stares at you as you sat down in the classroom

michael brown.
eric garner.
freddie gray.
sandra bland.

another fallen black body,
another white male in blue dress begging for a plea
another,
i felt in danger
and another—
they had it coming.

you thought it would get better,
thought that maybe trayvon martin was the mistake the government would learn from.

thought that maybe they'd see how much heartache killing one black boy would cause.
you thought that maybe they'd see the tears on his mother's face,
and the bag of skittles left on the ground, and get the message for once.

you had hope this time.

and even though you'd already memorized all of the words that were about to come out of the judge's mouth,
you still had hope.

you know the lines all too well
you can see the headlines already.
you can see the judge's face,
and try to resist the urge to punch it.

you wonder if this will all be in the history books,
if your children will only have to read about all of this injustice,
instead of actually live it.

that they won't have to look twice around them,
and keep still to prevent from being a target.

LOADED

AMY FLYNTZ

As I wrote this essay, I was struck by my own evolution: the twenty-one-year-old me in the piece has become much more curious than fearful. I now realize this boy could have been part of a revolution in Turkey in 1997. I wish I knew.

A palmful of metallic fishiness. My sole souvenir from scaling the towering wrought iron gates and breaking into Kensington Gardens last night.

My tongue, still swollen with wine, peels off the roof of my mouth with a muffled *cluck*. I burrow my face into my palm and inhale again the dank odor. There were four of us. Or five? Fogginess, an effect of the alcohol or adrenaline or both, makes it difficult to piece together the events of the night. I know it began with us having drinks in his dorm room. It seems to have ended with the motorized squeal of the motion-sensor cameras as they trained themselves on our advancing bodies, the soft click as they drew us into focus.

The open window by my roommates' beds whistles against a damp gust of wind. I pull the plaid blanket closer to my chin and roll over, tucking it against my cheek. The lumpy outlines of their bodies are barely visible in the grey light that has begun bleeding upward to overtake the dark. Jonell moans softly across the room, her mattress creaking as she shifts.

Britain doesn't have a Bill of Rights, I recall. *Who was it who told me that when we first got to London? If we were arrested—and Princess Diana just died. What were we thinking, breaking into Kensington Gardens?*

And now, I remember the framed photograph in his dorm room.

He is a full-time student, here from Turkey, whom we met in the cafeteria a couple of weeks ago. He's different from many of the American students in our program: He maintains eye contact during conversations. He is curious. Worldly.

You're so lucky, I've told him. *You get to stay here after we all finish our semester.*

In the photo, he is on a rooftop—or was it a balcony?—overlooking a Turkish city. He stands next to a man, squinting against the sun, their shoulders nearly touching. They both wear patterned scarves, but this is not their most striking similarity.

He noticed me staring and handed me the photograph for closer inspection. "My father and me," he said, brushing the glass with his index finger. I nodded. When I looked up, his broad smile had reached his enormous brown eyes, crinkling the corners. He held my gaze. I smiled back, my lips stretched tight against my teeth. I looked away.

I know when I see him in the cafeteria in a few hours, he will laugh about our adventure last night. I will again offer him a closed-mouth smile, my eyes fixated on his chin or cheek or worse, over his shoulder. I will pretend I need to study. I will brush off his thoughtful questions with one-word answers. Then there will be an excuse each time, until the invitations stop coming.

I will never admit that the machine gun in the photo, identical to his father's, is what ended our budding friendship.

KIZZY NELSON

YEARS AS MENTEE: 1
GRADE: Junior
HIGH SCHOOL: Urban Assembly School for Green Careers
BORN: Port-au-Prince, Haiti
LIVES: New York, NY
PUBLICATIONS AND RECOGNITIONS: High Honor Roll, Spanish Award

MENTEE'S ANECDOTE: *I am from Haiti, where parents are strict, but then I had to move to New York, which is where everything began; I was shy and barely talked. With my mentor I not only learned how to put my emotions on paper, I also learned what it was like to discover new places, stand up for myself, not be afraid. She not only became my mentor but an older sister that cheered me on and helped me pursue, and not give up on, my dreams; I've learned a lot of things with her, which I am grateful for.*

SOULA HARISIADIS

YEARS AS MENTOR: 1
OCCUPATION: English teacher, LaGuardia Arts High School
BORN: New York, NY
LIVES: New York, NY

MENTOR'S ANECDOTE: *A moment I'll always remember is standing in a store in Koreatown with Kizzy. The books, the posters, the music—she just drank it all in. I admire Kizzy's interest in Korean culture, and it's been a blast trying new foods and learning about K Dramas. Whether it's writing her latest novel or trying kimchi, Kizzy is full of an enthusiasm that is contagious.*

JANUARY 12, 2010

KIZZY NELSON

January 12, 2010 was one of those historical days for the Haitians that remains to be remembered; some of us are still traumatized, and a lot of families have been affected. I am leaving this message hoping to find peace after six years.

Does anybody remember or am i the only one?
i feel myself getting stronger every day
But once that day replays back into my memories
i don't really know what should i do
or how to hide the tears that remain to be slides
Cry, scream, or act like i don't understand what's going on
i can't act like i don't know
Because this is part of my story
A story that will remain in our memories, us Haitians, a memory that will
make us believe in our strength
A memory that demands to be remembered, felt
We are humans too, you know
Some people will not remember or know about this
But my mom taught me how to respect my ancestry and the ones that
fought for other people's lives.
January 12
i remembered you

i remember you
i will always remember you and the one that died, all those people that survived
or fought to see a new day.
They all deserve a silent day.

All those dead people, the smell of the blood, their screams under the buildings, they needed help but nobody could give it to them until they also died or some of them couldn't breathe clearly. Some of us are heroes from that day; we saw things that some people would be scared of seeing, or who wouldn't fight, like some of us did, just to see the sun again, one more time, before dying. That is why i call them Heroes. I still get traumatized by the effects, sometimes when people shake the table i still think it's happening again, i do not like tall buildings because i do not want to experience what those people did, what i saw, what i heard. January 12—it's a memorable day for the Haitians who did live that day, it is a silent journey, a break when we cry, scream, for the one we lost, a day when our souls give up on trying to be strong about everything.

I JUST DON'T WANT TO INSULT THEM

SOULA HARISIADIS

This piece was inspired by the Spoken Word Workshop and by my mentee Kizzy's bravery. Kizzy amazes me as she pushes herself to try new things while sharing her emotions and experiences in her writing, even when it's scary.

How about: he insulted me.

How about he was fourteen.

How about I was ten.

How about you left me alone with him.

How about I trusted you, and him.

How about, it wasn't one day, but many,
 one day after the next, after the next.

How about, the way he looked at me hurt.

How about, the way you didn't know about my hurt.

How about, when I told you, it had to be a secret.

How about, if we told *Yaiya*, the family would fall apart,
 but instead I fell apart.

How about, instead of, you never have to see him again,
 he apologizes.

How about someone acknowledges it.

How about someone acknowledges me.

How about you. How about you look me in the face,
 how about you give me a hug,
 how about you slap him across the cheek,
how about you all say,
"I'm sorry."

ASHÉ NERVIL

YEARS AS MENTEE: 2
GRADE: Junior
HIGH SCHOOL:
Democracy Prep
Charter High School
BORN: New York, NY
LIVES: New York, NY
**PUBLICATIONS AND
RECOGNITIONS:** Stanford
University Invitational:
semi-finalist in JV
Dramatic Interpretation;
fifth place in Spar

MENTEE'S ANECDOTE: *My writing has evolved this year through expanding the imagery and the amount of wordplay in my poems. It is through the expansion of my literary devices that I've been able to send a clearer message to my audience. Also, I am getting closer to a point where what I write on the page reflects what is going on in my mind. J M's critiques and advice have helped me get there. She's an awesome and exhilarating woman who never fails to bring a smile to my face.*

J M STIFLE

YEARS AS MENTOR: 2
OCCUPATION: Writer
BORN: New York, NY
LIVES: New York, NY
**PUBLICATIONS AND
RECOGNITIONS:**
Wrote video scripts for
Scholastic's Read 180
reading intervention
program; short screenplay,
Mortification of the Flesh,
was a second rounder at
the Austin Film Festival's
Screenwriters competition

MENTOR'S ANECDOTE: *I would say my time with Ashé this year has been more evolutionary than revolutionary. It's gotten deeper and richer. My favorite times have to have been when we did non-writing things. Like the Met Museum last summer. Between our time there and dinner after, we must have spent five hours together. And I can say, there are few people with whom I can stand to spend that much time, let alone discuss art and life with. She got me to explore parts of the museum I hadn't been to in years, or maybe ever.*

SHINING NIGHT

ASHÉ NERVIL

Slowly, I am discovering who I am, not only as a person but as an artist. This year I've been reflecting on my surroundings and myself. It is through this reflection that I am learning to embrace who I am.

Why must darkness be dark
Why must light be bright
Why do we always acknowledge the stars and not the infinite dark sky
For without darkness the star won't have their shine

People always look at stars as a beacon of hope
I too see hope
But it's false
Fake
Not raw
But the darkness
The dark sky
I know will accept me
Because darkness is quiet
Is an underdog
Is humble
Is a mystery that everyone is afraid to unlock
And I am stuck in that cage
In that category

I am darkness
I am the awkward mystery no one seems to want to figure out
I am hair to body
I am touch to sensation
I am question to confusion
I am particle within shadow
I am spectrum in light
I am important
But hidden
Not seen
Not respected
Not cared for
Not seen as important
But unlike darkness
It's hard for me to be humble
To let things run me over
To be fine with being ignored
Belittled
I am tired of hiding behind a smile
A laugh
A corny joke
I am tired of this mask that is stuck to my face
So darkness
Help me be humble
Help me unlock the voice that is screaming to be set free
And to ignore the voices that whisper deadly curses into my soul
Darkness
My bittersweet darkness
Teach me to embrace myself so that I too can shine without anyone else's
confirmation
Like you

A & J RiFF: A SKETCH IN SEARCH OF A PUNCH LINE

J M STIFLE

After a year and a half, I have begun to see how much Ashé and I have in common. I don't mean life experience or background, but similarities in emotional makeup, interests, personality. So, I began developing a kind of sketch that highlights those. The idea is to finish it together.

A:
What could a sassy young lady . . .

J:
and a cranky old bitch . . .

A:
possibly have in common?

J:
Well, we're both . . . what's the word?

A:
Forgetful?

J:
Could that be because neither of us . . .

A:
gets enough sleep? Could that be why—or because—it's one of our favorite activities?

J:

That's some deep wordplay.

A:

Another mutual favorite.

J:

And while we're on the subject of favorites, I can think of at least one activity we both would like to engage in . . . before we die. Something that would be a first for you.

A:

And a last for you . . .

J:

(sigh) Which brings me to unfavorites . . .

A:

The Kardashians. All of them.

J:

Stupidity . . .

A:

The Kardashians. All of them.

J:

We laugh at the same jokes!

A:

The Kardashians! All of them!

J:

And recycle the same punch lines . . .

A:

To be continued . . .

ROBERTA NIN FELIZ

YEARS AS MENTEE: 4
GRADE: Senior
HIGH SCHOOL: Manhattan Center for Science and Mathematics
BORN: Willemstad, Curaçao
LIVES: Bronx, NY

MENTEE'S ANECDOTE: *Jalylah and I first bonded over our germaphobia and our hand sanitizers in our bags. Over our next four years together, the various commonalities in our lives would fade in and out of our conversations and writing, often grounding us through hard times. Every meeting with Jalylah introduces me to a new fact about her family, her personal life, and her dreams, and I think that's a sign of a lifetime relationship. I'm lucky enough to have found someone who continues to inspire and motivate me even after four years, and who has chosen to share her life with me.*

JALYLAH BURRELL

YEARS AS MENTOR: 6
OCCUPATION: Educator and writer
BORN: Tacoma, WA
LIVES: New York, NY

MENTOR'S ANECDOTE: *A brilliant, disciplined, and ethical young scholar, artist, and servant-leader, Roberta is the most impressive young person I have met in my career as a writer and educator. I am grateful for the journey Girls Write Now set us on four years ago, and I am excited to witness her gift and grace transform the world for years to come.*

FiGHTiNG BACK AGAiNST MY CULTURE BY RECLAiMiNG MY CURLS

ROBERTA NIN FELIZ

Transitioning my hair allowed me to embrace and love my natural hair pattern, which I hated for a lot of my life. By embracing my hair, I was able to love myself more, practice self-care, and connect with my identity as an Afro-Latina.

This piece originally appeared in Femsplain.com.

I am a natural-hair-care-productaholic. I spend, on average, $100 a month on hair products (which is a lot, considering I still live at home). I have tried everything from Kinky Curl to DevaCurl, because of course finding the right products for my 3B/3C hair is essential. Not to mention, knowing when to take products out of my weekly rotation, or when my hair is tired of the same product, also requires experimenting with different brands. Keeping the curls bouncy, luscious, and moisturized ain't easy.

But besides keeping my hair healthy, I like looking at the mirror and being met with a mane of spirals and curls bordering my face. I love the compliments I get when my hair is "on fleek." I love the elasticity of my hair after a deep treatment of Shea Moisture's Yucca and Plantain masque. I love my hair. I am determined to take the best care of it because there was a time when the spirals and coils on my head were limp, heat-damaged strands.

For most of middle school, I had an obsession with straight hair. I went to the salon every week to sit under the hairdryer for an hour and get my hair blown out for another thirty minutes. Honestly, it was excruciating. I hated the heat and the waiting and the loud Dominican women gossiping about who got the latest liposuction or whose husband cheated. But I frequented the salon every week because I thought I looked beautiful. I thought straight hair was beautiful. I don't remember when I stopped liking my curly hair, but now that I'm older, the root of my obsession with straight hair is clear to me.

In the Dominican culture, Eurocentric and anti-black ideals of beauty have always been praised. There were the omnipresent rules and boundaries set for the women in my family not to date black men (which I broke) in order to preserve the whiteness of the race. We women were to always make sure our hair was done, and a portion of our weekly allowance was just for getting our hair silk pressed and flat-ironed, with a side of charred ends. My nieces, cousins, and sisters always had their hair straightened. My nieces, in particular—who have kinkier hair than me—would spend hours with a relaxer in their hair. My mother, whose curls clung to her head, also texturized her hair. And so, when I began to flat-iron my hair everyday, I was just following the women in my family. To them, straight hair was beautiful. And I wanted to be beautiful.

Because my hair was not "coarse enough" for hair relaxers and texturizers, the flat-iron would become my weapon in combating the curls on my head. I flat-ironed my hair every day before going to school and every night before I wrapped my hair. If it rained and my hair frizzed up, I made sure I flat-ironed it until my hair smelled so burnt that no amount of hair grease could cover the smell. It got so bad that my mom had to hide the flat-iron from me, and when I went to the salon, my hairdresser was like, "Girl. . . maybe you should stop straightening your hair." But I only realized I had to stop once so much of my hair had fallen out that the hair in the middle of my head was nine inches shorter than the rest of my hair. It was like a layered haircut gone wrong.

After that, I stopped straightening my hair altogether. I cut off most of the damaged hair and started transitioning. I like to think I went natural before going natural was cool. Besides providing me with beautiful curls, transitioning allowed me to really appreciate my Dominican features. All the women in my family sport beautiful curls and cinnamon skin—features we were taught to hate. As I transitioned my hair, I realized I wanted to end centuries of anti-black sentiment in my culture. Loving my curls and refusing to straighten them are things I can do to tap into my identity as an Afro-Latina without the additional standards of beauty imposed on my already beautiful features. Texture transitioning allowed me to realize that oftentimes the most beautiful parts of ourselves as people are the parts we try to hide the most.

Going natural's taught me a good lesson about loving myself, especially the parts of myself I cannot change. It's also taught me to appreciate the diversity of my culture and know when I should fight back against ideals rooted in outdated and prejudice claims. It's enabled me to indulge in myself unapologetically and unconditionally. So, who cares if my hair products are too expensive? My curls deserve the best.

SHEAR

JALYLAH BURRELL

Roberta's reflections on her hair journey prompted me to revisit flash points in my evolving relationship with my own willful strands.

I cut myself bangs last January. I opened my trifold vanity mirror and selected an unused straight razor from a box I had purchased for use in my callous shaver. I extended my wet spirals to tautness and sliced with the authority of a stylist I had seen on a makeover television show. Fashioning myself an organic hair professional, I cut what strands of my freshly-washed hair naturally fell forward. I attempted to graduate the bangs as the blade approached my temples, hacking more judiciously as the spirals contracted into naps. In a concluding ritual, I shook my thick mane with the relief and confidence of model in a Head and Shoulders commercial.

I had for years combated my naps, laying my wet edges down with gel and the bristles of a boar bristle brush. Their silken sheen would elicit comments attesting to the "niceness" of my mane. As a freshman in high school, I remember walking into my private school's gym as the boy's junior varsity squad prepared to take on a public school rival. My shoulders scrunched as I marched past the opposing team's bleacher section, preparing for a snide remark at the hands of girls of variegated brown and verifiable cool. A voice erupted from their huddle and struck me immobile. "You have pretty hair." I hurried to their midst, smiling at the unexpected invitation.

My hair's currency is not so much a testament to its proximity to the straight hair ideal but its distance from the beadie-bead nightmare, the hate that hate made. For those who, like me or my wavy-haired father or cloud-crowned mother, beauty is a partial mistress, and her lash an extension of the one that broke Patsey's spirit by Solomon Northrup's harrowing account.

ELSHAIMA OMRAN

YEARS AS MENTEE: 3
GRADE: Senior
HIGH SCHOOL: International High School at Lafayette
BORN: Alexandria, Egypt
LIVES: Brooklyn, NY

MENTEE'S ANECDOTE: *I trust Stacie with all of my secrets. I tell her everything that is happening to me, and I am confident about it. This year we have talked about a lot of things that changed in my life. We shared our ups and down. Due to the theme, Stacie and I have talked about times when we changed, and those were great conversations with her. I love talking about anything with her, because somehow we always have something in common. Like when we talked about our mothers and we noticed that we both have so much love for our mothers.*

STACIE EVANS

YEARS AS MENTOR: 3
OCCUPATION: Policy Advisor, NYC Mayor's Office
BORN: New York, NY
LIVES: Brooklyn, NY
PUBLICATIONS AND RECOGNITIONS: Publication in *After Ferguson*, anthology from Mourning Glory Press; acceptance into NYC cast of *Listen to Your Mother*

MENTOR'S ANECDOTE: *Shaima and I have been writing together and getting to know one another for three years. I can't believe it's only three years, however. I feel as if we've known each other so much longer. Sharing in Shaima's writing discoveries has been wonderful for me, and the time we've spent talking— about school, family, current events, books, friendships—has been even better. Shaima's expressiveness on the page has developed dramatically over this time, as have her clarity and confidence in her ideas.*

I WONDER

ELSHAIMA OMRAN

The poem I wrote is an idea of (r)evolution because people stereotype Muslims, and in my poem I wrote the solution I thought would be helpful.

I am a Muslim
In Allah I praise
My voice I raise
Saying in one god I praise
In one god I believe

He is the lord of the universe
He is compassionate to me
His prophet Muhammad
My father I never met or saw

He taught me all the way
To be honest and thankful
To be the right Muslim
He taught me to be fair with people
Throughout every day of my life

When it comes to the Holy Quran
my heart and face is full of happiness
For life this book is my guide
I will follow what it says

Islam is my religion
It's all about mercy and kindness
Islam led me to the right path

Allah showers us with his grace
Islam doesn't care
What color, nationality, or race you are
Working together with hope is Islam
Islam
It's full of love and peace

So I'm sick of you calling me a terrorist
All media is leading you to believe
Hurtful lies
Lies
That rip apart our loving community
Lies
Turning the whole world against Muslims
But my question is
Why do you always lie?
And say all Muslims are terrorists
I am Muslim
In Allah I praise
Why there is so much hate toward us
But first you must know us
You are all wrong
secured and covered

You are protecting yourself by blaming Muslims
Can't solve your problems so you blame Muslims
I am so ashamed of you
Sitting there and saying
"All Muslims Are Terrorists"

Every day I pray
That one day you will see the misguided ways
That you will stop pointing at and disgracing Muslims.

Maybe
Just maybe we can forget about our differences
Save the world together instead of fighting every day

Can you do it?
Can you reach out your hand?
Try to be one nation, one world?

But until that time
I will always say
I am Muslim
In Allah I praise
And I am not a Terrorist

BECOMING BLACK: UNWRAPPING THE GIFT

STACIE EVANS

I was inspired by Elshaima's poem. In it, I felt her strong, proud stance—her refusal to let anyone make her ashamed of her faith and her culture. The strength of her voice led to my exploration of the change in my writing voice.

Last summer, after Sandra Bland was murdered in that Texas jail, my mother was in New York. We were talking about Bland. I was angry and said something I would later develop into a piece about what I'd want people to know about me if I ever died in police custody. Whatever comment

I made, I said it with a head motion, one I'm sure I'd never made before, and certainly couldn't make now if I tried. My mother listened to what I had to say, responded, and then smiled.

"I think you just became Black," she said.

And we laughed, because, really, there isn't much question that I've always been Black, but I knew what she meant. I also know that it didn't happen in that moment—that it had been growing in me for a while.

When George Zimmerman was acquitted for stalking and murdering Trayvon Martin, something inside me shifted. I didn't "wake up." I've been woke for a long time, pretty much since childhood. But my response to that miscarriage of justice was different. Not the pain and sadness, the garment-rending wailing and despair of other responses. Yes, I was still in pain, but I was angry, beyond angry. Filled with a flaming rage I'd never felt before.

I almost turned away from it, almost doused it. That was fear. I've never had a good relationship with my anger, have always feared what would come out if I let myself feel it fully.

But in that moment, when I would normally have turned away, I faced those flames, inhaled their power and sweetness, understood what Zach de la Rocha whispered between beats twenty-five years ago: anger is a gift.[11]

I unwrapped that gift and have used it over and over in the two years since that hateful verdict. I've let it sink into my writing and crush my rage and pain into eloquent, multifaceted diamonds on the page.

Anger has changed the way I write, the way I think, the way I see the world. The voice I've found in these two years of rising up against state-sanctioned murder, the thoughts and feelings I've refused to shy away from expressing, have definitely ushered a new version of me into the world. And to call this me the fully Black me isn't a mistake. My anger has done what I always feared it would: opened my chest like a rib spreader and exposed my grieving, tender heart to the world.

And I've survived. I'm still here, still writing, still fighting. To quote my prose poem, "I Am Beautiful when I'm Angry"—

> This rage—rich and thick, with the sweet burn of cayenne
> chocolates and tamarind candies, no less potent for surfacing
> in words. Delicious. Mine.

---

11   Rage Against the Machine. "Freedom." *Rage Against the Machine.* Epic, 1992. CD.

KATHERINE ORTIZ

YEARS AS MENTEE: 4
Grade: Senior
HIGH SCHOOL:
Metropolitan Expeditionary
Learning School
BORN: Azua, Dominican
Republic
LIVES: Queens, NY
**PUBLICATIONS AND
RECOGNITIONS:** Scholastic
Art & Writing Award:
Honorable Mention

MENTEE'S ANECDOTE: *Wondrously brilliant, Joy inspires and motivates me to be the woman I am meant to be. Without her guidance, humor, and care, my outlook on life and my future would be drastically different. Thank you for three wonderful years. You'll be mentor, friend, and practically second mother forever.*

Y. JOY HARRIS-SMITH

YEARS AS MENTOR: 3
OCCUPATION:
Postdoctoral Teaching
Fellow, Princeton
Theological Seminary
BORN: Bitburg, Germany
LIVES: Queens, NY

MENTOR'S ANECDOTE: *It is said that the pen is mightier than the sword, and those words ring true when the pen is in Katherine's hand. It has been my pleasure to watch the beautiful flower Katherine is bloom over the past three years as a young woman and a writer. I am grateful to her and Girls Write Now for giving me a front-row seat to a wonderful experience.*

UNTITLED

KATHERINE ORTIZ

Inspired by the discovery of a foreign land where I was not only embraced by the culture, but found friendship that left me breathless with certainty. When my past was plagued with a stream of not cohesive, toxic relationships, France led me to friendship laced in humor, care, and most importantly, happiness.

"*Vous avez la pêche?*" Nathalie's voice awakened the sleeping bodies atop bus seats. My head lolled forward, sleep burning at my eyes. That morning's breakfast sat in my stomach uncomfortably, the back of my new sneakers tore at my skin. So, "*Non, je n'ai pas la pêche*, Nathalie."

"But we're in France," a meek voice argued, and although my spine ached beneath the milk of my skin, and the contents of my head rattled behind my pupils, I grinned to see that French fields lay in patterned quilts through the window pane.

So I found myself chanting, "*Oui, nous avons la pêche!*" along with a chorus of once asleep voices.

As we descended from the bus onto Normandy grass, Josh trotted beside me, a Canon hanging artistically around his neck. I knew then he held aspirations to be a photographer, even if he sort of just aimed his camera and hoped for the best. Of course I pretended I could professionally take pictures just as Josh could (even when he wasn't really trying), so I held my camera tightly against my palm, photographing the grinning boy clad in an engine red jacket.

Tall cathedrals met the sky, people littered at its base; everything was wondrously gorgeous. I didn't really think of God much, but in France I thought he meant for the world to look exactly like this.

Anyway, Normandy consisted of days tasting cheese that was beyond my palate, because honestly it was kind of disgusting, and *a lot* of walking and *a lot* of not enough sleep. And even though France held sights enveloping history and blood bubbling through stone streets, I find my happiest memories trotting through inclined French roads, bodies pressed against uncomfortable bus seats.

I've always believed friends are like water: you can feel them against the skin of your palms, but you can never *really* grasp them. They pool in drops against your knuckles, and dry into air. Maybe I was born lonely. A womb plagued by a thick isolation that seeped into the flesh of this newborn. I'm diseased in the truest form of the word. I sleep with words and wake up to the castings of the moon against my skin, alone.

But Josh was different. You could never really take him seriously, literally everything he said was meant to cause the ends of your lips to quirk upwards. Of course, I enjoyed this. My storybook had been retellings of too-serious moments with too many silences, and finding someone who was endlessly friendly was a relief.

And sometimes you can't imagine people with stories and lives and families and *hurt* to be so carefree. It was as if nothing burdened him, and I found myself wondering whether sadness ever bloomed in his chest, because my heart was a fucking garden. And how could someone just be *so happy*?

I thought maybe this friendship wouldn't survive in an endless stream of lightheartedness. But I am self-sabotaging, diseased, so I convinced myself depth wasn't necessary, not with us. Not everything has to be so fucking personal, Katherine, god.

But one day it just became that. Because as we sat in bus seats with legs curled and sweaters draped across our laps, craters were dug into an earth once so solid. Of course everything was painted in humor, a delicate lining of easiness, but our relationship was just that way: painted in humor, easy.

We spoke of our fathers, and although he was unburdened, nothing tainting the flesh of his heart, he had once been *hurt*. And even though he had once been hurt, sadness didn't constantly bloom in his chest. But it was as if every day was spring within my rib cage. I just didn't know how he trod through life so carelessly, lifted into an endless embrace of joy.

I just wished I could be embraced by life the way he is.

We fell asleep, connected by the lyrics of songs I didn't recognize, heads tilted onto shoulders and limbs aching. And everything felt airy, like fog and silk, and I realized maybe these burdens had dissolved into nothing. Our friendship was just so *easy* and *simple* and everything else seemed unnecessarily difficult in comparison.

Josh is contagiously happy, and every day I'm glad that it's so contagious. Because sometimes I just really need it.

CAN YOU STOP?

Y. JOY HARRIS-SMITH

This piece is about speaking truth to power.

Can you stop, government-sanctioned violence against black and brown bodies
Can you stop, dropping your eyes when you walk past me on the street attempting to deny my existence
Can you stop, offending me and then being surprised that I'm offended and telling you off
Can you stop, commenting that I "speak so well"
Can you stop, only acknowledging me when you need directions on the street
Can you stop, acting as though all of your policies and procedures apply only to me and never to you
Can you stop?!

VALERIE PEREYRA

YEARS AS MENTEE: 2
GRADE: Senior
HIGH SCHOOL:
The Beacon School
BORN: Queens, NY
LIVES: Brooklyn, NY
**PUBLICATIONS AND
RECOGNITIONS:** Scholastic
Art & Writing Award:
Honorable Mention

MENTEE'S ANECDOTE: *I am so happy to have gotten paired with such a cool and understanding mentor. Our conversations vary from the latest music (that Drake song) to existential questions of everyday life. But it's the feeling of these conversations—not the topic—that I remember most. My final Girls Write Now year is bittersweet: I got to meet Steph, someone with whom I have a lot in common and look up to as a writer. Sadly, our time together is limited. All our moments have been special in some way, whether it's sharing a bagel, laughing about our sense of direction, or dissecting a poem.*

STEPHANIE DEL ROSSO

YEARS AS MENTOR: 1
OCCUPATION: Playwright,
teacher, and editor
BORN: Silver Spring, MD
LIVES: Brooklyn, NY
**PUBLICATIONS AND
RECOGNITIONS:** Selected
as Playwright in the SoHo
Rep Writer/Director Lab;
Finalist for the Leah Ryan
Fund for Emerging Women
Writers; Semi-Finalist for
Page 73's Playwriting
Fellowship and Clubbed
Thumb's Biennial Commission

MENTOR'S ANECDOTE: *There must have been some telepathic magic at work in the Girls Write Now offices when Valerie and I were paired. The moment I met her, I was floored by how much we had in common (from coffee addictions, to older sisters, to travel, and writing interests) and how much our personalities clicked. It is no exaggeration to say that whenever I spend time with Valerie, my day improves. Our senses of humor are nearly identical, sure. But more importantly, Valerie is a tremendously mature and compassionate person and a gifted writer. I can't wait to see where the world takes her.*

MY HAVEN

VALERIE PEREYRA

*This poem—which I worked on with my amazing mentor—
deals with the evolving theme of learning to love and appreciate your own body and, essentially, your own being. Growing
into the person you want to be and realizing that your body is
your own safe haven is a work in progress.*

Let me close my eyes
to silence the throbbing in my forehead,
temples,
behind my eyelids I can still feel the ache in
my neck,
shoulders,
lower back.

My knees don't curve the way they used to
and I'm afraid they will snap like old wood,
giving splinters to those who run
their fingers along
trying to find the spot where my knee caves in
deeper than the holes in my ribcage
where nothing stays

because food doesn't feel the same
gliding down the pipes of my throat

jutting out whenever I breathe,
in a continuous sigh,
acidity pooling in the hollows of my cheek.

I never noticed how bitter my mouth tastes,
when it hasn't said the word "happy" for a while.

But it could be the leftover coffee from my chipped mug,
banging into my chipped
front teeth,
as I gulp down the frothy blackness.

My teeth are stained a vivid yellow
that is putrid
against white walls,
not a sunshine yellow, because sunflowers can't grow
in between the gaps of my baby teeth
still crooked
like my nose from the time
a girl punched me,
(I deserved it)
but my back straightened,
I stood taller,
when a man tried it.

He shrank back to the rut that he came from
with his misconceptions
his underestimations
and his audacity
to claim what wasn't his.

I JUST WANTED TO SAY

STEPHANIE DEL ROSSO

I wrote this piece during the Girls Write Now Memoir Workshop and was inspired to continue working on it thanks to Valerie's encouragement when I shared it with her. Revolutions take many forms, I've found: sometimes the smallest, seemingly mundane ones feel the most significant.

My dad hates phones. I don't mean that he is resentful of technology; I mean that there is something about the intimacy of a call: the narrowness of it, the possibility of being misheard, maybe. Dropped signals, garbled speech. This notion makes him anxious.

Perhaps. We've never really talked about it.

We e-mail. When I got into college, when I got my first job, he e-mailed congratulations.

On birthdays: e-mails. A mundane question (about health insurance, holidays): he will pose it in an e-mail. Sometimes I print them. I'm not sure why. They sit in a stack in an old shoebox, proof of something I don't know what to name, or why I need to. I am, after all, no good at candor either. It's a quality that I've inherited.

When I missed a call from my dad last week, I panicked. This meant disaster—I was sure. The red letters signaling "voicemail" glinted almost garishly across the screen. Did something happen with his job? My mom? My mom's mom? Worst-case scenarios spooled out of me like an endless cliché. I pictured fluorescent-lit hospital hallways, heard siren whirs. It began to rain. It was all some cheap tragedy, a movie that I was starring in against my will. I sat at my kitchen table and dialed.

"Hi Steph."

His voice didn't sound strained. It didn't sound dampened by sadness or sickness. But I figured it was imminent.

"Dad, what's wrong?"

There was a pause.

"There's nothing—there's nothing wrong." He laughed a little. "I just wanted to say. Hi.

To see how you were doing."

I sank back into my kitchen chair.

"Hello?" he asked.

"I'm here. Hi. I'm good, Dad," I answered.

"Is it raining there?"

ANGEL PIZARRO

YEARS AS MENTEE: 4
GRADE: Senior
HIGH SCHOOL: NYC iSchool
BORN: New York, NY
LIVES: New York, NY

MENTEE'S ANECDOTE: *This year has been a big transition in my life into young adulthood. My mentor, Kaitlyn, has shown a great amount of support and care when I needed it most. I appreciate all the advice and guidance she has given me throughout our year at Girls Write Now. Our meetings at the local coffee house truly lift my spirits after a long week, and I am grateful for all the conversations and personal moments we share.*

KAITLYN GREENIDGE

YEARS AS MENTOR: 1
OCCUPATION: Curriculum Developer, Amplify, Inc.
BORN: Boston, MA
LIVES: Brooklyn, NY
PUBLICATIONS AND RECOGNITIONS: *We Love You, Charlie Freeman,* published by Algonquin Books in March 2016; essays and fiction in Salon.com, Buzzfeed Ideas, Lit Hub, and *The Offing;* 2016 NEA Fellow in Literature

MENTOR'S ANECDOTE: *Angel is a curious, empathetic, and inquisitive teenager. My favorite times with her this year have simply been our conversations about writing and life. Recently, we were talking about her Modernism class. She told me she was studying Picasso's "Les Demoiselles d'Avignon" and had to write a response piece to it. "So I want to write about misogyny," she explained, breaking down that piece much more quickly than most writers I know. She's a really wonderful person and writer and I'm excited about all the great things she'll write in the future. I can't wait to read them!*

WOMEN OF OPPRESSION

ANGEL PIZARRO

This poem reveals the feelings that I have suppressed over the years. I wanted to bring awareness to how women are still affected daily by gender roles and inequality. It is an issue that continues to impact our lives.

I am a woman of oppression
Possession of the mind, body, and soul
By the chains of society
By its suffocating hold
I try and try desperately to break free
I'm not even close as I would like to be
Confining me
They tell me how to dress, how to act, how to speak
Weak is for those who try to stop us being
Feeling intimidated by what we think
What we believe
Misconceive our words
Ignore our blurbs
Treat us like we're not a part of this world
There's a restlessness deep in my soul
A loudness in my head
That I can't seem to control
Every night I fall asleep
But can barely make it through the week

I am fed up
Approaching the peak of the hill
That grows with anger
They want to suppress with a pill
Am I wrong to feel what I feel?
He told me stop being such a girl
That it's not such a big deal
He spits the words at me with venom
As if there's a dirty taste in his mouth
The rage inside of me reached an incredible height
Bite down on that tongue
Save it for another night
A daily fight I have tried to prevent
frequent arguments that don't seem to end
I am wounded
I am just another victim he will offend
Tell me what defines a girl in your mind
Remind me of why you are so disgusted by the label assigned
Are you more of a man now?
Does that measure masculinity somehow?
I was told to keep it in
Close my mouth but raise my chin
Swallow the words down with a small smile
Bile is what I end up trying to keep down
Meanwhile he is free to vomit his speech
Without even a moment to really think
About what he has said
I think it's time we allow ourselves to speak
Teach those who are unaware
Declare our liberties just as they do
Break through limitations
Our frustrations need to be heard
They can't hold us back anymore
Or tell us how we're supposed to act
Because we are women of oppression
And we will fight back

A TRICK OF THE DESERT

KAITLYN GREENIDGE

This is an excerpt from my novel We Love You, Charlie Freeman *(Algonquin Books, 2016). The narrator, Charlotte, is describing what it was like to first make friends with the only other black girl in her class, Adia Brietling, and her mother, Marie.*

It was exhausting to be with the Breitlings. Black people could love Joni Mitchell but still claim to hate white singers. It was one of an elaborate set of rules that Marie imparted to Adia, who parroted them back to me as if I had not been in the room at the same time she heard them. It was a long list, the work of many years' worth of debate.

We'd had our own version of these rules back home in Dorchester, but they had been rules of what you weren't supposed to do in public, what you weren't supposed to do around white people. Laugh too loudly, show anger, dress raggedy, show any sign of disorder or chaos. Fit perfectly—without strain—into space.

The Breitlings' list was different. According to them, these were the things black people did not do: eat mayonnaise; drink milk; listen to Elvis Presley; watch Westerns or *Dynasty*; read *Time* magazine; appreciate Jack London; know the lyrics to Kenny Rogers's songs; suffer fools; enjoy the cold or any kind of winter. Here were the things black people did do: learn to speak French and adore Paris; instinctively understand and appreciate anyone from a small island or a hot place; spank their children; obsessively read science fiction and watch *Star Trek* episodes; prefer sweet foods to salty.

The debate over whether or not black people were natural swimmers was a very old one between the two of them, an argument that was full of in-jokes and constructed of rhythms I could not follow.

Living in all-white Courtland County, Marie gave her daughter these specifications so that Adia could spot a real black person as soon as they came along, avoid all the mirages. That's what I thought it was at first, and it put me on the defensive, because surely, in this analogy, I—in my tennis shoes and wannabe white-girl bangs—would be the mirage. And who would ever want to think of themselves as not really water but actually a trick of the desert?

As I got to know them better, I realized the rules were for Adia herself as much as they were for the world around her. Marie nursed Adia on a bitter pabulum of omnipresent, always-lurking oppression. To ready her daughter for the assault on her rights that Marie was sure was coming, she had given Adia a very simple list of instructions on how to be black. All Adia had to do was follow them and her whole self would be secure. It was intoxicating. I wanted them to tell me their rules forever.

YESMIL POLANCO

YEARS AS MENTEE: 2
GRADE: Senior
HIGH SCHOOL: NYC iSchool
BORN: New York, NY
LIVES: New York, NY

MENTEE'S ANECDOTE: *My revolution was when I told my mentor about my past and she encouraged me to be a better person. She gave me the strength to be able to overcome other obstacles. We have been through so much. She listens to me and I love that. I love hearing her stories. She inspires me so much. Her positivity makes me feel so much better about life. I feel like we balance each other out, and I hope we stay in touch after high school. Heather is such a great advisor, her advice really helps me and I love that about her.*

HEATHER KRISTIN

YEARS AS MENTOR: 9
OCCUPATION: Writer
BORN: New York, NY
LIVES: Brooklyn, NY
PUBLICATIONS AND RECOGNITIONS: Interviewed by Oprah live on-camera, in *Elle* Magazine, on Latino NPR, and on Huffington Post Live with host Nancy Redd; speaker at The Get In Touch Foundation Summit at the Omni at Yale University; 2016 keynote speaker at The Mill River Country Club for The Sterling House Community Center

MENTOR'S ANECDOTE: *Yesmil opened my eyes to what it is like to be a Dominican living in New York. For her, it's huge family parties, taking care of each other, and comfort food, but also there is an element of gun violence and the glamorization of thug life. When Yesmil goes to college in the fall it will be a revolution because she will be the first in her family to do so! I'm proud of her evolution into intelligent business-woman who knows and loves her culture, and who isn't afraid of making her own mark on the world.*

MiEL

YESMIL POLANCO

This piece is close to my heart. It represents the struggles that many people go through when they leave their homes to come to a new country. In this poem, the girl mentioned is having a revolution with herself and is struggling to adapt to a new environment.

I.

a holographic sky,
the stars are clustered in groups.
happiness is a constant dream.

hiding in the midst of smoke,
finding a way out is a burden,
i only know sadness.
it's been embedded in my heart for a while.

it only gets worse,
tiring,
my hand can't hold these strings no more.

string by string,
my heart keeps playing,
this game of happiness is taking a toll.

II.

we ain't know this girl no more.
her eyes are matte,
tears dry, hair up

her skin was the color of honey,
beautiful and warm.
she left the caribbean,
but the caribbean didn't stay with her.

no light is here.
she grew up, she says.
her life turned from stars to complete darkness,
in a blink of an eye.

she tries playing the game for too long,
poor her,
she ain't know.
it's an illusion.

she wants it so bad.
oh honey,
happiness was once a thing in this world.

sinking deeper and deeper,
she thinks about mangos and coconuts,
to remind her of her mami.

yaileen is like her mami,
she's gonna end five hundred feet
below the ground.
the game of happiness ain't a game no more

DADDY'S DEAD

HEATHER KRISTIN

My poem "Daddy's Dead" was inspired by Grace Dunham's talk at the Girls Write Now Poetry Workshop. She told the group to write down a list of things we hated and things we loved. My list was most passionate about my mother, my father, and my past.

Coffee in the morning
Vodka in the night
This is how I simmer
When I remember family fights.

Fights about poverty, paternity, poetry.

Mamma said, "We're gonna be homeless. Put that book down. Daddy's dead. Daddy's dead. Did you hear what I just said?"

"He's a pop in a box," she yelled.
We grabbed our socks
And carried them to shelters, subways, and stranger's beds.
Stability became a wish and some days we starved.

Fights turned to survival, sacrifice, secrets.

Is it revolutionary or evolutionary that today my children are fed and my mamma is almost dead?

MEHAK RAO

YEARS AS MENTEE: 1
GRADE: Junior
HIGH SCHOOL: International High School at Lafayette
BORN: Malka Hans, Pakistan
LIVES: Brooklyn, NY

MENTEE'S ANECDOTE: *My revolution with my mentor was when we first met in the Girls Write Now office. Every week it kills me to come to 7th Avenue, but when I meet my mentor, it gives me excitement. Our first meeting was awkward. Then we started talking more and all the laughing made us closer. Even my friends want to be with my mentor because she can speak Korean. I just like my mentor, and I feel closer to her since she knows about me and my experience being in this country. I feel lucky to have her. I trust her now.*

ESTHER KIM

YEARS AS MENTOR: 1
OCCUPATION: Assistant Publicist, Columbia University Press
BORN: Yonkers, NY
LIVES: Brooklyn, NY

MENTOR'S ANECDOTE: *My personal revolution with my mentee was meeting her for the first time at Brooklyn Central Library. She shared her love of K-pop and updated me on the newest boy bands, like BTS (who knew Big Bang is ancient history), and her favorite foods, like kheer (a rice pudding dessert). She shared the story of how her family of nine moved from a plantation farm in Pakistan to Coney Island, Brooklyn when she was ten years old. I was and am still so encouraged by her strength and positivity.*

LAZY TO ACTIVE

MEHAK RAO

I wrote this piece to inspire my friends, so they can know that the Girls Write Now program can be fun and make your life busy.

Last year I was fifteen, this year I am sixteen, big difference. To think about it, I have changed from a lazy to an active person. Sometimes I try to save time just to stay home and spend some time with my family. I remember last year when I used to spend my time watching drama and wasting time at home getting yelled at by Mom, who'd say, "Do some work go outside of the house, lazybones. Lose some weight." Now I only hear Mom saying, "Outside is more important than family? Stay home." But because of Girls Write Now I feel like I have become more busy. Before it used to be home, before school, school, after school, and then back to home. Now it's home, before school, school, after school, mentoring, and then home. Since I am in eleventh grade, I feel like giving up, it's too much work. In school, I am involved in some activities I can't even skip that are a lot of work.

Since I am in the Girls Write Now program, I say to myself when I feel like quitting, "Mehak! You are working too hard, but it's worth it." Right now too much is going on, but I know I can do it, and I am happy that I am busy instead of wasting time. Now I like the way I am working hard instead of staying home and wasting time. I am not a lazybones anymore, as Mom says.

BLONDE

ESTHER KIM

This piece was written while sitting in Prospect Park on a spring day, reflecting on the changes—to my sublet, to my family, to my hair—I'd experienced over the course of a short six months.

Since I started Girls Write Now this September, my hair's changed from black to ash blond. I dyed it on Valentine's Day, and that change was inspired by the end of my first serious relationship. After the hair change, I got a promotion at work and a new, my first, intern—a Finnish student who shares the same shade of blond hair as me. My family moved back into our house in Long Island after five months of living in a hotel, only to decide that they want to move to the Canadian border. And I moved into my fifth apartment in two years.

The sand beneath my feet shifts, but my weekly meetings with Mehak remind me that a girl can go through big, painful changes and become all the stronger and wiser for it. I'm grateful for that.

JADE RODRIGUEZ

YEARS AS MENTEE: 3
GRADE: Senior
HIGH SCHOOL: Bronx Studio School for Writers and Artists
BORN: New York, NY
LIVES: Bronx, NY

MENTEE'S ANECDOTE: *My mentor and I have a very simple relationship: we're very open with each other. We first started connecting over our mothers and how we dealt with them. Linda has taught me to open up more and express my feelings toward everything. I am more open and well developed due to her.*

LINDA CORMAN

YEARS AS MENTOR: 3
OCCUPATION: Freelance editor and writer
BORN: Newton, MA
LIVES: New York, NY
PUBLICATIONS AND RECOGNITIONS: Recently, Knowledge@Wharton, the online journal of the Wharton Business School

MENTOR'S ANECDOTE: *The pivotal moment in our relationship came when we both started talking about our mothers. It helped me to know that sharing my own troubling experience with my mother was helpful to Jade in dealing with her relationship with her mother. Over the years, the high value I've placed on our relationship has taught me to be a little more patient, generous, and understanding— not just with Jade but also with myself, and, I hope, other people.*

GROWING UP IS HARDER THAN IT SOUNDS.

JADE RODRIGUEZ

I decided to use my friends as inspiration for this piece. I put them in situations that they have never been in, and I enjoyed seeing where it would go. I wanted readers to decide where the story ended. This relates to revolution because I would never have done that before.

High school is over and it's time for me to move on. I'm tired of walking past the same people and doing the same thing every day. I've always imagined myself packing up and never looking back. I have the money and I am ready. But the girls will be sad to see me go, especially Jackie. We've recently gotten closer but I need to push that from my head. Still.

"What's wrong, Liam?" Rose asked as I sprawled on her couch.

"Jackie."

"You feeling her or what?"

"I think I am, but Rose, I'm leaving. Once summer ends."

"Finally getting out of this town, I see. Anyway, talk to her."

"She will want something serious. It will end badly."

"Don't let it end badly. Tell her straight up and go for it. You will deal with leaving when that time comes, but just take a risk bro."

After leaving Rose's, I texted Jackie, asking her to meet me at the park. I arrived before her and sat down on our favorite marble bench. I looked up and saw her coming down the walkway. Chestnut hair curled to perfection, her face makeup free, making her even more beautiful.

"Liam, what's up?"

"I need to let you know how I feel about you."

"What do you mean?"

"I like you, Jackie, a lot. I don't know where these feelings came from, but they're here."

She didn't say anything, so I kissed her, and she didn't pull away. I looked at her to say something and all she said was, "I have to go."

After I got home, Rose texted me to come over.

"What's up?" I said.

"So, Jackie came over earlier."

My eyes opened wide. "When, today?"

"Yeah, she came over and told me what happened. She ran away because she is terrified, Liam. She felt something from that kiss but didn't know what to do, so she left. But she likes you, Liam."

I'd never felt so happy.

"So here's the plan, I'm going to tell her to meet me at Zulys, but instead of me going, you're going."

When I got to our favorite coffee shop she was already there, sipping coffee. I could drink coffee with Jackie every day for the rest of my life. The way she wipes the cream off her upper lip when she takes her first sip is my favorite.

I walked in, scared.

"What are you doing here? Where's Rose?"

"She's not coming. This was setup so we could talk."

"So you both lied to me?"

"We had to in order for this to happen. Please don't be mad."

"So talk."

"Oh, I didn't think I would get this far," I said with a nervous chuckle. "Anyways, I want you, Jackie. I felt something from that kiss. I'm pretty sure if I did, you did."

"Liam—"

"No, don't. I know you're scared, but you don't have to be with me. I won't hurt you. I promise."

Jackie didn't say anything after that. She just got up, moved next to me, and leaned in for a kiss.

"I want to be with you, Liam."

I smiled and deepened the kiss.

A month later, we were having coffee again, something we'd done almost every day.

"I haven't been this happy in a long time," she said.

"Me, too," I said. Then, "I have some news. I bought my ticket to Copenhagen."

Jackie didn't say anything.

"I thought your plans would change when our relationship changed."

"It has. This relationship makes me want to explore more."

"That's really fucking selfish! You make me fall in love with you, then you plan to leave me. You promised you wouldn't hurt me."

"I'm not being selfish, Jackie. Come with me."

"What am I going to do in another country?"

"Be with me."

"I start school in September. I have plans, too! I have to go."

Once again I let her go. I don't remember the walk home at all, but I got there quickly. I dozed off and when I woke up, three hours had gone by. Why hasn't she called? Did I lose her? Then I heard a pebble click on my window. I went to see who was there, and she was looking up at me.

"Come down."

My Jackie was sitting on the front steps, looking so beautiful in the moonlight. Her smile just popped out.

"Come sit down."

I sat down on the steps and looked her way.

"The moon looks so nice tonight, don't you think?"

"Yes, it does, but that moon's beauty has nothing on yours."

She blushed. "I'm not mad or hurt, Liam. I just don't want to see you go. But I had a talk with Rose . . ."

"What did our unpaid therapist say?"

"To stop being a bitch."

"What?"

"She said don't hold you back, because if the situation was reversed, I would hate you if you acted the way I did."

"You're a great person, Jackie."

"I'm just saying I need to stop being the selfish one."

POINT OF PRIDE

LINDA CORMAN

Although we originally decided to write short stories, we've mostly done personal essays. This spring, we decided to return to story writing, but ideas weren't coming. So we wrote character sketches, emphasizing what our characters most wanted. From these, we developed stories around our characters' conflicting desires. Here they are.

Maury watched Rachel let the royal blue silk dress slip down over her mannequin-like figure, her brown curls falling around her face as she smoothed the fabric. He buckled his belt and, shirtless, put his arm around her waist, caught her hand, and led her in a fox trot, humming something Frank Sinatra–ish.

She resisted slightly, then gave in to his lead. He was a good dancer. It was one of the things she loved about him. He had nothing to add to a discussion of the Beethoven piano sonatas she still played with the prodigious skill inflicted by the fearsome Madame Dentrovich, but he had rhythm, and he worshipped her piano playing.

"Maury, please. Let me finish getting dressed," she said after they'd made several turns back and forth in the narrow space between their bed and bureaus. She squeezed his shoulder and smiled to reassure him she really wasn't pushing him away.

As she tilted her head from side to side to put in the screw-on white drop earrings he had given her for their 20th anniversary the previous summer, she watched him thumb through the stack of mail she'd left by the phone on the bedside table.

"What's this? It's been more than twenty years since you were at Simmons College."

"Oh, nothing." She could have lied and said it was probably a fundraising letter, but it was a point of pride with her not to lie unless it was absolutely unavoidable.

"So, you don't need it?" he said, tossing it in the woven straw waste basket they'd picked up on their vacation the previous winter in Haiti.

"No!" she said, her emphasis giving her away.

"What is it?"

"It's my acceptance letter for the master's program in social work," she said, almost whispering. She might as well have been admitting an affair.

"What the hell? What do you need that for? I work my damnedest to give you a good life . . . move to this town with the fancy schools . . . that's not good enough for you?"

"It's not because of money. I want to do something . . ."

"You do plenty. You yourself are always complaining you're too busy. The School Committee . . . League of Women Voters . . . the kids."

"I want to have an a—a profession." She suppressed her amusement at her own near Freudian slip.

"What for? I do pretty well. Hey, I can't buy you a fancy car and we don't belong to a country club like the Hartwells do, but we do pretty well."

It seemed unlikely she could make him understand. But she was going to enroll anyway. She would use the money her mother had left her.

CATHIOSKA RODRIGUEZ

YEARS AS MENTEE: 2
GRADE: Junior
HIGH SCHOOL:
Bronx School for Law,
Government, and Justice
BORN: Bronx, NY
LIVES: Bronx, NY

MENTEE'S ANECDOTE: *Knowing I can count on Jen to not always be there for me for gossip, writing, my health, and myself means the world to me. I can also count on her to buy me my favorite soda, Dr. Pepper. I love her.*

JEN ORTIZ

YEARS AS MENTOR: 1
OCCUPATION:
Senior Editor, *Marie Claire* magazine
BORN: New York, NY
LIVES: Brooklyn, NY
PUBLICATIONS AND RECOGNITIONS: Published in *Marie Claire,* most recently an interview with actresses who have portrayed superheroes in films and TV as part of "Girl Power," a March

MENTOR'S ANECDOTE: *Cathioska is leading a one-woman revolution—she's fighting every day for a future that she wants more than anything. And damn, it's awesome. She's committed to so many extracurricular activities, it's hard to keep track. (Not to mention homework, mentorship programs, SATs and state tests, and life in general.) All for one goal: college. Correction: kicking college's ass. And to create a life that's all her own, on her own terms, with success at the finish line. And yet, every single time we've met, she's laughing, filled with energy, and never backs down from a challenge. Thanks for the inspiration, girl.*

2016 feature piece celebrating the impact of superheroes in pop culture; MarieClaire.com, most recently an essay titled, "I Went to a Super Cheesy 'Couples-Only' Resort So You Don't Have To"

MORE THAN "SOME ASSISTANT"

CATHIOSKA RODRIGUEZ

In relation to our theme of (r)evolution, I wanted to write a historical fiction piece about the transition of females joining the education system as students.

"Another effin' rejection letter?" I asked no one in particular. My husband walked over and stood behind me. He softly massaged my shoulders.

"It's just unusual for a female to be applying, Beth," he told me for the twentieth time.

"They should accept based on intelligence, not on my gender," I replied.

"One day, honey . . . One day." He kissed my forehead and walked outside to smoke a cigarette.

"You'll die because your lungs are going to rot . . .lay off the cigarettes, Tom," I called out. He waved me off and sat on the porch, a cloud of fading gray smoke surrounding him. As I continued to shuffle through the mail, I found another letter from Geneva Medical College in New York. I didn't want to get my hopes up, but butterflies came anyway, awaiting the "Congratulations!" or "We regret to inform you." I prayed it was a "Congratulations!" but I knew, in my heart, it probably wasn't.

I opened it delicately, handling it with care.

There it was: "Congratulations!"

"Tom! That 'one day' is today! I got in!" I yelled excitedly. His head popped through the door, his face showing his surprise. He dropped his cigarette, ran to me, picked me up, and spun me. I held his neck, giggling.

"My lovely young wife is moving on to big things," he whispered before kissing my lips.

I drew back in disgust. "Ugh, cigarette breath!" I scrunched up my nose, hoping the smell would vanish as quickly as the cloud of smoke did.

The class started promptly at 8:30 P.M. This college only offered night classes, because men had to work very long hours to support their family. It was only 8:20 P.M. The room was filled with at least six men. I was the only female there. And they definitely noticed that too. My husband had warned me I'd be the black sheep of the class. ("You don't have to go, you'll stand out.") Who knew it'd be this bad?

"Are you Mr. Johnson's assistant?" one of the men asked me. I gave him a questioning look for a moment, then realized they'd never seen a female in a classroom—until now.

The classroom was smaller than I'd expected. There were wooden desks with black chairs, a chalkboard with words partially erased.

"No, I'm one of his students," I replied calmly.

And that's when the chaos began. Before walking into class, I'd already learned one thing to be true: men will always be immature, no matter their age.

"Are you fucking *kidding me*?!" one man—er, boy—asked.

"Girls are too stupid to learn! They only know how to change a diaper and bake a pie!" another boy said.

I rolled my eyes at the discriminatory comments and took a seat front and center . . .still ignoring them, of course. I came here for a reason, they accepted me for a reason, and they won't stop me.

They can't stop me from something that's already begun.

HOW TO BECOME
A NOVELIST—
BEFORE ANYONE ELSE

JEN ORTIZ

Two things happen whenever Cathioska and I meet: we laugh, we talk pop news. (Did I mention how much fun we have?) So naturally, a Buzzfeed listicle inspired this historical fiction (Cathioska's favorite genre): "12 Historical Women Who Gave No F*cks." Here's to the women who started their own revolutions!

Stupid boy, Murasaki thought to herself as she pressed her ear against the red wooden door towering tall above her. Some days she'd imagine that the door stretched high above her home, high above the walls of the Japanese Imperial Court, high above any structure anywhere on Earth, touching the clouds and catching the sun's rays before they even had a chance to reach the ground below. She'd daydream about skipping along the clouds, leaping gracefully from one foggy white poof to the other. Up there it didn't matter that she was a girl. Or, as her father would say, "just a girl."

"Wrong again, boy!" she hissed quietly to herself. She rolled her eyes and allowed herself a sigh, low enough that only she could hear. She backed away from the door and couldn't help the small smile that crept along the lower half of her frustratingly childlike face. (She hated being seen as "just a child," too. She was so much greater than those two little words combined—why didn't anyone else see it?)

Beyond the great red door were her father and younger brother. The two of them were sitting across from each other, she imagined, at her father's ornate, and intimidating, desk. Her father, eyes narrowed, nostrils flared, fingers tapping in frustration atop the glossy wood that separated them. She could picture her easily distracted brother, eyes gazing toward the sky in mid-daydream, pondering what snack he might indulge his fat face with when this was over.

"Concentrate!" she heard her father yell as she walked down the hall toward the entryway that led to her bedroom. "*But father*—why doesn't Murasaki have to do this? It's not fair!" her completely clueless brother whined. She felt her face flush with anger, vowing to pay him back with a swift kick to the shin. But then her heart dropped. She felt tears well up and instinctively shut her eyelids to trap them. "Because she is *just a girl,*" her father answered, his voice thick with impatience. "She will become someone's wife one day and that's *it*. That's all she will be. No one will expect anything from her. They will expect *everything* from you—to be smart, to be clever, to honor your family. What a pity she was not born a man. Now, pay attention!"

She rushed inside her bedroom, quietly shutting the door behind her. *Wouldn't want to get caught eavesdropping on Father and his great, adored son*, she thought bitterly, wiping away the one tear that escaped. Her father was teaching her brother Chinese, the written language of the government—the same language women were excluded from learning—as preparation for a future career she could never imagine. Her brother had been taking lessons for months now. And for months now she'd asked, then begged, then pleaded with her father to let her sit in on the sessions. *I wouldn't make a sound, promise! You won't even know I'm there. Please, please, please?* It was always the same disappointing answer.

And she'd cry until her hot tears turned into anger, which she often took out on her younger brother, whose cries were quickly hushed by their strict attendant, a sullen older woman who rarely spoke and never smiled. She believed children should be seen, never heard, and wasn't going to let these two children make her look bad, she often reminded them. Murasaki both despised her and was grateful for her silence because, well, she never got in trouble.

Finally, Murasaki stopped asking. She hadn't given up, like her father assumed. No, in fact, after her brother's lesson was over, Murasaki's lesson would begin. As soon as she heard that large red door close, and the bickering voices of her brother and father faded down the hallway, she'd sneak out of her bedroom, slip into her father's study, and look at his notes. She'd study the lessons he'd written down for her brother, sometimes sneaking a sheet of paper from his pile to read later—and then destroy, of course, wouldn't want her noisy attendant finding it—under her bed where no one could see. Before slipping back out (stay too long and she'd risk getting caught), she'd look up at the scrolls stacked onto the shelves that lined the far wall. *I'll have my own writing on that shelf one day*, she thought to herself, *I'll show them*. Then the knob turned, and she was gone.

LUNA ROJAS

YEARS AS MENTEE: 2
GRADE: Junior
HIGH SCHOOL:
Cobble Hill School
of American Studies
BORN: New York, NY
LIVES: Brooklyn, NY
**PUBLICATIONS AND
RECOGNITIONS:** Scholastic
Arts & Writing Award:
Honorable Mention

MENTEE'S ANECDOTE: *I would begin this sentence with "My (r)evolution this year has been," but the truth is it hasn't been just my revolution. This year was our (r)evolution. It has been exciting and groundbreaking. My mentor Sarah and I have broken ground together, exploring themes and genres I haven't had the confidence to explore before. Sarah has a brightness to her that will never dull, and I'm more than glad to have had the privilege of working with her.*

SARAH TODD

YEARS AS MENTOR: 1
OCCUPATION:
Deputy Editor, *Quartz*
BORN: Summit, NJ
LIVES: Brooklyn, NY
**PUBLICATIONS AND
RECOGNITIONS:** Published
in *Inc., The Atlantic, Quartz*

MENTOR'S ANECDOTE: *I think that Luna should run for president of the United States one day, and if she does I'll be her number one supporter. She's got more ambition, insight, and drive than most adults I know, not to mention a vast imagination that imbues her work with empathy for people from all walks of life. She's a constant source of inspiration to me. "This summer is going to be great," she told me recently. "I'm going to get so much work done." I grinned and said, "That's the most Luna sentence I've ever heard." What I meant was, "Teach me your ways."*

INSTRUMENT OF THE HEART

LUNA ROJAS

This story began with an observation on the subway. The universe gave me a small moment, and I'm giving this story in return. Do we acknowledge the roles our parents play in our lives, how they change the way we see the world? "Instrument of the Heart" explores this idea.

"James."

"James."

"James!"

The sound of my name came into focus. I could feel Carina tapping my shoulder. I sat up on the couch.

"Yes?"

"Your father is calling you to dinner."

Our housekeeper had kind eyes and long hair that was always shiny. "Ah, *gracias* Carina."

I headed across the hall into the dining room. Saturday evening dinner was an important ritual for the six parents there. Sandwiched in between each pair sat their golden child.

"James—there he is."

"Darling, please take a seat," a voice sing-songed from the corner. There, glistening with pearls around her neck, her hair brushed back in loose curls, sat my mother.

"Your mother decided to make an appearance," my father said.

A guest chimed in, "Ah, yes, well it is looovely to see you Vivienne."

"It's lovely to be home, naturally," my mother said.

My father gave her an odd glance before raising his glass. "As you all know, this weekend James will be performing at Carnegie Hall. And this might come as a shock to you, my guests, but I can say whole heartedly that it's no surprise to me that . . ."

At this point, I stopped listening. I knew why my father made these speeches. I'd known ever since I was eight and stumbled upon the newspaper clippings lingering in the back of his sock drawer. My father's name blazed across the headlines. The photographs showed him seated at a piano, looking unrecognizable. I'd never seen him smile like that before.

Meanwhile, my father's mouth kept moving, his hand still holding up his wineglass in anticipation of a toast. I wondered what our guests would think if they'd seen him the day before.

After practicing the Moonlight Sonata, I'd moved away from the piano, letting my fingers graze the wood, shutting the keyboard. I walked over to the window and closed the curtains that draped so obnoxiously. I hated those ugly curtains. They were old, but nothing close to dingy. In fact, Grandmother's estate appraisers would have probably deemed them "marvelous." To me they were just preserved, a pathetic attempt at reviving a lost time.

I lay down on the sofa and closed my eyes. The foyer doors opened instinctively, and the flip of the light switch was accompanied by a stern voice.

"James, what the hell? I'd think the piano lessons you've had since birth would have helped you remember proper posture. Neanderthals hunched less than you do. And I'd appreciate if you didn't let your wrists and forearms dip below the keys like a common fool. What insufferable habits you've taken to."

Back in the present, the clinking of wineglasses brought me back to the dinner at hand. As I stared blankly at our guests, I felt the nudge of my father's knee, beckoning me to raise my glass and toast—toast to all his glory.

DEFINE YOUR TERMS

SARAH TODD

This spoken word poem was inspired by two people—both thanks to Girls Write Now. Grace Dunham's moving talk about taking ownership of your identity at a Saturday Workshop got me fired up. And Luna's clarity of purpose constantly encourages me to fight for the right to self-definition.

In the taxi on the way home from our college reunion,
late night spinning to bluegrass in the basement of our old dorm,
my friend A. tells that me it's funny how I work in banking.

And I say, *But I don't work in banking.*

And she says, But you write about banks,
and bankers pay to read your words,
and so: You work in banking.

I want to tell her that she doesn't have a clue
about what I'm working for,
about my late nights writing poems and essays
that will never pay the bills,
to name the stories I have published in magazines
I know she knows the names of.

I don't want to tell her that I'm scared she's right:
I am farther from myself than ever.
There is a system in this world
that values profits over people
and it wants all of us to come work for it,
but some people know better than others
how to say no thank you.

But what she doesn't know is that we can change,
and I am proof, because in five months
I'll have a job that sets my veins thrumming;
that what I learned poring over quarterly reports
will make my mind so sharp and hot it slays.
And I don't know that either.

So instead I just fight with A.
the whole way back,
our faces light and dark and red and white
beneath the streetlights
and the righteous glow of Circle K,
saying *I do not* when all I mean is
No one gets to tell me what I am.

DIANA ROMERO

YEARS AS MENTEE: 1
GRADE: Junior
HIGH SCHOOL:
The Beacon School
BORN: Santiago,
Dominican Republic
LIVES: Bronx, NY
**PUBLICATIONS AND
RECOGNITIONS:** Scholastic
Art & Writing Award:
Honorable Mention

MENTEE'S ANECDOTE: *I am proud to call Jan Alexander my mentor. She is a very hard-working woman who has helped me evolve not only as a stronger writer but a stronger woman. I know I can count on her to support me in everything that I do. Together we have revolutionized the way we see the world; whether it's by bringing life to objects by the dock or telling compelling stories through works of art, Jan and I have had the best of time working together and opening up our hearts to the stories that define who we are: writers.*

JAN ALEXANDER

YEARS AS MENTOR: 2
OCCUPATION: Senior Editor,
Strategy+Business magazine
BORN: Chicago, IL
LIVES: New York, NY
**PUBLICATIONS AND
RECOGNITIONS:** *Ms. Ming's
Guide to Civilization*, a
novel, appearing in
serialized installments at
www.sparklit.media;
"Perfidy," short story,
in *34th Parallel*, Issue 32

MENTOR'S ANECDOTE: *From our first meeting, we decided we'd stage our own (r)evolution by looking at the whole world in new ways. Diana has shown me how to open my eyes. We've written about inanimate objects and strangers in the coffee shop where we meet, and we've imagined ourselves as completely different people surviving an apocalypse. I love the way Diana finds creative inspiration in everything.*

THE DREAMS THEY CARRIED

DIANA ROMERO

*I come from a background of powerful women who overcame
struggles and proved victorious in creating survivors/warriors.
I feel empowered to share my story of evolution through my
grandmother and mother's journeys in pursuing their dreams,
and my hopes of fulfilling our destiny.*

MERCEDES: THE LOST DREAM

952 full moons ago, I was born on a small island in the Caribbean, in an
even smaller town in the middle of nowhere. I, Diana Mercedes Santana,
was born into the dark era of Trujillo's dictatorship. My father's manip-
ulative mindset was carved into his DNA by the depraved morals of the
Republic. He's been corrupted by the ideals of the leaders of this nation,
he's strong, and he's strict. I've grown up trying to be the perfect daughter
he wants, the perfect daughter he *needs*.

I tell myself that deep inside there is still a chance that he loves me.
"He just doesn't show it," I try to tell myself. But I am a woman, no longer
a little girl. I'm blossoming into the maturity of life, and trying to live with
purity and innocence—you have to hold on to that for as long as possible
in this world. But here, girls like me are a worthless piece of flesh formed
under the creation of a man.

I can't dream. Each night is an endless void of darkness. I am not
allowed to dream, because I have to work. I have to work hard to earn the
value of the sweat on my forehead. But when I do dream, I sing. I imagine

serenading the birds and bringing life to the empty fields. I imagine singing to the wind and lifting the heartache in my spirit. But then, without warning everything disappears. And I'm left struggling in the dark. Working.

JOSELYN: THE FALLING DREAM

About 1,290 days ago, God carefully crafted my beautiful self. Born and raised a *Quisqueyano*, I lived a blessed eleven years of my life. In my father's eyes, I was a queen. I meant the world to him, and he was my galaxy. Lepido was the greatest father in the world. I never felt unprivileged or deficient in his eyes, I felt like the richest girl in the world. He named me Santa because I was his Saint. Living in a world with only men, having a daughter was a blessing.

My mother . . . she is lost. She has lived my entire childhood with a wall wrapped around her heart; she doesn't let me in, and I don't ponder. She loves me, I know she does, but she loves me in her way. It's been difficult for her, losing every single one of her husbands, including my father.

I was eleven years old when he passed away. It's been years, and the damaged wound keeps getting bigger and the pain getting stronger. I lost everything that night, without even realizing it. I never got to say good-bye. I was covered in dark for an entire year, but I still feel like the veil has yet to be lifted. I miss him. My mom is still lost.

But I dream. I dream I am standing in front of a prominent educational institute, with the founding president by my side. I'm holding my diploma for "Honorable Educator." I am proud. But daydreaming is for confused children. I am a grown adult and I'm struggling to make ends meet in a different culture. I'm afraid my dream of teaching has been lost forever. Now, conformity is my best option.

FRANCHESCA: THE NEW DREAM

I was born in the Dominican Republic just in time to say good-bye to the twentieth century. Whenever people ask me where I come from, I tell them that I come from a warrior. And when they look confused, I tell them my mother was a warrior. She reminds me every day that I need to keep my feet on solid ground and stand up for what I believe in, while never giving up on my dreams. She had a dream once, and it was taken from her. She had to literally pack up her dreams and walk on to an entirely distant world, all by herself. And she was never given a second chance. Until I came along.

Before *I* packed my bags and came to New York, my Grandma told me that with God, everything was possible, and that no dream was too big or too abstract to exist in your imagination. She told me she was proud of the girl I was, and the woman I will soon become. I am my mom's second chance, just like my mom was Grandma's second chance, even if they never knew it.

Here I am, sixteen years later, realizing that the future is in my hands, that my dreams will not only fulfill my fate but unite our destinies. I dream of writing in the stars, and inspiring those with voices to tell their story, and their passions. It's in my hand to rewrite history, one word at a time.

THE REVOLUTIONS THEY GAVE ME

JAN ALEXANDER

Diana and I found a lot of parallels in the generations that came before us. Our grandmothers both had dreams but lived in worlds where women did their duty. Our mothers broke away. We both carry the things they taught us—and keep searching for life's big truths.

Daisy: On a sultry day in North Carolina, I married my handsome prince. I was nineteen. In our wedding photo, my sweetheart—I'll call him "Daddy" in front of the children forever after—is already embracing patriarchy, his collar starched, his jaw firm like the name they'll etch on his office door. I am looking away. As if I can see the nights that he'll come home late.

My house will be big, with a garden of roses. We'll have three fine boys and a girl who doesn't trust me.

There will be nights when he's very late. Men must have their fun. And proper ladies never complain. On those long nights I will go to the place I love most: the corner where my piano sits. I will bang out Mozart as if the world has ripped in two and only my playing can fix it. I will trill my fingertips across a bawdy world of jazz. I will thunder through that lively tune they play in my world.

I sense applause.

No, it's a glare so fierce you can hear it. My daughter, Elizabeth, has crept downstairs. "Mother," she scolds, "no one should ever play 'Dixie'!"

Elizabeth: All my family's sins rest on my thin shoulders, because I'm the only one who cares. Why are some people rich while others are poor? Why do those of color live on a different side of town? Why does my mother prattle on about fashion and recipes when people are starving? Why does Daddy tell her wear this, cook that, grow red roses, vote this way, and she does what he says?

I'll die if I don't get out of here. I'll go up North. I'll marry a Jewish intellectual. We'll take our children on family demonstrations for civil rights, against the bomb, against all wars. We'll teach them that what's important is asking questions, not making money.

Jan: When I was sixteen and my friends were getting cars, my mother, Elizabeth, said, "Why don't you start a clean air movement? Why don't you ride a bicycle like they do in China?" I expected nothing else.

We had a farmhouse in Canada where American boys came so they wouldn't have to go to Vietnam. We grew vegetables and didn't buy anything processed with chemicals by the government/military/corporate conspiracy.

"Why," I asked my mother, "do you never let up?"

She had an answer: "Because life should be fair."

I had to get away because she never let up. I moved to New Orleans, LA, New York, and Hong Kong, and back to New York. I rode a bicycle in China. The air was like sludge and the people couldn't wait to trade in their two wheels for BMWs and SUVs. I searched for my mother's revolution everywhere I went.

I wrote my mother's epitaph: "She lived to make life fair." And I keep looking for songs that she'd applaud.

SHANIA RUSSELL

YEARS AS MENTEE: 1
GRADE: Junior
HIGH SCHOOL:
Bronx Academy
of Letters
BORN: Bronx, NY
LIVES: Bronx, NY
**PUBLICATIONS AND
RECOGNITIONS:** Scholastic
Art & Writing Award:
Honorable Mention

MENTEE'S ANECDOTE: *Our first meeting was at a place called Filicori Zecchini—which I still can't pronounce—and most of what I remember is my nerves. I remember I was shifting from foot to foot, staring blankly at a menu I could hardly comprehend, feeling ridiculous and out of place, when Carol turned to me and prompted out my order—and then I was excited again. And that's our relationship: it's art galleries, blackout poetry, museums, and readings; it's being thrown into new situations without the fear of scrambling for my place. And I've loved every second of it.*

CAROL PAIK

YEARS AS MENTOR: 1
OCCUPATION: Writer
and editor
BORN: Lowell, MA
LIVES: New York, NY

MENTOR'S ANECDOTE: *When Shania and I met around Halloween, she arrived a little late, in full vampire costume and makeup, out of breath and out of sorts because she's never late. She sat down, composed herself, and said calmly, through dark purple lips, "I don't recommend riding the subway in a cape." Every time I see Shania, she'll very quietly say something unexpected, hilarious, thoughtful, truthful. She writes the same way. She's authentically her own person—willing to try anything, but also sure of who she is and what she likes. She makes me laugh, and she makes me think.*

FROM AN INTROVERT

SHANIA RUSSELL

Generally, I avoid getting personal at all costs, but when the prospect of writing an op-ed was presented, I knew this was too important for me to hide from—so I took it head-on. I vented, but I also tried to push myself beyond my singular point of view.

From an introvert to the general public,

Let me begin by assuring you that I am not clinically depressed. From experience, I assume you are not convinced, and all I can do is continuously push this point: *I am not depressed.* As hard as it may be for you to believe, when people sit alone at lunch, stare at the floor during a discussion, or break out the headphones in a social situation, these are not cues for alarm bells to go off in your head. There is no reason for you to whip out antidepressants or ask the dreaded *Are you okay?*—at least, not necessarily. In these situations, while it does not automatically rule out the possibility that we might be sad, it also does not automatically call for anyone to leap to the conclusion that we are stewing in some sort of impossible inner turmoil. There is always plenty rattling around in our heads, but it is not always something to be concerned about. And that is just what I mean to clarify here: that we really are okay.

To be fair, the confusion is common and perhaps even understandable. For some people, the connections are very simply made: when they are happy, they are talkative, expressive, and seek out social situations—

because their happiest place just happens to include interaction. Naturally, this means that when they are in the opposite place—upset, unhappy, sad, and so on—they avoid people. They want to be alone, they keep to themselves, and they keep quiet—because that is just their natural reaction. Judging by social norms, these people appear to make up the majority, and this makes it easy to forget about all of those even slightly different from that majority. It also doesn't help that many people remain unable to wrap their minds around the fact that not everyone is exactly the same. Not everyone has had the same experiences, not everyone thinks the same way, and not everyone's actions mean the same exact thing. This means that for some people, when they keep quiet or keep to themselves, they are not necessarily "going through a tough time" and "need to talk." Some are just content to sit alone; they are comfortable observing, rather than contributing to the conversation; they do not just plaster their happiness on their face; and there is nothing wrong with any of that. They do not need to be carted off to an asylum, and they don't need the next appointment with the family psychologist—they probably just need you to take a moment and breathe. They need you to remember that they are okay, and maybe not look at them as if you've just received news that they have twenty-four hours to live.

It's important—in fact, crucial—to remember that this goes for all people. You know the five-year-old on the playground who sits on the bench watching the other kids' intense game of kickball? Maybe you're right and she's a bit shy, or maybe she's having fun observing the game. Whatever the case, it's probably not a good idea to jump to conclusions and start hiding crushed-up pills in her mashed potatoes. And the teenager whom you haven't seen smile in the past week? Sure, they might be a bit stressed out; or maybe they're just not as expressive as you are. And if you're really worried about them dying internally, maybe don't pester them about their feelings. As for the adult who had lunch alone or sat with the group without saying anything—maybe they like their space or had something on their mind. And maybe you should call off the intervention.

Make no mistake, this is by no means true for every self-declared introvert out there, nor is it true for every single situation. Like anyone else, we have moments where we claim that we are "okay" or "fine" when in reality we are lying through our teeth—but there are other situations, the everyday sort, where we act a certain way and others jump straight to "worst-case scenario" conclusions. But in reality, not every action we make and word we speak is a cry for help.

FiRST VIEWING

CAROL PAIK

I never imagined I would ever write (let alone show anyone) anything that could be called Dystopian Flash Fiction (I tend to write Plodding Realistic Nonfiction), but I started this in the workshop and then Shania made me submit it. That's a significant evolutionary leap for me, thanks to her.

The day I aged to sixteen was the first day I saw my own reflection. We had all been carefully prepared, all the girls in my level. We had been through the training, which started when we aged to ten, so we knew, more or less, what to expect. Still, I was not completely prepared. The First Viewing affects different people in different ways. Some people fall into a kind of love with their reflection, cannot take their sighters off the polished surface of the Reflector, cling to it a little as it is taken from them and re-covered at the end of the allotted thirty ticks. Others are repelled, or frightened, or overwhelmed, have to look down, thrust the Reflector away.

Of course, none of us were complete strangers to our faces. We all had caught shadowy outlines in the occasional rain-puddle, bloated versions in the enameled side of a vase, suggestions of shapes in the depths of our mothers' sighters. Some of the more daring of us had asked others to tell them what they saw—but this was understood to be an infraction, and you had to be very careful whom you asked. Even so, we lacked the vocabulary to adequately convey what we saw in another. Those who asked were very rarely satisfied with what they heard; usually, they heard only enough to make them wish they hadn't asked at all.

For the most part, what I saw in the Reflector was in keeping with what I already knew. Having explored with my touchers, I knew the top part of my face was wide and marked with little bumps. I knew the hook and flare of my breather-smeller. I knew the taster had a thin top part and a pillowy bottom.

But I was surprised by the color of my sighters. I had thought they were dark, they had always seemed so in the quick glimpses I'd gotten, but it must have been the substrate that reflected them that was dark, because they themselves are not. They are pale, paler than the sky on a cold late-cycle day. It seems to me that with such sighters the world should look lighter to me than it does, for surely the hue of the lens should affect the light that passes through them.

But I barely had a chance to register this surprise before the Reflector was taken. The Second Viewing will not occur for sixteen more cycles, and I will have had plenty of time to absorb the new information that the Reflector revealed. But I find myself impatient for the Second Viewing in way that I was not before the First. Before that, I did not believe there was anything important about myself that I didn't know, couldn't learn. But now I wonder. I wonder all the time.

FAREENA SAMAD

YEARS AS MENTEE: 2
GRADE: Senior
HIGH SCHOOL: Hillside
Arts and Letters Academy
BORN: Queens, NY
LIVES: Queens, NY
**PUBLICATIONS AND
RECOGNITIONS:** Scholastic
Art & Writing Award:
Honorable Mention

MENTEE'S ANECDOTE: *Without Nan, I would not be the same person as I was two years ago. In our second and final year together, our relationship has evolved. Nan broadened my world perspective through art and culture, which inevitably led to our dual focus on writing and getting to know one another. In our escapades around the city we've created memories. How could I forget about the chocolate chip cookies she snuck away just for me? Or the time we tried to freewrite in a library filled with screaming children? My senior year has been incredibly special thanks to our relationship.*

NAN BAUER-MAGLIN

YEARS AS MENTOR: 2
OCCUPATION: Professor
and Academic Director,
CUNY (retired)
BORN: New York, NY
LIVES: New York, NY
**PUBLICATIONS AND
RECOGNITIONS:** Coeditor
of *Final Acts: Death, Dying,
and the Choices We Make*
and four other books

MENTOR'S ANECDOTE: *Two years together . . . how lovely! We worked hard this year: on Fareena's college essays, on her Scholastic portfolio, on new writing. But we could also relax and explore the city since we now knew each other, so we went to the Whitney Museum and the Rubin Museum of Asian Art; we looked at where the many immigrant workers jumped from the windows of the Triangle Shirtwaist Factory to escape the fire of 1911. Our relationship has evolved, as has Fareena's writing: she takes more risks in her writing, and she has a new, fierce confidence in her voice.*

37TH STREET

FAREENA SAMAD

On my way to the Girls Write Now office in the garment district, I admired all of the shimmering little dress shops. On one visit, I came face-to-face with the city's most hidden jewel, which I memorialized through this piece of writing.

I turn to look across 37th Street and there it is: a pretty little dress shop. I walk up the battered concrete and admire from far away. The sequins and glitter shine under the bright display lights. I lurk for a few more moments and contemplate whether or not I should walk in. Mother is waiting for me; she trusts me to quickly return home.

The pretty little dress shop stands out from the blandness of the rest of the block. It's brightly lit and neatly arranged. Dresses are gracefully exhibited throughout the store and behind the display window. The store looks empty, as if no one was worthy to enter. Except for me; I'm worthy. Every other shop on the block is dull upon comparison. Murky, grey clouds hover above me, leaving the whole city in a dark, cloudy funk. But the pretty little dress shop is the pearl among a sea of clams on that block. I want that pearl.

I stalk the pretty little dress shop for another few seconds. Five dresses dance in front of me. I see a coral pink starfish with a pattern of sequins flowing from the middle to the end of its legs. I see an endless and infinite *azul* sky glittering in broad daylight. I see an orange tabby cat watching its reflection, twirling the skirt of its dress to see how it fits. I see an apparition of the upcoming bewitching hour flashing its abundance of stars, glowing and twinkling under the somber sun, baffling even to the most knowledgeable scientists on Earth. I see its younger sister, the velvet night, waving to her friends and flashing a quick, secret smile to her crush. Each dress is shamelessly seducing me, begging for me to enter.

Is this how it feels to go window shopping?

I turn away from my treasured boutique and walk toward 7th Avenue. I get lost on my way to the subway station. I try to wipe away the glitter that's swirling in my head. The fleeting faces and the odd items being sold on every sharp corner only add to my creeping melancholia. I pass another dress shop but do not feel the same magnetic force as I did before. Its modern fashion and expensive, classy presence fail to beckon me. It's not my pretty little dress shop.

And so I make my way home to obey Mother, too much of a punk to go rogue.

THE WITCHES BEHIND WALMART

NAN BAUER-MAGLIN

Merritt Tierce's review of Witches of America *by Alex Mar (New York Times* Sunday Book Review, *10/27/15) describes the occult practices of modern-day witches, some of whom gather on the hillside behind a local Walmart. My mentee and I began a freewrite using that image.*

Who are these women who meet behind Walmart? Are they old? Ugly? Do they have magical powers? During the day, do they lead quiet lives as mothers and wives, wearing aprons and baking cookies? Or are they spinsters and widows with no ties to anyone, with bloodshot eyes and shrill voices? Who knows what they do during their weekly meetings on the hillside behind Walmart? Light fires, dance madly around the flames, uttering curses and throwing spells?

Maybe they are employees fired because they tried to make conditions better for all those men and women who work long hours, have few rights and no healthcare, stock shelves, stand eight hours, pressured to work faster while always smiling at the customer.

What is it they chant? Do they want to change the world or change their lives? Or is this their way to find company, to hold hands, to sing, dance, and dream of the future? Do they commune with nature or howl to the moon, or simply pray for more worldly goods, goods that they may commandeer at Walmart with their otherworldly occult powers?

These witches, these women, who are they and what do they do?

ROSALYN SANTANA

YEARS AS MENTEE: 1
GRADE: Senior
HIGH SCHOOL: Academy for Young Writers
BORN: Brooklyn, NY
LIVES: Brooklyn, NY

MENTEE'S ANECDOTE: *My mentor Lauren is not just titled my mentor for no reason. Together we can talk in depth. She is very helpful when I am stuck and can't get things on paper. She is helping me evolve as a writer. She makes me feel comfortable expressing personal things and writing about them. Lauren helps me learn things about myself that I didn't even know. With her, I want to evolve as a writer. I will come to her in the future whenever I need help with any writing. Together, we shall evolve!*

LAUREN ROSENBLUM

YEARS AS MENTOR: 1
OCCUPATION:
Adjunct Professor, Writing and Literature
BORN: Huntington, NY
LIVES: Brooklyn, NY

MENTOR'S ANECDOTE: *Rosalyn and I talk a lot about the different meanings of feminism. One idea we keep returning to is how the women in our lives influence us. But while maintaining this connection, Rosalyn is certain of who she is and what she wants. She's taught me that being revolutionary means both embracing where we have come from and being honest about who we are.*

BETTER TO BE KEN THAN BARBIE

ROSALYN SANTANA

This piece is special to me because it shows how, throughout life, we evolve within ourselves. We learn to find and accept our true self and be proud of it. I want to evolve with my talents and inspire others to do what they love by doing what I love as well.

When my mentor first told me we would be writing a piece on evolution and/or revolution, I automatically thought about the evolution of human beings and how we evolved over time. I was thinking too hard about the topic when I didn't have to. I learned that evolution and revolution can be present in many different forms. I thought again about it because evolution has to do with changes made and how things develop over a period of time.

I thought about an example in my life that could be considered an evolution or revolution. I thought about myself from my early childhood into my teenage years and how I have come to really have this self-acceptance with myself and my homosexuality.

When I was young—about seven or eight years old—and in elementary school, my mom would dress me and do my hair. I also had tons of Barbie dolls that I never played with unless my neighbor came over and wanted to play. Although I was young, I did feel different. I was more interested in the things my brothers or uncles wore and the things they did. I was comfortable in jeans and sneakers and I liked simple things. I was not comfortable in skirts or dresses, but I had to deal with them because I was young. Whenever I played with Barbie dolls I was always the Ken doll—or, when we played house, I would play the father. It was what I felt fit me the most. I wanted to be a tomboy, and as I grew older and began to evolve, that is what others began to identify me as.

When I got to junior high school, I was sort of shy and couldn't completely express myself through my clothing. I didn't exactly wear boy clothes, but I wore what was still comfortable for me and what I felt was the closest to what I actually wanted to wear. I used to claim I was bisexual so it would seem "normal" or acceptable. I've dated guys before, but deep down inside I knew I wanted to be the boy in the relationship. My mom was already aware of the way I was, the tomboyish type. I never really had to "come out" to her because it was pretty obvious. By the end of junior high school, I knew what I was and I didn't care anymore what others would think. I was done beating around the bush. By the end of junior high school I knew what I was and that I was only attracted to my own. I had evolved within my self-acceptance and I now was able to be who I'd always wanted to be and wasn't going to hide anymore.

For my eighth grade prom I did not go in a dress like the other girls. I wore a black button-down shirt, but under I had a red, black, grey, and white striped shirt. I wore corduroy pants with some Nikes that matched my shirt. I walked into my eighth grade prom very proud. I automatically felt different and stood out because I was the only girl in this type of wear. The point is that I was evolving within myself, and with my self-acceptance.

There are many forms of evolution. I feel like you can evolve into many things in life. But I have evolved within only this part of my life and I plan on continuing to evolve throughout my future. I want to evolve as a writer, I want to evolve my knowledge, I want to evolve as a musician, and more. Now I am in twelfth grade almost about to graduate high school, so I will be entering a new chapter in my life. It is okay to feel different sometimes, because you never know if that feeling could turn into something good and help inspire others to have self-acceptance. In life you should want to evolve, even if you don't exactly know where it will take you.

PAPER INHERITANCE

LAUREN ROSENBLUM

Rosalyn writes easily about relationships with her family—
something I find challenging. Inspired by her and by Sarah
Kay's "If I Should Have a Daughter," which we watched at
the Spoken Word Workshop, this piece considers how it feels
to be a motherless daughter, and the mother of a son.

Her hands were paper thin.
No.
Her hands were made of paper.
No.
Her hands flaked like powder.
No.
Her hands were paper. They smelled like sour milk.
Mixed with powder.
The paper cracks. The powder falls. She disappears.
A release from aging. A relief from suffering.
Or so they say.

I barely remember the feel of the paper now;
loss transforms memories into fear
that my child will not see me grow old
- crack and crumble -
That I will not grow old enough for him to worry about my aging.

I have her face, her ass, her impatience.
But my hands are dark. Defiant. More like pleather. But not so soft.
PVCs take a long time to shred.

This should be one of those poems that says,
Live for the moment!

No.
Kiss your baby!
No.
Embrace the everyday!
God no.
There is always tomorrow.
I procrastinate the end.

MAEVE SLON

YEARS AS MENTEE: 1
GRADE: Freshman
HIGH SCHOOL: Harvest Collegiate High School
BORN: New York, NY
LIVES: New York, NY
PUBLICATIONS AND RECOGNITIONS: "The Owl," poem, *Skipping Stones* magazine

MENTEE'S ANECDOTE: *I often write little sentences late at night, or on the subway going to school, or in class when I'm supposed to be paying attention to the teacher. Like every first draft, they are not very good. If it were just me on my own, the words would never see light or be transformed into something I was proud of. But I have Vivian. Vivian, who I meet at the cafe filled with children and nannies. Vivian, who makes me want to share my work. Vivian, who inspires me to keep writing. Because of Vivian, I now write with courage.*

VIVIAN CONAN

YEARS AS MENTOR: 4
OCCUPATION: Librarian, Westchester County; freelance copyeditor
BORN: New York, NY
LIVES: New York, NY
PUBLICATIONS AND RECOGNITIONS: Fellowship in Creative Nonfiction, New York Foundation for the Arts

MENTOR'S ANECDOTE: *"It's missing something here," Maeve says. She places her fingers on the keyboard, and when she lifts them, I see that what she added was just what was needed, in exactly that place. "It needs a pause here," she says, and I know she means a comma. Maeve paints with words and punctuation. I'm in the presence of an artist. She inspires me, especially in the way she trusts her reader to grasp nuances and doesn't overwrite. When I edit my own pieces now, I think, What would Maeve do here?*

SALTY SMiLES

MAEVE SLON

I wrote this poem when winter was thick and I escaped to memories of the beach.

Screams of joy and people talking
disappear when waves go crashing.
Silk and ice on my hot face,
Salty blue lifts my body
And fills my ears to water rushing.
I hold my breath and grip the sand,
Not getting caught by the cold hands.

When the waves pass
and it's time to come up
I do not appear.
It's peaceful under here,
and the loud sun is up there.

Eyes search for me
over the salty blue,
too many heads.
I disappear

I am losing air,
my head is going to pop.
Still I hold my breath,
not wanting to come up.

Next wave comes crashing,
throws me to the shore,
where people scream and talk with joy.
Eyes come running towards me
with salty lips and wet brown hair.
I smile, too, because the hot sun touches my face.
We go back in.
I hold my breath once more.

A CAREER LAUNCHED
BY A THREAT

VIVIAN CONAN

*Some people choose their life's work, some fall into it. This is
how mine evolved.*

"If you want to live in this house, you have to get a job or go to school,"
my mother said. She wasn't smiling.

It was August 1964. Since I'd graduated from college eight months
before, I'd worked for two weeks as an elementary school teacher (I quit
when I couldn't stop the kids from chasing one another across the desk-
tops), and four months as a substitute in a nursery school. Now it was
summer, and between office-temp jobs, I lolled on the beach. Life was
good. Until my mother's ultimatum. I was so upset that I considered can-
celing my dinner date with friends that evening.

In retrospect, I'm glad I went.

We were beginning the main course when I said, in what I hoped was a casual voice, "My mother wants me to get a job or go to school. Otherwise, I have to move out."

"What are you going to do?" Susan asked, crisp and practical.

"I don't know." That an event so terrifying could be reduced to ordinary words in an ordinary restaurant made it seem less scary.

"Why not go to school to become a librarian?" Louise asked.

I looked at her across the candle flickering in the Chianti bottle. As far as I knew, all librarians did was mark the due date in the back of a book with a rubber stamp attached to a pencil eraser. "Do you have to go to school for that?" I asked.

"You need a master's. It would be a good career for you."

I did like libraries. And reading.

"I once thought I wanted to be a librarian," Louise went on, "and I sent away for library school applications, but I changed my mind. Would you like them?"

"Okay," I said, brightening. A life raft.

The next day, she gave me forms for Pratt, Rutgers, and Columbia, all the library schools within commuting distance. I put Columbia and Rutgers in the "no" pile, because they required the Graduate Record Exam. Pratt requested only a college transcript and the names of three periodicals I read regularly. I listed *The New Yorker*, *The Atlantic Monthly*, and *Saturday Review*. I never actually read them, but they would give the impression that I was literate.

Because the term was starting soon, Pratt interviewed me before receiving my transcript. After a few questions about my education and work experience, they explained the registration procedure. I figured that meant they planned to accept me.

"I got in!" I told my mother when I came home, more excited about being able to stay in my room than about becoming a librarian.

"Good," was all she said.

My first term was dull: mostly reading and papers. At the start of my second term, I moved into an apartment with Susan. I also got a job as a trainee in the Pratt Library and found that I loved connecting people with the information they were looking for.

Fifty years later, I'm still loving it.

MEEK THOMAS

YEARS AS MENTEE: 2
GRADE: Junior
HIGH SCHOOL: Uncommon Charter High School
BORN: Brooklyn, NY
LIVES: Brooklyn, NY

MENTEE'S ANECDOTE: *My mentor Carlene and I meet whenever we can at a dimly lit café in Brooklyn. This spring we both challenged ourselves to speak more in public and ask for help when we needed it. I'm so glad this year to be paired with Carlene once again, because we both are very similar in our fears and desires. She has made such a positive impact on me these last two years, and I'm so glad to continue to learn more about her as we grow in writing.*

CARLENE OLSEN

YEARS AS MENTOR: 2
OCCUPATION: Graduate student, Columbia School of Journalism
BORN: New Haven, CT
LIVES: Brooklyn, NY

MENTOR'S ANECDOTE: *If Meek and I could pick a superpower, it would definitely be the ability to be in more than one place at the same time. This year, our schedules are really hectic—grad school for me, high school for Meek, plus all of her after-school activities, like cheerleading, choir, and taking on leadership positions in her church youth group. Meek juggles a lot of responsibilities, and she is a constant inspiration to me. I feel lucky to have such a talented mentee who enjoys a good laugh, especially when words just won't come out on the page.*

OPENING UP

MEEK THOMAS

This year, Carlene and I have made it a resolution to begin opening up. I'm passionate about these pieces because they show our struggle asking for help, and how just a little effort can go a long way.

Ms. Sears, our school's guidance counselor, greets me with a smile—protocol, I'm guessing, because no one is ever that happy, especially not someone whose job is to help a bunch of kids going through rough times. She reaches out to grab my shaky hand. I don't know why I am nervous. I scheduled the appointment. It's probably because I'm scared my mom might find out and think I'm seriously depressed. I'm not.

My hands clam up and twitch vigorously the closer we get to Ms. Sears's office door. She finally lets go to open it and steps aside, the jolt of her head silently letting me know it's time to come in. I cross the threshold, but remain in the doorway. The red walls are the first thing I see, covered in inspirational quotes. One in bold font says: "Don't become the person that hurt you." No one hurt me—that's the first thing that comes to mind.

"You can sit anywhere you want," Ms. Sears says. I pick the farthest beanbag chair from her desk and plop down on it.

"Nya, right?" she asks. Of course she calls out the wrong name. I sigh at her mistake, already regretting my decision to speak to her.

"No," I say, and my voice cracks a bit. "My name's Meek."

"Ahh, yes. I'm sorry, hon." Ms. Sears scribbles something down on her clipboard and I repeatedly crack my knuckles, a nervous habit I've picked up over the years. "So, what did you want to speak to me about?"

I'm terrified, I don't know where I'm going. I'm lost, and I'm hoping you will just give me the answers to all my problems. "Oh, um . . ." I clear my throat. "I guess I was feeling a bit overwhelmed," I say flatly. I'm careful not to show emotion.

"Hmm." She nods. "How so?" She picks up the clipboard and pen again, awaiting my answer.

No one cares what I'm feeling. I've been living to try to please others my entire life and now I seem to have completely lost touch with myself. I want to go away for a bit. "School," I blurt out. "It's hard."

Ms. Sears looks up at me with a raised eyebrow, silently condemning my reluctance to open up, then sighs and walks my way, green Post-it and pen in hand. She plops down on the beanbag chair next to mine and sits there quietly. *Really, lady?* Time goes by and neither of us has made a sound besides my occasional sniffle, and I begin to wonder if I'm wasting my time by coming here. Then I find the courage to look her way. She has four Post-its placed in a line on the white board next to us.

"I heard you like to write," she says. My heart leaps in my throat and I nod. "So write what you're feeling."

For the next thirty minutes I write how I am feeling toward family, school, relationships, and inside.

My mom only cares about my grades. "How'd you do in school today?" is different from "How was your day?" She doesn't pay attention unless I'm failing.

"I just want to graduate, but I don't know what comes next. I mean, I know I'm supposed to go to college, but what if that's not for me? Can I study what makes me happy or what makes money?" I think of dropping out every day.

My boyfriend loves me. He's told me multiple times. I love him too, I think. He really does care about me and has pushed me the most to get some help. He's special, but I feel like I'm waiting for him to screw up, like all the others do.

Ahh, internal stuff. I know nothing about myself except for my name. I think I'm going through that "finding yourself" stage. I Googled symptoms of depression again last week just to be sure things haven't gotten worse. I think I'm good. Is it normal to be strangers with yourself?

I drop the pen in the beanbag chair. I don't realize I'm crying until Ms. Sears hands me a box of tissues. "Thanks," I sniffle.

"We've all been in this place, honey," she begins. "And sometimes it takes crawling through a whole bunch of mess, but we eventually get through it. This is part of growing up; we realize that the things around us aren't always as they seem, and right now you're just swaying in the middle of child and adult. You're a promising girl, and I know you're going to be something real special. You just gotta pick yourself up."

She steps closer to hug me and I open my arms to embrace her. When she pulls back I begin to chuckle through my tears.

"What's funny?" she asks.

That was the best Disney advice I've ever received.

"Thanks for today," I say. "Save some more Post-its for next time."

THE COUCH

CARLENE OLSEN

Meek and I wrote about the revolution of self-care by describing our first experiences talking to a counselor/therapist. I feel so honored Meek feels comfortable opening up to me, and I love working through challenges together. As we know, it takes major guts to ask for help!

I never imagined seeing a psychologist, especially not one with an office in a midtown apartment building. But I felt stuck, a few years out of college and in the midst of the quarter-life crisis. My friends had exhaustedly doled out their advice and I still had no idea how to fix things—how to get back into the writing career I left to explore Europe, how to salvage or say good-bye to my volatile relationship, how to feel more in control of my day-to-day routine and be available to support friends and family.

Everything unraveled so quickly, and here I was sitting on a couch—*the* couch—though the office was more pleasant than I expected, like stepping into an aunt's living room rather than a therapist's lair. Dr. O sat in a chair across from me. We stared at each other blankly, each sizing the other up. Then she broke the silence.

"Tell me about your parents."

Why? That's not why I'm here.

"Why are you here?"

To talk about my relationship.

"Okay, tell me about that."

We have a lot of problems. It's complicated, kind of a *West Side Story* situation, but with more layers.

"I once dated an artist who was much older than me—a very passionate affair that ended badly. I get it."

I thought we were here to talk about me?

"Sometimes it helps to hear someone else's story, for empathy, don't you think?"

Depends. I've never been to therapy before, is this how it works?

"Let's talk about you."

Do you watch *Mad Men*, the show?

"You're not the first patient to mention *Mad Men*. Why did you bring that up?"

Because a lot of people think that's an anti-feminist show, but I disagree.

"Why?"

Well, Don Draper's wife—Betty—is incredibly smart. She knows he's cheating and she knows how to use that information to her advantage.

"Is that what you're afraid of, cheating in your relationship?"

I'm afraid I'm not doing what I want.

"What do you want to do?"

I want to write. I want to travel and write about interesting people and places in the world and, ideally, I want people to read my work.

"Do you know how many people come to me in their twenties because they have no idea what they want to do with their lives?"

A lot?

"A *lot*. You're very lucky to know exactly what you want."

I think it's a blessing and a curse to know what you want, because if you're not doing that thing, you don't feel satisfied until you find a way to do it.

"So find a way."

Well, it's not that easy.

"No one said it was easy. You want to write? You're sure?"

Yes, that's all I've ever wanted to do.

"What did you study in college?"

Journalism.

"You want to write *and* you have the skills and background to succeed at this, but you're not writing now?"

Well . . . yes.

"Well, I suggest you write."

I should write.

"So write."

And in that moment, Dr. O told me exactly what I needed to hear.

CHARLENE VASQUEZ

YEARS AS MENTEE: 2
GRADE: Junior
HIGH SCHOOL: Bronx Career College Preparatory High School
BORN: Bronx, NY
LIVES: Bronx, NY

MENTEE'S ANECDOTE: *Caitlin is such a sweetheart; it's monumental for me to have been able to work with her for two years! The world rotates on devastating events and inhumane activities, so I feel fortunate to be working with Caitlin for an hour a week; it is such a refreshing opportunity, for sure! She's so positive and full of nothing but beneficial things to say! It was her idea to write about the topic of my piece, and I went in for the kill. Thanks, Caitlin!*

CAITLIN RIMSHNICK

YEARS AS MENTOR: 2
OCCUPATION: Adjunct Instructor, Columbia University; tutor, BMCC Writing Center
BORN: Denver, CO
LIVES: New York, NY
PUBLICATIONS AND RECOGNITIONS: Published a review on *Bookslut*

MENTOR'S ANECDOTE: *One of the first things my fabulous mentee wrote in our peer sessions was, "The name's Charlene, but I think it sounds like the name of a businesswoman." This quirky line perfectly captures one aspect I love about Charlene (and her writing). She has a unique way of looking at the world, not to mention an enviable sense of humor. Charlene consistently strives for originality in the way she writes and lives, and she inspires me to do the same. I am so lucky I get to be her mentor!*

WHY I BELIEVE IN STEVEN (AND YOU SHOULD, TOO!)

CHARLENE VASQUEZ

What's revolutionary about Steven Universe *is that it's a cartoon Rebecca Sugar created to illustrate what real love is, and how it's super important to love, not loathe. In a world so cold, I thought I'd express how this is revolutionary in the world of mainstream entertainment.*

It was around the end of the summer when my cousins introduced *Steven Universe* to me, and I loved it. I first watched "Giant Woman," episode twelve of season one, and I was intrigued. I was inclined to watch the pilot all the way to the latest episode. I loved the innocence of it. I didn't really pay mind to the darker sides of the show until much more recently. It was because of school (and lack of cable) that I couldn't catch up with the show, but *SU* continued to bloom, and its fan base is still growing to tremendous proportions. And I swear, the crew of the cartoon knows how to grab hearts and keep them. I, for one, feel so happy that the Internet is raving about this show.

Every episode is a joy, and every protagonist shows their vulnerability very well. Look, I'm talking about a cartoon that's about aliens and half-aliens trying to prevent other aliens from destroying the Earth. When you put it that way, it sounds cliché. And you know the heroes always win. And yet, somehow, Rebecca Sugar, the creator of the cartoon, warped this cliché idea and turned it into something so much deeper, and so much more "slice of life" than, let's say, *My Little Pony: Friendship is Magic*. This speaks volumes, too: Lauren Faust, the creator of *MLP: FiM*, desired to break stereotypes and bring out the family on cotton candy horses, which she did. That fan base grew bigger before everyone's eyes, and even the haters made its popularity grow stronger. It's a beautiful, phenomenal cartoon. So how does *SU* break this barrier? I'll tell you how.

This cartoon destroys a bunch of stereotypes: chubby, curvy women are represented in a good light; women heroes and villains appear often; there's diversity, including homosexuality (although the Gems are gender-less, their representation is explicitly homosexual, which is still a touchy subject in other countries of the world); and lessons are portrayed that go farther than telling you why family and friendship are important— they *show* you why. The cartoon breaks down these things implicitly and explicitly, and in every way. From there, I think that's why this cartoon is gaining popularity. It's fresh and new, even though it's not. It's considerably bold of Rebecca Sugar to do this, and in such a clever way. Now I'm not saying this while bashing other cartoons out there—there is tons and tons of entertainment that speaks about these things. *SU* is not the only show in the world. And yet, I glorify this cartoon in ways I don't other things. Why? Why do I feel so good about this show?

The answer is simple: the cartoon is real. I don't mean "non-fiction." I mean that it touches home base on a lot of real-world problems, from morality to growth, you name it. And the writers are cunning while doing so. The jokes are humorous and the acting feels so genuine it's scary. I can go on and on praising this cartoon. So, instead of that, let me get to the point. This show has a way of turning insecurities into strengths for me.

It's not just how gorgeous Rose is, even though she's fat, or how Amethyst breaks down crying over how she was born. It's the messages, like, "Nobody is perfect—that's what makes the challenges of life great," and "Being strong in the real way" comes in different forms. Hell, I feel most closely related to Steven Universe himself because he's a prepubescent boy trying to get by with something foreign, with a paradigm he knows yet doesn't understand. He's completely alien to the majority of other people, despite being half-human himself. He's flawed. It's not necessarily a bad thing, though. When people see change, they charge it down. Humans hate change. Non-humans, as told by the Gems's story, hate change too, and Steven being the only hybrid on their Earth is a scary change, and yet it's something that affects their everyday lives. That in itself inspires me, to believe that a hero can't save everyone, that there's still good in the world, that we can trudge on however it suits the situation, that you should love your surroundings, etc. The amount of love I feel for this show changes me. It makes me want to be better, feel better, love better, give more, and cherish my family and friends much more. All the people I fight with, that I fall in love with, they come and go. One day we won't live to see another day, but that's why we try. That's why we continue. That's why we fight bad guys and then, of course, go out for pizzas. And I laugh after I feel like crying, just by watching this show. I have never, ever experienced entertainment so revolutionary to the point where it changed my life. It's truly a beautiful cartoon, something so raw and loving visualized with simple yet beautiful characters. This is why *Steven Universe* is so highly anticipated— and why I believe in Steven. Do you?

CRAFT

CAITLIN RIMSHNICK

"Hey, look," Charlene said on our way to the workshop, pointing out a statue of a giant needle and button. I'd walked that route countless times but had never noticed. Charlene reminds me that a writer pays attention to the little details, as I tried to do in this piece.

It was a small moment. One fall day, I was walking down Broadway, I am not sure doing what. Maybe I was heading home from the graduate school where I studied creative writing, or maybe I was walking in the opposite direction, leaving my apartment on a rare break from my desks: two glass modern-type deals, one in the bedroom and the other in the living room. I would wheel my single comfortable chair back and forth between them, chasing my muse; sometimes I'd find it in the solitude of the bedroom with the door shut, other times I liked to write out in the open to the background noises of my husband's puttering. Wherever I was situated, my brain was constantly grasping for just-right words, the kind that would make my readers lean forward into the pages I wrote, the kind that would move them. But back to that moment.

I'd seen variations of the moment many times before—a disheveled man crouched near the sidewalk holding a piece of cardboard. But this was a little different. This man had a marker in his hand and was staring at a tan blank slate, a contemplative look on his face. "Wow, this is the moment, before the sign gets written," I thought. "I've never seen it." I imagined the various word choices he might be debating, how surely he too was imagining his audience's response. I felt a particular brand of guilt, the one I always feel when I pass a homeless person and wonder if I should give a dollar, or a granola bar, or smile, but in a bout of indecision generally do nothing. I felt a new feeling too: an appreciation for the act of creation, from one writer to another.

JAELA VAUGHN

YEARS AS MENTEE: 2
GRADE: Junior
HIGH SCHOOL:
Richard R. Green
High School of Teaching
BORN: Bronx, NY
LIVES: Bronx, NY
**PUBLICATIONS AND
RECOGNITIONS:**
Scholastic Art & Writing
Award: Gold Key

MENTEE'S ANECDOTE: *Laura has really helped me find my voice for writing, as well as helped me edit my work so that my message/tone/voice conveys to the reader what I want it to. She has been my biggest supporter, and I am glad that she continues to expose me to new writing styles and literature, and that she is all around awesome. Meeting her and becoming her mentee is my (r)evolution!*

LAURA BUCHWALD

YEARS AS MENTOR: 2
OCCUPATION: Writer
and editor
BORN: New York, NY
LIVES: New York, NY

MENTOR'S ANECDOTE: *My work with Jaela is especially rewarding when I see the progress that she continues to make as writer, and as a young woman who is developing her very strong voice. Getting her to love the editing process as much as I do has been challenging. That she worked hard on several drafts of her Scholastic submission and was subsequently awarded the Gold Key is a triumph for us both—and a testament to the creative power of editing!*

UNLIKELY FRIEND

JAELA VAUGHN

Billy, the black sheep of his workplace, finally makes a friend of his own after being ignored by his coworkers yet again. I like to write about characters who march to the beat of their own drums, the "misfits" and "outcasts" who make the world interesting.

Billy stared sadly at the colorful man playing the flute. He was wearing a geometric suit, his jacket blue on one side, red on the other. His shoulders formed sharp edges, his arms holding the thin instrument that covered his "O"-shaped mouth. His fedora was small and bright in color. He looked every bit the well-dressed man; if it weren't for the triangular holes littered across his body, you might not realize he was a statue.

Taking another swig of his drink, Billy asked himself why he'd come to this godforsaken party. He was the tagalong, the plus one, the person that you bring just so you won't seem so lonely. One of his "buddies" from the office brought him, the one who thinks his name is Richard, despite having worked with him for more than ten years. He took another sip and turned to stare at the group of people huddled together in their best formal attire, smiling and laughing while he sneered in disgust. There was nothing that seemed faker to him than an office party. Nobody liked one another, this was all an attempt to look good in front of their boss, who cared little for them either way.

"What do you think of this?" Billy joked with the statue. "Doesn't it make you sick?"

The silence from the flute player came as no surprise to him. He would need another drink soon.

"Look at them all." He turned the man to face the others. "Kissing up to him like this'll do anything to change their lot in life. At the end of the day, we'll all come to the office tomorrow, and nothing will be different. We'll all still be miserable, and no amount of fancy dinner parties can change that."

"You're awfully pessimistic."

His voice sounded smooth, like a cat who plays jazz. It wasn't Billy's voice, and there was absolutely no way that the others had heard him talking.

"Either you just spoke or I've had a bit too much," he joked to his painted wooden friend.

The flute that crossed the statue's mouth did little to render him speechless. *"What's the matter?"*

Billy was bewildered, and a little amused. "Oh my God, you are talking."

"And you haven't answered my question."

Billy stared down at his drink. He couldn't even bring himself to walk over there and refill his glass of champagne. He couldn't stand the sight of them. "You know, you're the first person . . . thing . . . to ask me that."

This time there was no response from the rainbow man, and Billy sighed and chugged the rest of his drink. He was sad it was gone. "They don't care a fig for me, you know. Hell, they don't even know my name. Richard, Rob, George . . ." Billy's mouth twisted to the side as he realized that he was holding back tears he didn't even know were there. "They know they're not right to me. You would have to be a fool not to realize that. They order me around, they mock me when they think I don't hear them, and then, on the one occasion when they remember me well enough to invite me to these . . . I don't know what to call them . . . they form their little League of Friends and don't even care enough to look my way."

"Surely there's someone who cares for you."

"Point me their way, then."

He looked up and saw the crowd had migrated from the kitchen to the living room. Their laughter rang in his ears, and his vision blurred with tears at the sound of their happiness. "Sometimes I wish . . . I wish that one day I could be there laughing with them. And not just the laughing where you don't want to look like a jerk, genuine laughter. Just once."

"I think I've picked up a few jokes in my time."

"Your time? You're joking, right?" Billy chuckled.

"Well I just made you laugh now didn't I?"

Billy's eyes widened, and then he laughed again.

"I guess you did."

"Now, I don't know what'll happen later, but for now, I could be your company for the night."

Billy's heart leapt at the suggestion. So what if the flute man was an inanimate object? He was the only one talking to him, and, if Billy wasn't completely out of his mind, he was the only one who actually *liked* him.

"Are you asking to be my friend?"

"If you'll have me."

Billy set his glass on the table beside him and grinned. He heard the others laughing again, and this time, this time the sound didn't bother him.

MR. BOJANGLES

LAURA BUCHWALD

I am currently in New Orleans working on the second draft of my novel, and this marks an evolution both for me as a writer and for this project. Prompted by a photo, Jaela's story rings with the kind of magical realism that infuses this very special city.

It's said that once you drink the water here you've no choice but to return; it becomes a part of you. It seeps into your soul, this magical corner of the world where the streets are paved with music and the trees drip Spanish moss, wind chimes, and Mardi Gras beads.

It's voodoo and gumbo and Zydeco, shotgun shacks and Creole cottages in purple, gold, and green, and every color in between.

Street corner musicians dance among black cats, and Indians, and the tarot card readers of Jackson Square.

It's a beautiful love letter to itself, this town, to its past and its present, to Louis Armstrong and Storyville, the Fleur de Lys and Marie Laveau.

Here the dead have joie de vivre, and the local spirits are as much a part of the fabric of life as brass bands, second lines, Dr. John, and crawfish.

Once you've been here, indeed, you can never forget what it means to miss New Orleans.

KRISTINE VERAS

YEARS AS MENTEE: 1
GRADE: Sophomore
HIGH SCHOOL: Uncommon Charter High School
BORN: New York, NY
LIVES: Brooklyn, NY

MENTEE'S ANECDOTE: *Being in Girls Write Now as a first year mentee can be very nerve-wracking. So it's nice to find out that your mentor is in her first year as well. From the first time I met Adina, she was always so open and nonjudgmental. Throughout our journey, we always talked, whether it was about life or current events. She definitely taught me to never be afraid to be who I am, to be spontaneous, to never fear taking new risks, and, better yet, to do what I want because I am in control.*

ADINA TALVE-GOODMAN

YEARS AS MENTOR: 1
OCCUPATION: Managing Editor, *One Story*
BORN: St. Louis, MO
LIVES: Brooklyn, NY

MENTOR'S ANECDOTE: *I thought my goals when I started Girls Write Now were going to be to build Kristine's sense of confidence, to make her feel as if anything is possible, and to make it clear that she is an exceptional writer—I didn't expect to change much in myself. But Kristine came into the program with a light and positivity that astounded me. I found myself having to catch up to her spirit. It continues to be challenging for me to share my work more, risk failure, and shrug off perfection but I do it every week because my mentee does it, too.*

SAY CHEESE

KRISTINE VERAS

This poem is a response to the many injustices I've witnessed over the past few years. I wrote it as a way of showing how these daily revolutions, changes in society, affect me. Adina and I spend a lot of our meetings talking about the themes in this poem.

And so I asked myself:

Why is it that the white man's rewarded for
building a nuclear bomb,
But the innocent Muslim kid
is the one with the cuffs on his arm?

They say 9/11 was the president,
so, why is anyone with a hijab
automatically a terrorist?

It's things like these
that deter us
from any chance of equality.

They also say we emerged from Adam and Eve,
but why do we uphold all these social hierarchies?
—Better yet,
why do we uphold the white supreme?

What really is a white supreme
in a world full of melanin?

They're constantly bashing Africa for being so "poor,"
yet they invaded the country and took all its gold.

They call our culture disgusting and ratchet,
but,
when Kylie Jenner wore her braids
it was "fashion."

Since when did these things happen?
Where we live in ignorance and oppression;
or as I like to call it—madness.

I just don't get it.

It was so easy to kill and frame Sandra,
But the minute you even bump a white lady,
you're a monsta.

Say it,
say her name.

Sandra, I'm afraid.
And why can't we say your name?
N why are things this way?
Did you really die how they say?
R.I.P., you deserve it
American "life"—is it really worth it?

Welcome to America,
where the only time our hands are up
is when we're about to be arrested.

Where police brutality overwhelms us.

Where they tell us not to fight back,
but how are we supposed
to feel, as a target
knowing we can't get our life back?

They seem to be missing the bigger picture.

They want us to look in the mirror and see a "nigger,"
but since when do outsides really differ?
We used to be brethren,
now it's
"Nah, he chocolate,
I'm light-skin."

But tell me—
Who really got the juice?
A brotha can't even get some juice
Without it being an invitation to shoot.

R.I.P. Trayvon.
We still can't believe you're gone.

Man, I'm charged up,
they wear that badge to protect us,
yet all they do is harm us.
They advertise
a country full of freedom—
but
how ironic is it—
we're not
free, because of 'dem.

Being treated different
for not being white
and penalized
for innocence
OH, America the great.

Click clack,
now it's too late,
he can't get his life back.
Put your hands up
FREEZE!
Get down on your knees.
Look at the barrel,
Say Cheese

BANG.

All he did was freeze.
And every single passing day it can be me.

LAYTON'S, AFTER MIDNIGHT

ADINA TALVE-GOODMAN

When Kristine and I met, we both said we'd like to write more poetry and work on being brave enough to share what we'd written. This poem came out of an exercise in repetition we did together, and the courage to share it came out of our sessions as well.

I remember my father holding me to his shoulder
I remember him walking me up and down our hallway
I remember fighting hard not to drift off to sleep.
I remember him finally whispering, *Okay, let's to Layton's.*
I remember walking into Layton's, after midnight.

I remember the diner décor being the same as it had been since the '70s

I remember *change* being a dirty word there.

I remember walking to our booth and ordering my usual grilled cheese, whole wheat

I remember splitting the pickle with my father, bite for bite.

I remember him asking how many espressos I'd had that day

I remember he said *I just wish you could sleep.*

I remember shrugging my shoulders and fighting to keep my eyes open.

I remember the waiter asking *Hey, are you Steven Spielberg?*

I remember my father saying, *Yes, it's me.*

I remember him signing the check *Steve S.*

I remember playing quarter hockey on the table until one in the morning.

I remember him saying some lies don't hurt nobody.

I remember walking out and the waiter asking

Are you really him?

No, not really. Have a good night.

MYA WATKINS

YEARS AS MENTEE: 3
GRADE: Senior
HIGH SCHOOL: Brooklyn Technical High School
BORN: Queens, NY
LIVES: Brooklyn, NY
PUBLICATIONS AND RECOGNITIONS: Scholastic Art & Writing Award

MENTEE'S ANECDOTE: *Meeting with my mentor has been such a fun addition to every week. From talking about politics to doing fun prompts like a selfie in a poem, being with Connie Mae is always great. I love responding to the many interesting prompts she brings to our meetings and the different poets she's introduced me to. She has helped me learn to edit my writing and write in ways I never thought of. Going to museums and the Hello Kitty store are just some of the fun experiences we've had together. Connie Mae has been an amazing mentor and an even better friend.*

CONNIE MAE OLIVER

YEARS AS MENTOR: 1
OCCUPATION: English Adjunct Lecturer, Brooklyn College
BORN: Valencia, Venezuela
LIVES: Queens, NY
PUBLICATIONS AND RECOGNITIONS: Poems have appeared in the *Brooklyn Rail* and *No, Dear*

MENTOR'S ANECDOTE: *Working on poetry projects with Mya this year has been absolutely wonderful. Her incredible poems tend to be about family, her impressions of the world, and personal meditations. Mya has not only been a phenomenal mentee but an enthusiastic peer with whom I've had the chance to collaborate and share a love of writing. It is my hope that she will continue to pursue creative writing throughout her studies and beyond; I believe that the world needs more sincere, gifted, and bold writers like Mya. I am looking forward to reading her first chapbook in 2016!*

YOU ARE NOT INVITED

MYA WATKINS

In a Girls Write Now Poetry Workshop, one of the questions was to write about what I am passionate about. This is how I responded.

When I graduate,
You will not sit in the audience
You will burn in Florida heat
Not knowing who I am

When I choose a college,
You will not be aware
You will stew in ignorance

When I get married,
You will not see my family
You will not, never will be, my joy
Our blood has never made us the same

When I have children,
You will never see their faces
You will not learn
So I will not teach you

When you die,

I will not cry
For what should've been
What you should've been
I will smile
Content that you will never leave
Another child fatherless

MATA HARI

CONNIE MAE OLIVER

"Mata Hari" is an allegorical and historical poem.

Tiny & the eldest   of four,
and for her neutrality   double, self-
coded and robed;   feathers only,   bandeau,

jeté'd over the   border with   papers you'd
think they'd   run   but the trial
        sepia   and pre

written, the   prance intercepted,
does it mean the body   is a facility
does it mean the oldest   form is facility

or code, if I remember—Thursday
night
classes   at the Jill Mallory
                 studio,

they told me to intuit
the paneling, touch

my nose

                                     to my knees,

                                     bend the arms and let
fold the knees, still,   by firing squad she fell &
how far indeed

                                     was the fall.

AMAYA WILLIAMS

YEARS AS MENTEE: 2
GRADE: Sophomore
HIGH SCHOOL: Manhattan Hunter Science High School
BORN: New York, NY
LIVES: New York, NY
PUBLICATIONS AND RECOGNITIONS: Editor-in-Chief of Student Newspaper

MENTEE'S ANECDOTE: *One of the major reasons I joined Girls Write Now is because I wanted to lend myself to a more rigorous program that would allow me to both write more and step outside my comfort zone. Meeting Nicole, however, was one of the best surprises that came with joining the program. She's blunt, hilarious, and treats me not only as a mentee but as a friend. She has pushed me to become more sure of myself and has coached me on how to impassion my writing. If I have accomplished anything in this program, it's thanks to her.*

NICOLE COUNTS

YEARS AS MENTOR: 2
OCCUPATION: Editorial Department, Spiegel & Grau, Random House
BORN: Princeton, NJ
LIVES: Brooklyn, NY
PUBLICATIONS AND RECOGNITIONS: Executive editor for *Lakota Nation,* a documentary on the Lakota people

MENTOR'S ANECDOTE:

Evolution, n, growing.
Revolution, n, a radical change.
Amaya, n, a mirror.

To my mirror—thank you for allowing me to see myself differently; thank you for showing me how to become a mirror and to look at myself and my own writing in a new way; thank you for showing me that what we see in the mirror is beautiful, whole, honest, and perfect as is; thank you for reminding me that to grow we must look inward; and thank you for showing me over and over how radical we already are—how all we need is our words.

SESAME SEED STREAMERS

AMAYA WILLIAMS

"Sesame Seed Streamers" is a satirical take on confederacy in America, and by extension, reveals my own (r)evolution about the knowledge of my heritage and my culture. I've learned that in my growth, it's become impossible to "turn a blind eye" to injustices in our society.

The dull blue cow was a humble, quiet cow who lived a humble, quiet life in his humble, quiet home. He'd lived in his home for many years, as did his parents and his grandparents before them. The pink fluorescent dog lived a boisterous, busy life; one far too busy for a wife or children. He was constantly traveling and roving about the pasture, which he shared with the dull blue cow—tidying his home and pampering himself. There was a startling contrast between their two homes: the long, tall grass the pink fluorescent dog left unkempt was most visually separable from the tidy crops lining the front of the dull blue cow's cottage. Between the two homes a tall flag flew, one that the pink fluorescent dog had stuck into the ground the moment he moved in. The flag—a picture of a burger, large and greasy—cast its shadow over the dull blue cow's sweet grass.

Every day the dull blue cow would wander outside of his home, either walking his young daughter to school or mowing the grass with his large amber teeth. Every day, like clockwork, the dull blue cow would gaze upwards into the azure of the hazy southern sky and grimace at the flag.

One day, when his daughter had been playing with a daffodil buried in the dirt in front of the fence separating the two homes, she'd stumbled across the flag—albeit not the first time, but the first she'd seen it in such tantalizing detail.

"What does that mean, Papa?" she'd asked.

It was in that moment that the dull blue cow realized he had no true answer. He could tell her truthfully, that the flag celebrated the herding and butchering of cows—but then he'd have to explain their suffering, and looking into her wide brown eyes, he didn't know if he could fathom it.

"It's nothing dear, trot back to the house and see if mother is done with dinner," he replied simply, his eyes cast determinedly over the shadow of the pink fluorescent dog's home, "Tell her I will return soon, I have some business to attend to first."

"Excuse me, Mr. Dog," called the dull blue cow from the pink fluorescent dog's porch.

The pink fluorescent dog stumbled out of his home clad in a gold satin robe, a pair of spectacles perched atop his snout. He poked his nose at the dull blue cow, gazing upon his figure first up, then down.

"May I help you?" he asked haughtily.

"I would like to ask you if you could remove your flag from our fence. I feel that it is an unsuitable message for my children, nor does it please me morally."

"*Morally*," scoffed the pink fluorescent dog.

"Morally," echoed the dull blue cow.

"I don't believe it's offensive," the pink fluorescent dog said shortly, his stance widening at the dull blue cow's allegation. "My flag's been flying for thirty-three years, and I'm not about to take it down. I have the right, as a pink fluorescent beef eater, to display whatever pleases me as long as it does not physically harm others," barked the pink fluorescent dog. "Good day, *Cow*."

Not much sooner was the dull blue cow facing only the door of the pink fluorescent dog's home.

How strange, thought the pink fluorescent dog as he strode back into his cottage, that one would ever consider his flag offensive. How odd that the dull blue cow would find the idea of a burger in front of his home distasteful and "unsuitable for his children." The pink fluorescent dog chortled to himself, plopping down into his La-Z-Boy and puffing smoke out of his pipe. He sat in his home—now quiet—watching the gentle sway of his delicious sesame seed streamer as the figure of the dull blue cow disappeared.

The dull blue cow sighed in his departure, trekked through the pasture, and reposed himself in his quiet, humble home. He kissed his delicate, hushed daughter on the forehead, and sat himself down at the dinner table.

"If only that pink fluorescent dog could have someone to love." He smiled, admiring his fine, amicable wife. "Perhaps he would hold less hatred in his pink fluorescent heart."

NEST

NICOLE COUNTS

Amaya and I both found different ways to express our voice this year, either through a cow or through a character named "girl"—and whether we used those voices to make a political statement or to understand our own emotions, we each found a way to give our voices power.

I was there when we fell in love.

* * *

On 16th Street, between Montgomery and Berks, Girl slipped out of a three-story brick row home, identical to the ones to her right and left. ÐÐÐ sat painted purple above the blue door, with a hawk and the words "Go Die" under it. Girl had felt disgusted at the sight of it, but that had not stopped her from entering a forbidden zone and coming out disgruntled and pitiful. The light from the track a block away shined down 16th, warding off predators.

It may have been thirty degrees out, but Girl's vodka drink draped her in a deep purple coat. It felt as easy as seventy. The cool, silver numbers, which looked odd on such old homes, branded the block as full of college students. *Where are they?* Alone on the sidewalk, she glided to the street, aware of the silence, the lack of cars, and feeling alone. Girl's mouth moved slightly apart, allowing a small smile to escape across her face.

Against the wind, Girl flapped her arms as hard as she could, *I'm a bird, I'm a bird*—her coat became a cape the faster she went—*I'm a bird, I'm a bird. Can you hear that, Boy? I'm a bird. I said, I'm. A. Bird.*

The red cup that had fallen on Girl's royal blue heels must have splashed on her face too. She could feel the dampness on her cheeks, nice in the cold. *How can I run this fast in heels? Look down, Girl, don't fall.* Black pavement. Pebbles, glass, weave, and chicken bone.

North Philly, you're a graveyard of college disasters, drugged up memorabilia, and empty cases.

I'm a bird, I'm a bird. Where are you, Boy?

Girl looked back and laughed at the orange moon hanging just above her, over the empty street cart touting fifty cents for Italian Ice and one dollar for a Sailor Moon– or Spider-Man-themed ice cream bar. The moon looked closer tonight, its edges blended into the black sky. *When did the moon become so orange? When have I ever been so close? Can flying be so good?*

Boy was running behind Girl. Boy moved closer to girl and stopped. Watching her watch the streetlight. Boy felt immense love for Girl, life-threatening love. Boy reached out and his hand went through her. Boy had given her the red cup. Boy had given in and escorted her out. Boy had taken every step he knew he shouldn't have taken. Boy knew better. Boy loved harder.

The moon turned red then blue then red then blue then red then blue. The pebbles crunched under Girl's feet. *They are so loud when they move. There is no wind, how are they moving? Am I moving?*

Boy is that you? Boy, my dear stop tickling me, it hurts. Why is your voice so loud dear, why is your voice so loud? Why are you yelling at me? Who? What? No, officer I do not need help. Boy is my boyfriend! I am a bird, leave me be.

Girl ran forward until running became running and her feet and legs sent signals to her brain that they were in pain and her hypothalamus activated and she knew that a dark street was not a good place to be and her heart felt heavy, too heavy to hold, too heavy to stand up with, she had to crouch, she had to bend forward, until she was no longer running, and Boy was standing in front of her.

* * *

Boy led Girl to bed. His arms were tired after her carrying her down Diamond Street, a left down 19th Street, just before Susquehanna. He led her up four flights and into his small corner room. She moved to his bed and huddled in the corner, in a ball, in her nest. He reached out to place his hand on her back and she screamed. A wretched, bloody murder kind of scream that he was afraid the cops that lurked around the block would hear and take him away for. Girl mumbled to herself. Girl thought of the other man's touch, her repeated "no." Girl muttered that he would not listen. Her tears had made puddles in the sheets. Her lipstick smeared over the pillow she drowned her head in. *I don't want to, I don't want to, No, No, No.* Boy tried holding her. She kicked him away. Boy got up off the wooden floor, his stomach throbbing and ass already bruising. He walked to the corner farthest from Girl. He looked down. He looked up. He looked left to right. He looked at Girl. He looked away from Girl. He closed his eyes. She was still there. In her nest.

Crouching down in front of her, eye level, he said, "What's my name." Girl did not respond or move. Girl sat frozen. *I don't want to hear you talk,* she thought. *I don't want you, I don't want this, Please go the fuck away, I don't want to, I don't want it, No, No,* "No, No, No," Girl said.

. . . "Please Girl, what's my name." Nothing.

. . . . . .

. . . "What's my name?" "Tell me my name." "What's my name, love?" *Boy, you are Boy.*

. . . "Boy."

. . . "Good, and where are we going to live when we are older." *I don't know.*

. . . "I don't know."

. . . "Yes you do, Girl, tell me what our house will look like." *Yellow*

. . . "Yellow."

. . . "With a wraparound porch that we can drink our tea on and watch our rain?"

. . . "Yyyes."

. . . "And what's our son's name." *I don't want to, I don't want to.*

. . . "I don't want to."

 . . . "Girl, it's okay, what's our son's name."

. . . "Thomas."

. . . "Yes, that's right, Thomas."

Girl looked up from the pillow. It was brighter than she expected. The overhead light right above her made her squint. The TV sat untouched, a cup of tea, half empty, was still on the nightstand, Girl's coat was left sprawled on the floor. Boy sat still in front of her. Boy moved to embrace her. Girl let him. Girl was in her nest. Boy was, too.

RUBY XIAO

YEARS AS MENTEE: 1
GRADE: Sophomore
HIGH SCHOOL:
Richard R. Green High
School of Teaching
BORN: New York, NY
LIVES: New York, NY
PUBLICATIONS AND
RECOGNITIONS: Internship
at Goldman Sachs

MENTEE'S ANECDOTE: *One of the first things Nancy and I worked on was writing poems in Starbucks! She always had a Venti iced tea and I usually got Frappucinos. I learned that poems don't have to be sentence-like—I struggled with that, because I felt every word was important. I learned the term deus ex machina, which means when the writer has God-like powers to the point that the story doesn't make sense. We visited MoMath (Museum of Mathematics), MoMa (Modern Art), and restaurants. I'd never heard of MoMath, and it was a fun experience. We scrutinized Picasso sculptures at MoMA.*

NANCY HOOPER

YEARS AS MENTOR: 8
OCCUPATION:
Writing teacher,
Success Academy;
cooking teacher, Agile
Learning Center
BORN: Minneapolis,
Minnesota
LIVES: New York, NY

MENTOR'S ANECDOTE: *When Ruby told me she loved math, I figured our pair relationship was doomed. I'm a sensitive English major! I hate numbers! But we've discovered a huge common trait: our HUMOR! Whether we are laughing about how "mathy" Ruby is, or how I like to throw around phrases like deus ex machina, we've discovered how to evolve as a writing team. She's taught me to use forms of language I'd forgotten—"gasp!" and "LOL!" and "whatever!"— and I've shared my secret for overcoming fear of writing on Sunday mornings: Starbucks's green tea Frappucino with whipped cream!*

GEOMETRIC PUZZLE
AT MOMATH

RUBY XIAO

*I love math because it's so easy! Nancy took me to MoMath.
I'd never heard of it! I became fascinated by the puzzle-making
station. It was cool watching the laser printer cut out the weird
puzzle pieces. Besides loving math, I love spending time writing
poems with my mentor! Gasp!*

We are in the basement at MoMath;
We mean Museum of Mathematics,
Not of Modern Art.

We see kids playing on a computer,
A small, old-fashioned, kid-sized computer,
Moving the lines of a polygon on a pad
With their fingers. By the way,
Poly in Latin means combining more than one,
Gon means many-angled.

I sat down in front of a computer
(My mentor stands behind me, confused);
I choose a random base made of repeating hexagons—

A hexagon is a polygon with six sides and angles;
(My mentor is more confused now and yawns).

The directions say to drag the lines of the hexagon in any way
So . . . using my finger, up, down,
Left, right, whatever (teen word),
I drag a random line up
Forming more angles and lines;
What is this polygon called?
Mentor is oblivious.

Now I am moving other lines
In all directions, one at a time;
Other lines move automatically, too,
Forming identical shapes;
Now we have twenty-one angles . . . but
How is that possible?
Mentor still discombobulated but asks,
What do you call that shape?

I say, it's a polygon that looks like a horse;
Mentor says, I see a bird in flight and
Shows me what looks like a beak;
I say, it's a polygon that forms a puzzle
With a rotational symmetrical relationship.

Mentor is tired and baffled and says
I give up. You are too mathy!
I laugh and continue designing my puzzle.
Finally, the laser cuts out the shapes
And I stare at it, amazed and excited!

Mentor says let's go to Starbucks . . .
My treat!
It's okay that you're "puzzled," I say.
Let's go. That was spontaneously fun.

MY MiNNESOTA MUTiNY

NANCY HOOPER

*During a pair session, we experimented with poetry by start-
ing with a line from a published work. I selected the opening
from W.H. Auden's poem "The Plains." It triggered thoughts
about where I grew up—terrible, hateful thoughts! Here are
three stanzas from my one-woman revolt against Minnesota!*

I can imagine quite easily ending up
In a two-bit thrift shop in Hell's Kitchen,
Fingering dirty lace blouses while detoxing
From gin and juice and dumpster scraps;
And I can envision myself living at Trump Tower,
Blonde, blown-out, and bored to death
By too much Bergdorf, Botox, and Big Daddy;
But I cannot think of Minnesota without a shudder—
"O God, please don't make me live there again!"

It's horrible to think what Minnesota comes down to,
That God-forsaken interstate of endless greenery and tar,
Where locals talk of seasons—summer and construction—
While sucking down Miller High Life, because this,
The Land of Ten Thousand lakes, is known for 3.2 beer
And Lutefisk and Bundt pans, Wheaties and Spam;
Such darned nice people, too. Yah, sure, you betcha!

Ponder, too, the mind-numbing landmarks:
Mall of America! Babe the Blue Ox! Gavidae Commons—
O geez, Margie, that's the Latin word for loon, our state bird;
And don't forget the World's Largest Twine Ball in a town called Darwin,
Or the inventors of the stapler and Scotch tape;
What's it really like to live in a state where skin congeals at 32F below?
Go ask Garrison Keillor. Or did he move away, too?

READY, SET, WRITE!

PROMPTS AND WRITING EXERCISES

FOR INDIVIDUALS AND GROUPS

Girls Write Now mentors and mentees are in a continuous state of evolution. As we have grown in our mentoring relationships and further developed writing skills over this past program year, we have engaged in our own personal revolutions.

In our pair sessions and group workshop experiences, we have identified and embraced our voices by navigating through the genres of flash fiction, personal essay, op-ed journalism, spoken word, speech writing, and sketch comedy. *(R)evolution* represents our growth as writers, women, and activists, as well as our ability to evolve and revolutionize with our words.

Use the prompts on the following pages to join our revolution to amplify your voice and ignite change within your own community.

—EMILY YOST, Senior Program Coordinator

JOURNALISM:

OP-EDS & THINKPIECES

In these exercises you will identify opinion statements that you can use to write a journalism thinkpiece. A thinkpiece is a form of personal journalism.

PART ONE: PASSION STATEMENT PROMPTS

Read the list of prompts below and choose one that interests you. Write a "passion statement" about one or more of the topics. For example, "I strongly believe _____" (including a "because" is suggested, but not required). You can use first person, you should use your own voice, and most importantly you should be firm in your opinion. Then expand your passion statement to 750 words.

1. What's the biggest misconception that teachers, parents, or the media might have about your generation?
2. What TV show or movie have you seen recently that you think is doing something new, radical, or progressive?
3. What's the most pressing issue facing young women today?
4. What concerns you most about culture right now?
5. What current fashion trend do you think is underrated? What looks should be brought back?
6. Who is the most overrated artist in music, and why?
7. What is the issue that is most important to you politically, and why should politicians in office pay more attention to it?

PART TWO: EDITING (PARTNER EXERCISE)

The scary part about writing an opinion piece for publication is that it can open you up to tough criticism. It takes courage to write about your personal feelings. Take a minute to re-read your draft. Then share your thinkpiece with a partner.

PARTNER QUESTIONS

What would a skeptical reader say about the piece?
What would a generous reader say about the piece?
What are your observations about the style and structure?

RECOMMENDED READING

Opinion Sections of: *The New York Times, Huffington Post,* and *The Toast*
See Shirleyka Hector's "Justice for All—the Ironic Song of America" for a thinkpiece response
See Shania Russell's "From An Introvert" for use of voice in an opinion piece

FICTION: FLASH FICTION

In these exercises you will create a dystopian fiction scene and then choose the most concise way to tell the story in order to produce a piece of flash fiction. Flash fiction is a fiction story that is written in 500 words or less.

PART ONE: FLASH STORY STARTERS

Select one of the prompts below and begin to write a story that is set in, or is about, a dystopian world. You can write this story from any point of view—it's up to you.

1. The end of the world didn't go down the way I thought it would.
2. The elixir would soon take hold. Nothing else mattered. Waiting, waiting. Counting each breath. Enduring each heartbeat.
3. The day I aged to sixteen was the first day I saw my own reflection.
4. Most girls would scream if they found a ninja assassin in their room, but Alexandra grinned. Finally, she was important enough to be found.

PART TWO: REVISION

Edit your piece into a three-paragraph or 500-word story. Be sure to include a beginning, middle, and end.

PART THREE: FLASH EDITING

Time to get "flashy!" Continue to edit your story so that it is only made of five tweets—140 characters, including spaces, punctuation, and letters. We've already mapped out the character spaces for you below. Hint: It may help you to first underline or circle which points of the story are most crucial.

MEMOIR: PERSONAL ESSAY

In these exercises you will reflect and define personal turning points in your own life in order to create a memoir. Memoir is a form of the personal essay with specific knowledge from the author.

PART ONE: REFLECTION PROMPT

Write a letter to a younger version of yourself.
What would you want her to know? What has changed since then?

PART TWO: PROJECTION PROMPT

Write a letter to your future self.
What will you be doing in ten years? What will you have accomplished?

PART THREE: THOUGHT QUESTIONS

1. What sensory details stand out and feel important?
2. How did it feel writing about a moment that has passed? Do you feel differently about it now than when it occurred?
3. Did you write with a specific audience in mind? What feelings do you want your readers to come away with?

4. Are there larger themes in your piece that feel universal or potentially relatable to other people?

RECOMMENDED READING

Crave: Sojourn of a Hungry Soul, Laurie Jean Cannady, craft talk speaker
Is Everyone Hanging Out Without Me? (And Other Concerns), Mindy Kaling
See Misbah Awan's "Adhan" for a memoir piece that sets the scene for the reader
See Diana Romero's "The Dreams They Carried" for a reflective personal essay

POETRY: SPOKEN WORD

In these exercises you will explore the social justice movements that resonate most with you and the words or phrases you would use to express your opinions. Spoken word poetry is a type of poetry that is meant to be performed for an audience.

PART ONE: SOCIAL JUSTICE PROMPTS

Use the questions below to help you articulate the subjects for which you must demand justice. Then try to write a short poem about your thoughts.

1. When has something in the news affected you personally?
2. What would you join a protest march about?
3. What is something that bothers you when you are in public?
4. What is the number one issue you think the 2016 presidential candidates should be discussing?
5. What is something you deal with in your own life that others should learn about?
6. What do you find yourself educating people about often?

PART TWO: BALLAD CHALLENGE

Challenge: Write a fourteen-line poem where every line is repeated. Read your poem out loud to see how your voice changes the meaning of the line.

RECOMMENDED READING

No Matter the Wreckage, Sarah Kay

See Rachel Aghanwa's "A Big Brother, A Big Mouth," inspired by the Black Lives Matter movement

See Mya Watkins's "You Are Not Invited" for a poem that exemplifies repetition

See Sarah Todd's "Define Your Terms," written after Girls Write Now's Spoken Word Workshop

ABOUT GIRLS WRITE NOW

Founded in 1998, Girls Write Now is New York's first and only writing and mentoring organization for girls. Girls Write Now has been distinguished twice by the White House and the President's Committee on the Arts and the Humanities as one of the nation's top after-school programs; twice by the Nonprofit Excellence Awards as one of New York's top ten nonprofits; and twice by the New York City Council as one of the city's top girl-focused initiatives. Our girls—over 90 percent high need and over 95 percent girls of color—have performed at Lincoln Center and the United Nations, published original work in *Newsweek, Elle India, AOL Cambio/Huffington Post*, and our award-winning anthology, and earned hundreds of Scholastic Art & Writing Awards. 100% of our seniors go on to college. This year's anthology supports the rollout of our innovative three-year strategic plan to double the number of girls we serve, and to enrich and extend our college prep and alumnae services.

Our annual anthology has received the Outstanding Book of the Year award by the Independent Publisher Book Awards, and has earned honors from the International Book Awards, The New York Book Festival, the National Indie Excellence Awards, and the Next Generation Indie Book Awards. The anthology has also received Honorable Mention from the San Francisco Book Festival and the Paris Book Festival.

PARTNERS

Alliance for Young Artists & Writer
AOL #BUILTBYGIRLS
AOL Cambio Huffington Post
Makers
Barnard College
Book Riot
Bust Magazine
Bustle.com
Children's Book Council
Chime for Change
Etruscan Press
Flavorpill
Fletcher & Co
Fusion
Hachette Book Group
HarperCollins
Hive Learning Network New York City
Houghton Mifflin Harcourt
Huffington Post
Hunter College
Independent Publisher
Knopf
Little Brown & Company
Macaulay Honors College at CUNY
MAKERS
McNally Jackson
Mentoring Partnership of New York
National Book Foundation
New York Women in Communications
News Corp
The New School University
Of Note Magazine
One Teen Story

Open Road Integrated Media
Outbrain
Parsons The New School For Design
PaperGirl
Penguin Random House
Poet-Linc at Lincoln Center
Poetry Society
Poets & Writers
Poets Out Loud at Fordham University
Queens Library
Riverhead Books
Rona Jaffe Foundation
Scholastic
Schwartz & Wade
She Knows
She Writes Press
Simon & Schuster
STARS Citywide Girls Initiative
StoryBundle
Student Science
Teen Voices
The Feminist Press
THINK
University of Pennsylvania, Kelly
Writers House
VIDA: Women in Literary Arts
Wall Street Journal
Women's eNews
Women's Media Center Live
Writers House
YesYes Books
Young to Publishing Group

GiRLS WRiTE NOW 2016

STAFF

Maya Nussbaum,
Founder & Executive Director

Tracy Steele,
Director of Operations

Maria Campo,
Director of Programs & Outreach

Emily Wurgaft,
Director of Development

Naomi Solomon,
Program Manager

Christina Drill,
Senior Program Coordinator

Emily Yost,
Senior Program Coordinator

Sierra Ritz,
Program Coordinator

Molly MacDermot,
Communications Advisor & Editor

Hannah Lythe,
Communications Manager

Suhaila Meera,
Senior Operations Coordinator

Amber West,
Senior Grant Writer

Sandra Pons,
Development Coordinator

INTERNS

Antonia Behrman

Kim Francisco

Camille Fung

Mikaela Houghton

Isabela Quintero

Jessica Risolo

Caroline Ver Planck

BOARD OF DIRECTORS

Gloria Jacobs,
Board Chair

Sandra Bang,
Vice Chair

Ellen Sweet,
Secretary

Kerry Smith,
Treasurer

Michelle Levin,
Acting Board Development Chair

Erica Mui,
Finance & Audit Chair

Laura Scileppi,
Fundraising Chair

Marci Alboher

Ellen Archer

Marie Dolan

Galina Espinoza

Faiza Issa

Justine Lelchuk

Maya Nussbaum

Chelsea Rao

Elaine Stuart-Shah

Kamy Wicoff

COLLEGE PREP EXPERTS

Juliet Packer
Joshua Morris
Chandra Smith
Suzanne Toma

POETS COLLECTIVE

Maria Dwyer
Jada Fitzpatrick
Shakeva Griswould
Shirleyka Hector
Muse McCormack
Bre'Ann Newsome
Angel Pizarro
Natalia Vargas-Caba

CRAFT TALK AUTHORS

Kate Blumm
Laurie Jean Cannady
Meghan Daum
Grace Dunham
Helen Phillips
Andrea Pippins
Jamie Serlin
Martha Southgate
Kamy Wicoff

CHAPTERS READING SERIES KEYNOTE SPEAKERS

Tanwi Nandini Islam
Mia Alvar
Angela Flournoy
Naomi Jackson

ANTHOLOGY SUPPORTERS

We are grateful to the countless institutions and individuals who have supported our work through their generous contributions. Visit our website, www.girlswritenow.org, to view the extended list.

Girls Write Now would like to thank Amazon Literary Partnership, which provided the charitable contribution that made possible this year's anthology.

SheWritesPress

The anthology is supported, in part, by public funds from the National Endowment for the Arts; the New York State Council on the Arts, a State Agency; and the New York City Department of Cultural Affairs, in partnership with the City Council; the Manhattan Borough President's Office; and the New York City Council STARS Citywide Girls Initiative.

CPSIA information can be obtained
at www.ICGtesting.com
Printed in the USA
FSOW02n0339030516
19859FS